Yes You Can

the working woman's guide to her
legal rights, fair employment,
and equal pay

EMILY B. KIRBY

A SPECTRUM BOOK

Prentice-Hall, Inc., Englewood Cliffs, New Jersey 07632

Library of Congress Cataloging in Publication Data

Kirby, Emily B.
  Yes you can.

  "A Spectrum Book."
  Bibliography: p.
  Includes index.
    1. Women—Employment—Law and legislation—United
States—Popular works.   2. Sex discrimination against
women—Law and legislation—United States—Popular works.
3. Equal pay for equal work—Law and legislation—United
States—Popular works.   I. Title.
KF3467.Z9K57 1984   344.73′014   84-11603
ISBN 0-13-972241-6   347.30414
ISBN 0-13-972233-5 (pbk.)

1 2 3 4 5 6 7 8 9 10

Editorial/production supervision by Chris McMorrow
Cover design by Hal Siegel
Index prepared by Jane Farnol

ISBN 0-13-972241-6

ISBN 0-13-972233-5 {PBK.}

For Frank, mentor and friend, with love and thanks.

Contents

Preface

Yes You Can is designed to make the working woman aware of her legal rights and to help her recognize and deal with any violations of them. Therefore, the book aims to increase understanding of laws affecting the legal rights of individual working women, so that each will know her legal rights and thus be able to exercise choice of action in the workplace, and to assist working women who want to take the difficult initial steps toward a strategy for achieving individual legal rights in the workplace.

What are these legal rights that working women could benefit from knowing about, understanding, and developing strategies to ensure? The legal right to equal pay for equal work, the legal right to equal employment opportunity, and the legal right to equal credit are three examples. These legal rights and others are treated in detail. In addition, every chapter includes pertinent observations, experiences, and methods found useful by working women seeking to have their legal rights respected.

Of course, the hope is that *Yes You Can* will help you avoid unpleasant situations. If you see something coming, you can prepare yourself well and snatch victory where the opposition had planned your defeat. When that is impossible, *Yes You Can* hopes to help you avoid panic and impulsive behavior.

One earns one's livelihood in the workplace; panic and impulsive behavior are usually counterproductive. They seem to indicate that important information and skills are lacking. Maybe that is why working women react in unbusinesslike ways when they become frustrated or feel that they have been treated unjustly. *Yes You Can* suggests that it is worth the effort to try another approach—one involving knowledge of workplace rules, practice of appropriate workplace roles, and devising of constructive strategies grounded in and relying on implementation of existing laws—to make that positive difference working women so earnestly desire. To this end *Yes You Can* contains many illustrations of ways to increase insight about workplace rules to enhance role effectiveness and personal satisfaction as a successful working woman whose legal rights are respected.

There are eight chapters in the book. Each begins with a "mindset" to prepare you for what follows. The first chapter presents an overview; it introduces techniques for understanding workplace structure and function. Chapter 2 focuses on the Equal Pay Act of 1963. Chapter 3 evaluates implementation of Title VII of the Civil Rights Act of 1964, emphasizing the role of the Equal Employment Opportunity Commission. The fourth chapter presents a novel way of looking at affirmative action implementation in your workplace. Legal rights related to education are examined next. Then, in Chapter 6, the Federal Equal Credit Opportunity Act and its impact upon working women is considered. Chapter 7 gives clues to why equal rights have not been achieved through a constitutional amendment by America's working women. The final chapter discusses contemporary options working women may decide to exercise.

Yes You Can is intended to stimulate your thinking, bolster your courage and self-esteem, and assure you that as a working woman you are not alone in the legal rights jungle. Your efforts, teamed up with knowledge from *Yes You Can*, ought to enable you to participate confidently, actively, enthusiastically, and fully in your workplace and in our democratic society.

Many people help an idea blossom and come to fruition as a book. Hundreds contributed to this one. Although they cannot all be thanked personally, their help was truly appreciated. Special thanks go to Dr. Ann Matasar, for highlighting the relationship between assertive and legal rights; my students in "Effective Business Roles" at Mundelein College's Weekend College, for their honesty, for sharing their experiences, and for identifying the need for this book; my supervisors—all male, all different—who taught me workplace strategies and encouraged the testing of some strategies included here; the seven men and one woman who reported directly to me, for constructive, corrective influences, and proving that men and women can work together even with a woman boss; women friends, who enriched this presentation and listened to or read the text—I hope you enjoy finding yourselves in these pages; the four women—Dee, Pam, Jackie, and Carol—who performed the nitty-gritty tasks I am genetically incapable of doing; Joe Cardillo, who encouraged me and initiated use of the book to help working women before anyone else did; all the people at Prentice-Hall who had faith in this book throughout its preparation; my sons and daughter, for sincere interest throughout; and my helpmate of thirty years, the book's literal (and literary) godfather, who helped in countless other ways, too. Thanks to you all! You deserve credit for whatever merit *Yes You Can* contains.

The first quotation on page 22 is used courtesy of *California Women*, newsletter of the California Commission on the Status of Women.

The excerpt reprinted on page 24 from *We Were There: The Story of Working Women in America*, by Barbara Wertheimer, © 1977, is used by permission of Pantheon Books, a Division of Random House, Inc.

The second quotation on page 68 is used by permission of Human Science Press, Inc. It is from Wilma Scott Heide, "Women's Liberation Means Putting Sex in Its Place," p. 15 in Mildred E. Katzell and William C. Byham (Eds.), *Women in the Workplace: Confrontation with Change*, (New York, N.Y.: Behavioral Publications), © 1972 by Human Sciences Press, Inc.

Excerpted material in Chapter 3 from *the Managerial Woman*, by Margaret Hennig and Anne Jardim, copyright © 1976, 1977 by Margaret Hennig and Anne Jardim, is reprinted by permission of Doubleday & Company, Inc.

The chapter opening quote on page 115 is from Mary Crawford's "Climbing the Ivy-Covered Walls," *Ms.*, Vol. vii, #5, (November, 1978), page 61, and is used by permission.

The first quotation on page 181 by Verna Jones, "A Matter of Survival: Feminists Pick up Where ERA Leaves Off," *the Chicago Tribune, Suburban Trib*, January 30, 1980, is used by permission.

The second chapter opening quote on page 205 is reprinted by permission of the *Wall Street Journal*, © Dow Jones & Company, Inc. (1981). All rights reserved.

'I don't know what you chicks are complaining about. We're just trying to protect your feminine mystique.'

Bill Sanders, *The Milwaukee Journal.*

Yes You Can

Since the beginning of the Republic, there have been 1734 Senators; of them, 14 have been women. Of a total of 9,699 members of the House of Representatives, only 90 have been women. It defies reason to believe that imbalances of this magnitude are not reflected in the outcome of the legislative process.

SHARON PERCY ROCKEFELLER,
as quoted in *California Women*,
May–June 1979, p. 5.

Statistics on the sex segregation of workers and on the undervaluation of women's wages suggest that many companies in the United States discriminate against women workers on a daily basis. . . Women have begun to fight against this reality, but the attack is still sporadic. Most women do not fully understand the mechanisms used to discriminate or the legal weapons available to attack them.

SUSAN DELLER ROSS and ANN
BARCHER, *The Rights of Women: An
American Civil Liberties Union
Handbook,* Revised *(New York:
Bantam Books, (1983), p. 15.*

The Contest
of the Workplace
an introduction

THE PLAYING FIELD

Mindset

After reading about the contest of the workplace, you ought to have a framework for thinking about working women. Several organizing concepts are provided for this purpose. One examines the workplace in terms of its structures and how they fit together; another presents the workplace as an arena of athletic and intellectual activity or conversely as a stage where dramas are acted out. The sports or games aspect of the contest reminds you that rules always govern action, while the theater aspect keeps you conscious of enacting a role in a drama (one that often benefits from rehearsal before appearing onstage). Yet another concept is historical; it tackles the question of how working women got to where they are today.

After reading this chapter, you should be able to chart the formal and informal structures of your workplace and to have begun analyzing your position in them. You should have begun thinking about your mastery of rules and roles pertaining to your workplace. You might be thinking about what can be learned from the lessons of history so that undesired outcomes are not repeated to eternity. If you took the Lawful Law Fool Quiz, (pages 13-14) you might be on your way to the library, or you might be getting comfortable for a night's digging into *Yes You Can*.

You may be feeling angry, anxious, or incredulous. You may feel a new empathy with all working women, or scorn for them. These are among typical reactions to the material presented. But actions, not reactions, have payoffs. You know that, of course, so when you finish reading the chapter, get out your pen and pad and start plotting your third act. The primary intention of this chapter is to arouse your purpose, your resolve to learn about your legal rights and how they can help you as you help yourself.

Taking the Measurements

Being a working woman automatically makes you a player in one of the world's most involved and engrossing games. The playing field is your workplace, the place to have fun while you accomplish your task and meet the goals you set. That's what the contest is all about. But we will exhaust ourselves and achieve few gains unless we discipline ourselves to concentrate on the playing field during working hours.

2

Those little Etons that train British boys—not exactly where we are—relate to our playing field and workplace analogy. Ball games at Eton teach boys behaviors that are rewarded years later on battlefields, in business, in government (or in marriage). "Come off it," you say. "American girls don't go to Eton." True, but you missed the point. What those British boys ingest through play is how to move successfully through the contests that are likely to arise during their adult working lives. American women have not learned rules through team sports, so they have had to memorize rules or learn them through concerted effort. Girls have been at a greater disadvantage because they have lacked team practice; this disadvantage even applies to girls who are superior individual players. Game rules are basic, but team practice adds another essential element.

Stated differently, being super at your job is not enough. Learning specific skills and the workplace rules enables us to do our jobs well. What is missing is the playful, real camaraderie of the workplace that makes it shine like a diamond. It's the magnetic part that attracts pleasant thoughts about work when you're elsewhere. It's what we've been calling the playing field. Concepts of workplace and playing field share similarities and differences. Both concepts may share the same location, taking their definition from the same place. However, as night and day shade into each other at dawn and twilight, so do concepts of workplace and playing field. Maybe you have some less pleasant thoughts about workplace and playing field.

Such thoughts may be justified, but they won't get you anywhere. Although there is no need to minimize working women's difficulties in arriving where the game goes on, or to deny that some women use self-defeating tactics, getting into the real game has not been easy. Men, accustomed to team play on the one hand and looking out for number one on the other, apparently make unwarranted assumptions about working women. Men may even assume that since no one told them the facts of work life and since they do know them, working women must be unmotivated, disinterested, or slow learners.[1] Some rare men might decide that the contest was loaded. Such men might help individual women to achieve a position closer to the infield. Yet most women must help themselves or go without, remaining to some extent helpless.

Words, rules, and roles. Linguistic usages and interpretations accentuate feelings of helplessness. That linguistic interpretations differentiate the sexes can be seen in Figure 1–1. You may have overlooked the

FIGURE 1-1 Source: Sex Equity Project, Richland Community College, Decatur, Illinois.

*Because of Sexism in Language.

effects of such utterances. They are powerful, nevertheless. Rules, too, are couched in words. We learn, largely through words, what the workplace game is and what our part in it is. Alert working women can and do use words to improve conditions. Let's follow an example to see where it can lead.

THE RULES

Pearl Bailey sang about the tug of war between men and women. Her frame of reference was the sexual playing field, not the workplace. Anything but helpless, she made up her own rules and advised women to follow them. One prescription suggested that women be steadfast in purpose, be constructive, do the unexpected, and discover the man's next move before they make a permanent decision. It sounds more like chess than romance, but it is admittedly a terrific ploy. Women have been using it for centuries, everywhere but in the workplace. Perhaps the workplace is the ideal location for the application of Pearl Bailey's rules—in translation, of course. The advantages would not be only getting the upper hand but also having important information about the other side. But best of all, you would have the opportunity of exercising your sense of humor while earning your living.[2] And while you are savoring this peak experience, your next move develops.

You might find you've got a real talent for throwing a curve, for swerving. That's fine as long as you know what you are doing, what the consequences might be, and if you are willing to take responsibility for your actions. Irresponsibility has no place in the working woman's world. Irresponsibility correctly implies loss of self-control. By contrast, what will aid women is increased self-control, including self-determination, on the playing field.

There's another important thing to consider. Men in the workplace define their tasks differently from the way women do. Men know the real rules of management, how to gain and use power. Women tend to believe that the essential factor is doing the task. Women are beginning to realize that the real rules have a lot more to do with how to plan and implement the plan than with evaluating the results. Women are beginning to understand the subordinate skills of delegation and supervision. Women are even starting to deal with the notion of accountability, which looms so large in the workplace. These skills go a long way, although most women find them hard to learn, harder to practice on the playing field. Most working women respond to cultural expectations of nurturing and for support when more energy spent on getting the job done would produce better results. Getting the job done would indicate ability to function within the rule structure and might even be rewarded with an occasional invitation into the inner circles of the power structure. Who knows, male coworkers might respond with the highest compliment of all: They might learn and practice the skills for which women are famous. But we don't see too many supportive and nurturing males yet; those behaviors have not left the counterculture of the workplace for the haven of sanctioned acts. So, working women must learn the real rules and, for the time being, park their caretaking cultural stereotypes at home. They need to concentrate on being effective rather than affective.

So much for introduction. We've used Pearl Bailey's approach as an example of the informal rules that govern interaction. We've talked about the approaches used by successful males in the workforce—efficient, effective, planned, evaluative—as examples of formal rules. Naturally, it isn't that simple. Let's look more closely at some facets of formal and informal structure in the workplace.

Formal Structure

Separating the formal (spoken, written) rules from the informal (understood, unwritten) ones requires a conscious effort. Still, an effort that needs to be made. How many working women have analyzed their playing field's dynamics and structures? Have you?

If you are unsure, you might consider the nature of the formal rules where you work. Formal rules may govern the range of procedural detail from protocol (who speaks to whom first, and what forms of address are used) to space location and allocation (where you are on the playing field, how much space and privacy you have) through use of authority or power (are you docked for lateness or dental appointments, and given compensatory time? are you chewed out publicly, praised only in private?). Comparing your situation with those of others in your workplace can lead you to see what the formal rules are and derive the resultant formal structure governing it.

Your organization will be unique in some ways. Still, a bit of thought will enable you to chart the positions to see where you fit and where you would rather be on the organizational chart, and to give you ideas of other positions for which you may want to obtain job descriptions. Of course, it is likely that an organizational chart already exists, but even if it does, you may want to do this exercise just to check out your perceptions. Whether you have seen such a chart of your organization's formal structure or not, you may discover new things that you can do from this exercise on formal rules. If you are a typical working woman, you are good for more than you thought, more than your organization has led you to believe.

The sample organizational chart in Figure 1–2 will get you started.

Use a large sheet of paper and begin with your position. You might work upwards first, then sideways. The finished chart will indicate how positions relate to one another within the formal structure of your organization. Formal structure is the foundation for formal rules. Here, we are discussing formal rules and positions or roles, not the people performing within them. Label each position by title. Put an X at your position.

You have now made a start on the most important rule for the playing field: objectivity. It is so difficult to learn objectivity that most of

FIGURE 1-2 Hypothetical Organizational Chart: Formal Structure.

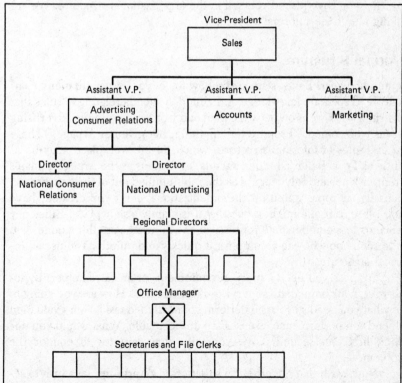

us never master it completely. All of us tend to let feelings, uncontrollable ones, pop up uninvited at awful moments. Don't despair. Working men suffer from emotionality, too. If you watch football or hockey on television, you've observed weekly demonstrations of lack of objectivity on the real playing field that is the professional athlete's workplace. But most working men do a good job of being objective during working hours. We working women can achieve the same alert calm. Keeping your cool in the workplace can be as important as getting the job done: It lets you observe what is going on around you. So does being alert.

Being calm, alert, and objective are useful attributes on the job; it is small wonder that men practice them. These attributes are so useful in sensitizing workers to what's really going on that it's a wonder all working women have not begun using them. What's really going on concerns the other piece of the organizational structure and function game. Properly put, how things really get done around here is what you want to know now that you have placed yourself in the organizational structure. We are talking about the informal structure.

Informal Structure

Remember Pearl Bailey's advice on how to get your way with men? Pearl Bailey had accurate knowledge of the hidden agenda relating to rules that governed what went on between men and women. So did the advertising genius who coined, "Promise her anything, but give her Arpège." These are examples of informal structure, which, in the workplace, may be as subtle as Pearl Bailey's hidden agenda, as devious as the Arpège adman's intent, as enchantingly magical as the rabbit pulled out of the hat. Formal channels, as represented on the organizational chart you created, have their place, but one might argue that it is mainly a showplace. Efficiency demands less cumbersome routes. When you want something done, you go to someone who can accomplish it quickly and quietly. You use an informal structure.

Suppose you need a piece of equipment, or an extra helper, by tomorrow. Your immediate supervisor is on vacation. How are you going to get what you need so you can perform your assigned task? Your evaluation depends on performance; excuses are unacceptable. What would you do? Think first, act second! Give yourself a few minutes to ponder the problem.

Now, with that hypothetical situation as a warm-up, let's turn to serious business. Study the informal structure given for a hypothetical organization in Figure 1–3. It provides an executive secretary's view of influence and information flow. As in the Figure, using your picture of the formal structure of your organization, show with dash marks (--) how influence flows to get jobs done where you work. Your two diagrams should represent the formal and informal structures you deal with every workday. Study them carefully. As you do, keep in mind that the informal structure is dynamic; it changes quickly and often, needing frequent updating, whereas the formal structure changes much more slowly, although it is by no means static. Treating these charts as maps to your organization and to your action within it may be worth thousands of dollars to you.

"Time out," you say. "I don't know enough about this place. I've worked here only five years (or months, or days)." That doesn't make any

FIGURE 1-3 Hypothetical Organizational Chart: Information/Influence Flow.

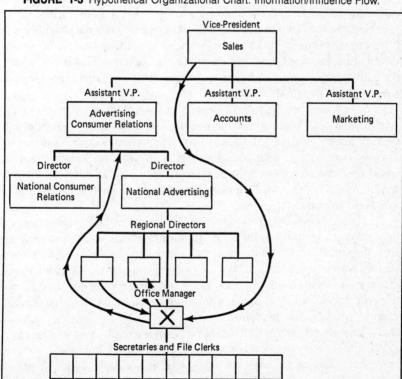

difference; now is the time to begin thinking about and diagramming these relationships. Try the exercise again later.

Comparative comments to assist you in your charting. As you repeat the exercise, you'll become aware of other patterns within the formal structure. It may strike you that large organizational units tend to be duplicates of one another; familiarity with one unit transfers easily to another more promising unit. The formal structures are so similar that the transition period should be relatively short. You may reflect that formal structures in organizations having the same purpose—for instance, two schools or hospitals or department stores—are often very much alike. This knowledge can be put to good use in lateral, or sideways, moves within a given field. Too few working women have fully exploited this aspect of formal structure and rules as they climb the career ladder. By contrast, most men maximize their success and experience by doing precisely that. They specialize in lateral moves until their careers take off.

Men also cash in on knowledge of informal structure. They find out early how information is transmitted, who has what reputation, and so on. Working women often feel at a disadvantage where informal structure and rules are concerned. That's unnecessary. It is not true that all important information becomes available only in male bastions. The ladies' room, the Tupperware party, and even the coffee break are great places for uncovering the formal structure.

Secretaries are important people in the informal structure. They work closely with key organization people; they know the formal rules and quickly learn about new developments. They expand their influence by sharing information with one another. Furthermore, most American working women have either been secretaries or have reported to them at some time; thus a natural foundation exists upon which working women can build informal structures.

The exercises help you to realize that formal and informal structures depend on rules; mysterious initially, rules gradually become second nature. For most working women formal and informal rules at first are completely implicit and covert. We learn to classify rules, to order them, rather than having them order us. However, formal rules are always more explicit, overt, and rigid than informal rules. Informal rules remain more covert, implicit, and flexible.

Formal and informal structures and rules complement one another, existing together within each workplace; and although important, they do not exert total control over the workplace or your fate within it.

The suprastructure: making and describing the model. Another structure exists. It originates outside all organizations, is readily available, powerful, yet relatively unknown. It operates on a higher level than the formal and informal structures, which we could now define as the infrastructure, the underpinnings. Now we are going to examine this new structure: the suprastructure.

Our laws are higher than or placed above other things we've built, including our organizations. Laws outrank the formal and informal workplace structures. This book's major focus is upon these codified rules: laws serving as work game umpires protecting fair play. Figure 1–4 illustrates the relationships between laws and formal and informal rules. If we could present Figure 1–4 in three dimensions the large circle labeled suprastructure would be above and surrounding the smaller circles labeled formal structure and informal structure. In Figure 1–4A, we have a model of a law-abiding organization; the formal and informal structures that display a moderate amount of overlap are within the suprastructure.

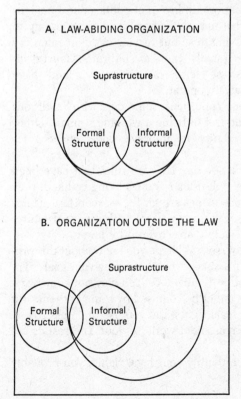

A. LAW-ABIDING ORGANIZATION

Suprastructure

Formal
Structure

Informal
Structure

B. ORGANIZATION OUTSIDE THE LAW

Suprastructure

Formal
Structure

Informal
Structure

FIGURE 1-4 Models of the Suprastructure.

Figure 1–4B is a model of an organization in which most of the formal structure is outside the suprastructure, while most of the informal structure is within the suprastructure. One would not expect such an organization to last for any length of time. One would hope that it doesn't.

The model must include some prosaic details. Even the suprastructure requires some hierarchy among its laws, which will soon be described, and some additional structure to manage the implementation of the laws. The implementation of our laws involves thousands of persons trained to deal directly (lawyers and judges) or indirectly (police and agencies of all kinds) with questions about the correctness of actions in terms of the laws. In general, we do a good job of implementing our laws. That ought to make us feel safe, and it does.

But some parts of the suprastructure are less well understood and less often enforced than others. Among these are the several types of laws that govern your legal rights as a working woman. Some depend upon where you work; executive orders from the president, for example, affect only U.S. Civil Service employees or employees of public educational institutions.[3] There are statutes that may differ from state to state, city to city. There are federal laws applying to all but varying in enforcement by jurisdiction and from law to law. Finally, there are Supreme Court decisions that set precedents, shape legal interpretations, and have nationwide effect on laws already in operation.

Some laws concern working conditions; some deal with conditions outside work stemming from the fact of being a working woman. Other laws deal with matters like ability to improve one's chances for advancement.

If you think about it, you'll see that laws are rules that have been codified and enacted. In games, rules don't end up being codified; they don't have to be, usually, because games are for fun—except war games and work games. Both of those eventually waft up to the suprastructure. Thus, most serious matters ultimately are covered by laws.

Take a breather and test yourself. What do you know about this protective suprastructure capable of assisting you in reaching your goals? Try the Lawful Law Fool Quiz found in Figure 1–5.[4] You may not know what laws relate to the statements or might be confused by some of them. But even if you do know all of your legal rights, can you use them effectively to make the system on your playing field work for you? The results are summarized in Appendix A.

Whether or not you could identify your legal rights, you probably

FIGURE 1–5 Legal Rights: The Lawful Law Fool Quiz

Determine whether the statement is true or false. Think about what laws may relate to the statements. If true, circle T. If false, circle F.

STATEMENTS	TRUE	FALSE
1. Before lending a woman money to buy a house, a loan officer may ask her what method of birth control she uses.	T	F
2. There is a federal law that makes all discrimination based on sex illegal within the United States.	T	F
3. Schools and colleges that refuse to send out student transcripts when ordered over the telephone are discriminating against students.	T	F
4. People who have honorable discharges from the military find it easier to get federal, state, and local government-sponsored jobs than do those who have always been civilians.	T	F
5. You have to spend as much on girls' sports as on boys' sports today if you run a school.	T	F
6. The federal government forces employers to hire women for the higher-paying jobs as a result of a law.	T	F
7. Some jobs, like secretary, if done by men should pay higher than when done by women. We have a law that makes this a reality.	T	F
8. The sex discrimination laws really don't have any teeth.	T	F
9. Good jobs are often advertised Help Wanted Male and Help Wanted Female.	T	F
10. While this is kept quiet, colleges and universities are well within their rights when they set admissions quotas for women so not too many women get in.	T	F
11. Bankers are wise to discount the wife's earnings in determining mortgage loan limits.	T	F
12. Affirmative action means a company must hire unqualified people to reach its quotas of women and minority group members.	T	F
13. The new laws make it acceptable to *plan* to hire, train, and promote members of underrepresented groups. You don't really have to *do* it.	T	F
14. The next worker in line must automatically be promoted, according to the law. One never needs to apply.	T	F

FIGURE 1–5 (Continued)

STATEMENTS	TRUE	FALSE
15. If you have been treated unfairly on the job and have filed a complaint, your employer can demote you, withhold your pay, or fire you.	T	F
16. Titles of jobs can be legally fixed so that men and women doing the same things are called by different titles and rewarded with different wages.	T	F
17. Without your knowledge, the personnel manager can place negative things about you in your personnel file.	T	F
18. It is acceptable to offer training to men only because, as everyone knows, they have to support their families.	T	F
19. It is a good idea to look at the firm's affirmative action plan before taking the job that is offered.	T	F
20. In moves to avoid government interference, larger, richer companies have become more likely to promote women to top-level management than smaller, poorer companies.	T	F

expect the suprastructure to function smoothly. It doesn't always. When it fails to, we are disappointed. Did we make the error of concentrating on the structure while ignoring the players?

Painful as it is, working women need to recall that those who shaped our nation's suprastructure were males. They created new roles and enacted them on a pristine stage. In time, those new roles became norms, expected, old hat, though they remained exclusively male. The same males who made the legal rules made the rules for sports and for dramatic action.

Working women tend to overlook history and, with it, men's intense proprietary feelings toward the workplace, which many of them apparently see as another sports palace, battlefield, pleasure dome, or stage. Here we are going to borrow those metaphors for activity in different types of places and use them to help us in the workplace. We become the players or the actresses, and we get on the court or tread the boards.

Work Sports and Work Drama

For more than 350 years, women in North America have been promoting women's legal rights. This uphill fight need not be rehashed here. (A short list of recent accounts may be found at the end of this chapter.) Women have accomplished much by sheer determination and effort. They doubtless would have gotten far more done had the suprastructure accurately assessed and acknowledged the value of their contributions. But that wasn't the custom when the stage was being set for women's legal rights.

So many women are convinced that the scene is changing—that women are in the workplace to stay, taking full responsibility for their careers, expecting the same opportunities, acceptance, and reward as all adult workers—that we've put together some general considerations cast in theater language. These stage settings, or asides, are intended to help women achieve their full legal rights in the workplace first by taking that giant step onto the stage; one might call this prompting or cueing the players. The underlying idea of the stage mechanics aspect is that all of us can—in fact, we must—learn new roles, new parts to fit into the new world exploding around us. But we have to practice so we can perform with assurance, saving our main effort for the job at hand. From that perspective, the dramatic analogy signals a need for rehearsal. It tells you that there is something to consider, try out for, and to perform smoothly.

By contrast, in this chapter, instead of viewing the workplace as a stage, it has been seen as an arena, a place of constant contests. We could have referred instead to the social, sexual, and intellectual tests working women face. Margaret Hennig and Anne Jardim, who describe them, advise, "Don't play the game."[5] Our advice is to learn the rules thoroughly and have fun with the game. Be playful and change the rules a little at a time so they work for you. You'll enjoy it if you do it skillfully, and others will enjoy working with you. Best of all, you'll position yourself to make sure that your legal rights are always respected. You'll soon find yourself helping other working women to play their roles better. And when you reach the final chapter, a few finishing touches are offered, while your stellar performance on stage, and in the game, is assumed.

WHAT WOMEN'S LEGAL RIGHTS ARE ABOUT

One could view the American woman's pursuit of legal equality as a play that falls apart at the third act (or as an inning in which the women's team rapidly makes the third out). Playwrights often stumble after act two, failing to achieve a satisfactory resolution of the plot. The same thing happens to American women crusading or campaigning for their legal rights.

Some Props

Insight into this situation may be found in the way Americans, particularly women, view the political events of their times. Contemporary Americans are possibly the last political innocents in the industralized world. American unwillingness to learn the coping strategies necessary for effective functioning in a democratic society can be a self-defeating tactic of mammoth proportions. As a nation, we repeatedly experience the distress that accompanies lack of political awareness at home and abroad. However, the majority of Americans seem to remain unperturbed, continuing to blame unpleasant national and global events upon others.

A general example, and one specific to women, will illustrate the problem. Self-report data on large survey samples help to reveal our pattern. A report on "education's contribution to the quality of life of a sample of 30-year-olds" dealt with how these young adults (surveyed first at age 15) evaluated important facets of their lives shortly after Watergate.[6] These Americans overwhelmingly ranked "participation in activity related to local or national government" lowest on their lists; family, friends, and recreation received high rankings. Had the study been confined to women, or had it been conducted this year, it probably would have produced identical results. American women, like American men, are ignorant about and apparently uninterested in their legal rights. It's a topic that arouses much ambivalance. The survey of 30-year-olds is our general example.

The specific example, chosen from many similar ones, appeared in a popular magazine article entitled "Is His Money Your Money Too?"[7] Two aspects of blaming others for our unpleasant consequences are represented. There is the woman who, having stopped working to become a homemaker, resented having to ask her husband for money; and there is the wife whose children reached school age, enabling her to go to work, who rejected the idea of contributing any of her earnings to the family upkeep. When the working wife saved all of her money in her own bank account while continuing to spend her husband's earnings, he remarked, "What's mine is ours and what's hers is hers."[8] Both of these women felt that they were not at fault; neither could understand nor come to grips with her anger and its expression in her behavior. You can easily think of some mature, face-saving solutions for the resentful wife and the stingy one.

Surely adults—American women—would work to handle money matters amicably, responsibly, maturely. Surely they would welcome responsibilities that accompany legal rights. Such a belief is even more innocent than the political naiveté mentioned earlier. The truth seems to be related to deeply ingrained ambivalence that is difficult to uproot. Such ambivalence manifests itself in myriad disguises.

The possession of knowledge, money, and a job cannot ensure that ambivalence will be resolved, that participation in the democratic process will occur, and that rights and responsibilities will become balanced. Emotions are a decisive element in the women's legal rights saga. Emotionality may lie at the heart of the ambivalence.

What we observe in American women today is nothing new. Why is it, one is tempted to ponder, that women get so close to their goals so often only to give up before achieving success?

SOME LEGAL ISSUES

Playbill Notes

America's founders wisely adopted a few potent principles rather than many, leaving interpretations and enforcement flexible. Women's troubles may have begun at that juncture. It was established that the United States would be governed by laws, not by persons. But women were not specifically included in the early documents.

The Founding Fathers made provisions for smooth transitions by and following elections, and for interaction among different levels of government and among different branches of government. Foreseeing such evils as usurpation of rights, the early legislators tried to prevent them and were remarkably successful. But the rights of women were never considered.

The Founding Fathers' failure to protect women (and children) and their rights is today viewed as vicious discrimination. More accurately, and perhaps with greater devastation, the evidence indicates that American women were simply ignored. What we are quick to label as discrimination never really came up. Women were taken for granted. They (legally) were essentially nonpersons. How can one discriminate against nonpersons? Isn't that the essence of nonsense?

Fortunately, nothing remains static. Change is an inescapable fact of life, whether the focus is fashion or fairness. The challenge is to produce constructive change and to provide for its continuity, growth, and development. Women tend to forget this, or at least those wanting to ensure that their gains would pass to their daughters apparently did.

When we examine aspects of working women's legal rights, we are struck by the success of the divide and conquer strategy that has often prevented passage of legal rights legislation. Yet women have rarely used this tactic to weaken opposition to proposed legislation. By contrast, nonworking women frequently seem to use their time to fragment and destroy support for legislation beneficial to all women. Meanwhile, working women rarely make their prolegislation views forcefully heard in time.

Alas, this is largely a rerun. The roots of efforts toward women's legal equality in America were sustained and nourished largely by justified anger coupled with absolute conviction. Today it is difficult to imagine the dedication of the women's legal rights pioneers in America. Small groups of women worked hard and long for legal equality, and small groups of women are still doing so. The difference is that today these women are also working outside their homes.

Why getting the vote, achieving financial independence, receiving fair treatment on the job, and granting equal educational opportunity to women should have appeared scandalous to so many fathers, brothers, sons, and husbands may seem a mystery. Perhaps it was the need for something constant in a world that saw home industry give way to massive factory operations, farm life being supplanted by cities, and the horse being replaced by steam and then by electricity, to mention a few inescapable changes.

Despite the changes, plots of recent dramatic struggles for the attainment of women's legal equality resemble past ones. Past and present, women technically won some battles, ended some scenes in victorious limelight. *Full legal equality* was not achieved by women as U.S. citizens under the laws of the land; the struggle continues, no less dramatic for its many repetitions.

Some victories were granted by default, or as magnanimous gifts, long after the active campaign ended. False complacency on women's part has resulted. Counterbalancing this are daily accounts of unenforced laws, of overt opposition to the laws, testifying to the power of opponents of women's equal legal rights. Mankind and womankind are divided among and between themselves. While many women oppose women's legal rights, many men support women's efforts. Many working women oppose equal legal rights for themselves and others; likewise, many nonworking women are staunch supporters of legal equality.

So much heat has been generated by the question of legal equality for women that one tends to forget that just causes do eventually change the norms of their society. Women's suffrage is a potent example of such change. Today nobody would question any American woman citizen's right to vote. But considering the proportion of voting women, an unbiased observer might say that American women are taking the vote for granted. It would be still more dangerous if working women took the vote for granted.

Perhaps because American women have been so apolitical, some legal rights remain insecure and others have not been achieved. This book will examine legal rights for working women, providing brief historical and contemporary background for each issue. It will focus on the legislation and offer ideas you can use or modify to promote your full legal equality as a working woman. After that, it's up to you.

The part left for you we've called the third act. We have cast it in theatrical mold for emphasis and because it fits.

The Third Act

You get to write the difficult, troublesome third act. What was self-evident in act one and unfolded in act two tends to dissolve in act three. The audience demands a worthy climax. It wants to applaud a wrap-up handed over on a glittery stage. Multiple curtain calls reward life-sized, not gigantic, stars. Each spectator expects to leave with a message of hope or new power bestowed by the play's magic. Your aim is to achieve that.

Real life and legal rights for women are not easy to portray. Drama resides in the pursuit and capture of legal rights. Moreover, neither plays nor laws are cast in concrete. Theatrical dialogue is open to new interpretations. Likewise, laws are amended, reinterpreted, repealed. Without changes, plays and laws would not serve their purpose. The legal rights drama will never be completed.

You, the working woman, need to use your talents in constructing, producing, staging, and directing scenes in the legal rights drama. The result can be acts played out wherever and whenever working women win a legal rights victory in the courts, legislatures, or workplaces of America.

This dynamic drama offers parts to novice and experienced players alike—opportunities to learn, to guide, and to lead.

The lights are dimming. The theater is hushed. Your turn begins.

ADDITIONAL INFORMATION SOURCES

Popular and semipopular books to fill you in on the historical perspective of women's legal rights (all available soft-bound):

BIRD, CAROLINE. *Enterprising Women*. New York: Mentor Books, 1976.

BLACKWELL, DR. ELIZABETH. *Pioneer Work in Opening the Medical Profession to Women*. New York: Schocken Books, 1977.

GRAY, DOROTHY. *Women of the West*. Millbrae, Calif.: Les Femmes, 1976.

GURKO, MIRIAM. *The Ladies of Seneca Falls: The Birth of the Woman's Rights Movement*. New York: Schocken Books, 1976.

HAHN, EMILY. *Once upon a Pedestal*. New York: Mentor/New American Library, 1974.

LERNER, GERDA. *The Grimke Sisters from South Carolina: Pioneers for Woman's Rights and Abolition*. New York: Schocken Books, 1975.

SMUTS, ROBERT. *Women and Work in America*. New York: Schocken Books, 1971.

STANTON, ELIZABETH CADY. *Eighty Years and More: Reminiscences 1815–1897*. New York: Schocken Books, 1971.

STEVENS, DORIS. *Jailed for Freedom: The Story of the Militant American Suffragist Movement*. New York: Schocken Books, 1976.

WELTER, BARBARA. (ed.). *The Woman Question in American History*. Hinsdale, Ill.: Dryden Press, 1973.

WERTHEIMER, BARBARA MAYER. *We Were There: The Story of Working Women in America*. New York: Pantheon, 1977.

NOTES

1. Robin Lakoff, *Language and Woman's Place* (New York: Harper/Colophon, 1975) gives rules for usage which help women present workplace concerns effectively. Chapter 2, "Talking Like a Lady," gives examples of language best avoided at work. Forms of women's language are summarized in pp. 53–57, while the topic is defined as "language restricted in use to women and language descriptive of women alone." It has, among its effects, that of suggesting "triviality in subject matter . . . uncertainty" (p. 7) and other inferior traits. Lakoff demonstrates that these linguistic imbalances "bring into sharper focus real-world imbalances and inequities," (p. 3). This is crystal clear on the playing fields of the workplace.

2. For instance, when a male supervisor is kept in the dark, as when you know he really wants to fire you and is seeking a cause which you refuse to supply, you can have a great time. Just find a new, superior job; then go to that evaluation interview where he expects you to be scared witless, and give a great dramatic performance. *You* know it's an act. Later, when you resign, all he can say is, "I wish I'd known earlier."

3. Chapter 9 of Caroline Bird's *Born Female* (New York: Pocketbooks, 1969) describes presidential actions in behalf of working women during several decades, in addition to presidential inaction. Information in the chapter relates working women's participation. See p. 162 for details of Lyndon B. Johnson's efforts. Higher education chronology appears in the footnote, pp. XXVII–XXVIII of Jessie Bernard, *Academic Women* (New York: Meridan/New American Library, 1974).

4. The quiz was taken by two groups of students plus their male and female coworkers. Two-thirds of the 227 participants were women. After trying the quiz, see Appendix A for the second report to quiz takers. Since then, some laws have been amended; some responses will have changed.

5. Margaret Hennig and Anne Jardim, in *The Managerial Woman* (Garden City, N.Y.: Anchor Press/Doubleday, 1977), tell "What Women Can Do" in Chapter 11, pp. 172–175.

6. John Flanagan, "Education's Contribution to the Quality of Life of a Sample of Thirty-Year-Olds," paper presented to the American Educational Research Association National Convention, Washington, D.C., March 31, 1975.

7. Sally Wendkos Olds, "Is His Money Your Money Too?" *Redbook* 149, no. 5 (September 1977): 120, 164–169.

8. *Ibid.*, p. 164.

The United States Senate pays its women workers 55% as much as it pays men, according to a report presented by the Capitol Hill Women's Caucus at a Senate hearing. This prompted Senator James Abourezk (D., S.D.) to comment that it is "the ultimate hypocrisy" for Congress to practice the same kind of job bias it has outlawed for the nation's employers."

California Women, July 1978, p. 3.

How much compensation is fair? What are you really worth? Your salary is a seal of approval, an index of your value to the organization you work for, but has little, if anything, to do with your worth as a human being.

RUTH HALCOMB, "How to Get a
Raise," Working Woman, June 1980.

The Scoreboard
fair employment practices and equal pay

FAIR EMPLOYMENT PRACTICES
AND EQUAL PAY

Mindset

This chapter is intended to make you sensitive to important distinctions between work life and work law. Some practices may shock you; they are the opposite of what the law endorses. An example concerns differential payment for men's and women's work.

The equal pay movement's course during half a century is provided in detail. You will consider recent attempts to change public opinion regarding the value of women's work. Such attempts to judge the inherent task value are gradually being included in interpretations of federal laws governing wages. The value of work question today encompasses equal pay, equitable pensions and comparable worth. These complex issues merit the attention of all working women. Choices for action are provided to help you move from thinking to doing something constructive about these issues.

Stage Setting

Institutionalized social customs, such as sex stereotypes and double standards, have powerful workplace effects. These effects are acutely felt by women workers where wages and job treatment are concerned. Employment unfairness is doubly serious in the United States, which equates personal worth with earning power. One may think such a standard is childish (that no woman could have dreamed it up); still, it exists. Determining a person's worth by earning power serves another purpose. It demeans the work women do and by contrast inflates the value of men's work. A more reasonable outlook would be to use importance of the task rather than sex of the worker as a measuring rod.

The chapter's governing concept is that all workers deserve equal job treatment and fair or equal wages for work performed. We will use the Equal Pay Act of 1963 (EPA) as our case history in examining background, current thrusts, and application of information presented.

Background on the Fair
Job Treatment Scene

Imagine that you worked with hundreds of women in a poorly lit loft. The hum of sewing machines was the only sound heard until someone's arm or hair got caught in a machine, or until something worse—something like the Triangle Shirtwaist Fire—happened:

> Workers at the Triangle Shirtwaist Company returned to work without a union agreement in February 1910. . . . The strike had been lost, largely because of the company's use of scabs. Two of their key demands, therefore, were never discussed with the firm: open, unlocked doors from the Triangle Factory on the seventh, eighth, and ninth floors of the Asch Building to the street; and fire escapes that worked.[1]

On March 25, 1911, 146 workers, mostly women, perished in the Triangle Shirtwaist Fire.

Safety precautions in American factories in 1911 were poor to nonexistent. Working women, who had learned political tactics during their struggle for acceptance as union members, waged an unending battle for occupational safety. They added a new dimension to the fight for working women's legal rights: the right to stay alive on the job. This demand was considered so outrageous that little was done to ensure its fulfillment.

Safety laws were enacted eventually, yet nothing changed. In 1958, barely half a mile from the Triangle Shirtwaist Fire site, another conflagration took the lives of 24 women workers who either jumped to their deaths or were incinerated.[2] The alarm had not been sent in promptly. The building, in violation of the city code, lacked a sprinkler system and had nonfunctioning fire escapes.

Between these preventable, senseless tragedies, some progress was registered by two New Yorkers: Franklin Delano Roosevelt and Frances Perkins, who were powerful enough to affect our national scene.

Fair Labor Standards Act of 1938: A Giant Step Toward Fairness

The struggle for job fairness got a big boost with enactment of the Fair Labor Standards Act of 1938 (FLSA) during FDR's presidency while Frances Perkins was Secretary of Labor. This act began regulation of minimum wages, overtime pay (time and a half for each hour worked beyond the 40-hour work week), equal pay, recordkeeping, child labor standards, and the concept of willful violations of the law.

Figure 2–1 presents the equal pay provisions, recovery of back pay, and other enforcement aspects of FLSA. The material is worth reading.

The FLSA acknowledged in law that working women needed pro-

FIGURE 2–1 Fair Labor Standards Act of 1938*

EQUAL PAY PROVISIONS

The equal pay provisions of the Fair Labor Standards Act apply to all employees subject to the minimum wage provisions of the Act and to every establishment where such workers are employed, as well as to executive, administrative, professional and outside sales personnel.

The provisions prohibit an employer from discriminating on the basis of sex by paying employees of one sex at rates lower than those paid to employees of the opposite sex in the same establishment, for doing equal work on jobs requiring equal skill, effort and responsibility and performed under similar working conditions.

For purposes of comparison under the equal pay provisions, jobs need only be substantially equal—not identical. Moroever, jobs may be compared where employees of one sex are employed to do substantially the same work formerly done by employees of the opposite sex.

A wage differential between men and women may be justified where it can be shown that the differential is based on a bona fide seniority system, merit system, system of measuring earnings by quantity or quality of production, or any other job-related factor other than sex.

The law prohibits any labor organization, or its agents, representing the employees of any employer with workers subject to the equal pay provisions, from causing or attempting to cause the employer to discriminate against an employee in violation of the equal pay provisions.

The law also prohibits an employer from reducing the wage rate of any employee in order to eliminate a prohibited wage differential.

RECOVERY OF BACK PAY

Under the Act, these methods of recovering unpaid minimum and/or overtime wages are provided:

1. The Division may supervise payment of back wages.

2. The Secretary of Labor may bring suit for back pay and an equal amount as liquidated damages.

3. An employee may sue for back wages and an additional sum, up to the amount of back pay, as liquidated damages, plus attorney's fees and court costs.

4. The Secretary of Labor may obtain an injunction to restrain any person from violating the law, including the unlawful withholding of proper minimum wage and overtime compensation.

An employee may not bring suit if he or she has been paid back wages under supervision of the Division or if the Secretary has filed suit to recover the wages due to him or her.

A two-year statute of limitations applies to the recovery of back wages, except in the case of willful violations for which there is a three-year statute of limitations.

25

tection of their legal rights which otherwise might not be respected. Figure 2–1 spells out the equal pay protections of FLSA as amended. A series of amendments (in 1961, 1966, 1972, and 1974) expanded coverage and revised definitions, thus bringing the majority of working women under FLSA protection.

The power of commanding an equal wage for "doing equal work on jobs requiring equal skill, effort, responsibility and performed under similar working conditions" should have been a boon to American working women. However, in 1939, when FLSA became effective, few jobs were available.

Nevertheless, FLSA was enabling, precedent-setting legislation, which stated that "jobs need only be substantially equal—not identical."

Further, when the sex of the workers doing a job changed—for instance, promoting men and replacing them with women—the jobs remained comparable; it became illegal to pay the new workers less than the former workers had received. An employer could no longer get cheap labor simply by hiring women (instead of men) for a job category and remain within the law.

Allowable wage differentials, by sex, were those based upon a good faith "seniority system, merit system, system of measuring earnings by quantity or quality of production, or any job-related factor other than sex." It sounds almost ideal. But how does this all function in real work life for the individual working woman? An example may shed some useful light.

Example: Some Personal Experience

Like most female employees, I was covered by FLSA but didn't know it when the events related took place. I had worked hard and well for the organization and loved my job even after my male boss was forced to resign. He was replaced by an unprepared, ineffective man who lacked the training to supervise my highly specialized work. The new boss refused to perform the required annual evaluation. But he did ask me to sign the evaluation prepared by my former boss. I was told that my signature only meant that I had read the evaluation and did not signify agreement with it. The new boss said, "That's a terrible annual evaluation."

Comparison of my evaluations for the current year and prior years revealed the newer evaluation's clear superiority. I know now that the second evaluation represented correct evaluation game playing: praise improvements over last year, encourage continued superior performance, suggest constructive activities. The new boss refused to play by these rules. Infuriated, and without guidelines for future performance, I retreated into planning my vacation, but I continued doing my work.

Returning from vacation, I found a contract accompanied by a sheet explaining that salaries had been computed by using an across-the-board percentage plus a merit increment. My calculator verified that I had not gotten any merit increment. Something was really wrong, since at no time during my stay had I gotten any complaints about my work.

My first thought was, "You don't need to let them do this to you." I called a lawyer for advice. My idea was to obtain information from someone knowledgeable and objective. I hoped the lawyer would be such a person.

The lawyer said a lot about how long it takes to get a case heard, what it costs, what kinds of legal rights cases are likely to succeed in court, and problems of getting court decisions enforced. While none of the comments related to FLSA or equal pay, the lawyer's advice was very helpful. Her best advice was to find another job.

The lawyer agreed to see me, however, and at our meeting she advised me not to sign the new contract for two reasons: signing it would signify my agreement and would bind me to its conditions, and that could be awkward if I accepted a new job. We also set up a series of memos, which I sent to my boss.

These memos, plus replies received, revealed a bad faith merit system. That means merit increments were subjectively, not objectively, determined. They were based on popularity (and political savvy), not upon productivity or organizational service. Some managers stated that the four most meritorious employees had received the highest awards (a $1000 increment), as follows: the first person "to bring his salary into line with competitive places," the second "because we couldn't give her an appropriate raise last year," the third "to keep the old VP's pay higher than the newly appointed VP's pay," and the fourth "because the president likes her." Almost unbelievable! My memos had respectfully inquired about the specific criteria used to judge my effectiveness. I received no substantive answers. Nevertheless, I truly enjoyed asking about the criteria used. Thus, merit increments functioned in that workplace as a kind of political patronage and were in direct violation of FLSA.[3]

I could have told my employers, "You don't have a bona fide merit system, and you cannot demonstrate that you do." I might have gotten a piddling merit increment (the lowest increment that year was $250). The male administrators would have backed down, paid up, and resented me mightily. By calling their bluff, I would have given them a real cause. They would have closed their ranks and their ears.

I could have used a different legal tactic. It might have been fun. But in those days I was not all that sophisticated. You, however, may find it interesting.

FLSA Penalty Provisions

FLSA could have dealt with situations similar to mine in another precedent-setting way. FLSA extended the statute of limitations to three years for recovery of back wages "in the case of willful violation." The concept of a greater penalty for willful than for nonwillful violation of the law was later incorporated into the Equal Pay Act of 1963, where intentional flouting of the law gets a stiffer penalty where payment to workers is the issue.

My boss, his boss, and the organization could have been brought to the bar for that. Using differential criteria for judging who gets the merit rewards is intentional, a willful act; it is the essence of inequality, exemplifying the bad faith merit system.

A bad faith merit system can operate to exclude, if not to punish, working women who do not fit into the stereotype of the manageable, well-behaved, good little girl. The willful violation of FLSA by use of that merit system thus was discriminatory. So was the parceling out of those merit increments: women received theirs (or didn't receive them) for behaviors different from those leading to rewards for males. Playing the game (male) and being pretty and malleable (female) during that year averaged out to $650 in merit increments. Alas, I didn't find out what the game was in time. I wasn't even on the playing field, let alone batting my eyelashes. I left the arena, got another job, and felt I had learned a lot from my personal experience.

At one time or another the majority of working women have suffered a similar fate. They have not accurately sized up the playing field. They also probably do not know that FLSA is part of the legal umbrella protecting them.

Or maybe they are outside FLSA's protection as is the Congress and its nearly 20,000 employees. The Congress exempted itself and its workers from the FLSA and the Equal Pay Act.

Example: Playing "The Emperor's New Clothes"

On the other hand, the country's largest employer, the federal government, is covered by all of the laws. The federal government states that equal pay and equal opportunity in its Civil Service antedate the federal laws. They do, on paper.[4] However, records document great need for improvement in Civil Service implementation. Although a few women in high government service classifications are featured as evidence of progressive federal government employment policies, approximately half of all government employees in the bottom third of the Civil Service ratings are women; yet roughly one-third of all federal employees are women. Something is amiss.

Federal government employees are located throughout the country and abroad. This has made it difficult for federally employed women to establish and maintain the cohesiveness necessary to effect and assimilate beneficial changes. Further, women employees work in many fields. The scientists and engineers work where the federal government has an embarrassingly poor record for promoting job equality and equal pay according to a National Science Foundation Survey based on 1977 data. A group of federally employed women in science confirmed the report's findings.

Women government workers have now organized to achieve equality with male coworkers. Their groups have scrutinized job entry qualifications that require college degrees when the work does not demand skills only taught in college (whatever such skills might be). Federally Employed Women (FEW) is one support group that may be contacted for current action agendas and other information. The address is given at the end of this chapter.

The federal government is not the only FLSA/EPA offender. Alas, union leaders have frequently been followers when it comes to fair job treatment for women. Working women did better in the International Ladies Garment Workers Union than in most unions. The outcome of successful clashes was that, while women's salaries improved, they invariably remained lower than those of male workers. Change inevitably takes place. It may be that one day we will be able to see the emperor's new clothes, and if we choose we can then behave like empresses. One assist, to hasten the day, is described in the next section.

Fair Employment Practices Commissions: How They Work and Can Work for You

In early 1941, another step toward fair job treatment resulted from political pressure—pressure not exerted by working women. A union leader seeking improvement in pay and job opportunities for black male union members promoted all workers' welfare by his action. A. Philip Randolph, who had affiliated his union with the formerly white American Federation of Labor, informed President Roosevelt that he was ready to march on Washington with his thousands of jobless, Depression-weary black union members to protest the New Deal's failure to provide for their employment. President Roosevelt quickly issued an executive order forbidding discrimination in defense industries and government bureaus, and created the Committee on Fair Employment Practice. This committee was the forerunner of state commissions, the Fair Employment Practices Commissions (FEPC), found in 1973 in 41 states.[5]

Today there are federal laws covering a host of potentially explosive employment circumstances; likewise, there is much useful state legislation. Are you aware of the merits of state legal aid in cases of unfair employment practices?

There may be advantages to the local approach to unfair job treatment. Practicing lawyers are both location-bound and specialty-bound. Each is expert in a legal field as it applies within a jurisdiction, such as a state. Some state laws in neighboring states differ; others are identical. Identical state laws are usually based on the same federal laws; laws that differ tend to have statewide application or to be those delegated by the state to its smaller units (counties or municipalities). How might the local approach help you in an instance of unfair job treatment?

Suppose your department had posted a job opportunity. You applied, ready for this promotion to unit supervisor since you had taken additional training. You were interviewed, but the job went to a 19-year-old male high school graduate. He found you motherly and confided his plan to "learn what the job was all about." He said he needed your help. While you smouldered, this coworker announced that the job interviewer had remarked that he had no intention of "promoting any damned-broads to unit supervisor." To make matters worse, this new, inexperienced unit supervisor was already being paid $1800 a year more than you were earning after three and a half years. Your burn speeded up; it felt like heartburn.

You called a lawyer, told your story, and asked, "Have I got a case?" You meant, "Do I need a lawyer?" You wanted the odds on getting a legal remedy for sex-related job discrimination. While the lawyer made suggestions, you began to learn the necessary legal vocabulary. In legal matters, the right words open doors and produce action. Such words must be used sparingly and at the right time; employers are sensitive to legal words, too. If you can tell an employer that he violated your right to due process, though he will hardly be delighted with you, he may attempt a remedy. Thus, that call to the lawyer, even if no legal action was recommended, provided you with practical information about handling your situation and gave you some choice words for later use. The lawyer may also have referred you to a federal agency.

If your state has an FEPC, you might be able to work directly through that agency. Your lawyer may have referred you to the FEPC because it is experienced in handling cases like yours. In states having small populations and few large cities, an FEPC may be the most efficient way to get action on your case. The backlog of complaints may be small, so handling of your charge may begin relatively quickly. (Relatively quickly in the law is not the same as relatively quickly in life.) However, it may take years to finish. Therefore, another advantage to utilizing the FEPC is your ability to monitor your charge. You would regularly remind your contacts at the FEPC of your interest and desire for results.

The FEPC will educate you and keep you current on legal rights for working women and aware of changes in your state law relating to employment discrimination. Some state FEPCs can initiate complaints in their own name. Can yours? It's a good question to ask. If yours can, why hasn't your charge been settled?

You'll need to know the scope of your state's FEPC, and you'll be interested in all laws that might bear on an employment problem involving you. For instance, consider the recent rash of cases in which overweight persons have been denied employment. Overweight persons are covered by legislation protecting the handicapped and prohibiting employment discrimination against them. An overweight woman can now aim two legal arrows at her employer: sex discrimination and discrimination against a handicapped person. Unquestionably, the more legal pressure that can be brought to bear, the more likely it is that the employee will achieve fair job treatment.

As we noted earlier, FEPCs were not originally established to deal with working women's complaints of unfair job treatment. FEPCs generally began with provisions for the "investigation and processing of employment discrimination charges based on race, color, religion, national origin and ancestry."[6] As new federal laws were enacted, FEPCs began to reflect them. Sex discrimination in employment was forbidden. The FEPC was extended to cover smaller employers (those with 15 or more employees), and protection was offered to the handicapped.

The FEPC is a big help to working women, as we have seen. But it is only fair to add that the FEPC has some disadvantages. First, the FEPC tends to be more conservative in interpretation of the same legal principles than the federal government, which may mean refusal of your charge, which may in turn mean that your best route to on-the-job justice is the lawyer.[7] Second, you may have to undergo personal incovenience to present your charge (and then it may not be accepted). Some states provide in-person, in-depth interviews that seem more like a modern-day Spanish Inquisition lacking only the Iron Maiden.[8] You may be required to present evidence backing your charge: names, dates, places, concrete evidence (memos, etc.). Third, you may be treated so impersonally that you freeze. You may have a strong case yet present it weakly (and it may not be accepted) because you find the procedure intimidating. If this might happen, having a lawyer handle your charge may be the best strategy.

Matters may be more complex if you work in a state without an FEPC. With one exception, North Dakota, states recently lacking FEPCs were southern states. But don't despair. If your state lacks an FEPC, there are federal legal remedies available to help resolve your sex-related employment discrimination problem. But now we'll look at Illinois' FEPC procedure, which parallels that found in federal laws. Illinois makes it illegal for employers, employment agencies, or labor unions to engage in discriminatory practices related to employment. Most prohibited aspects are beyond the employee's control; one cannot choose one's sex, race, or national origin. The FEPC reasoning seems to be that society must take responsibility for production of discrimination rather than addi-

FIGURE 2–2 How FEPC Works

FAIR EMPLOYMENT PRACTICES ARE REQUIRED BY LAW IN ILLINOIS*

It is ILLEGAL if, for reasons of your race, color, sex, national origin or ancestry, physical or mental handicaps unrelated to ability, less than honorable discharge from military service, or arrest record:

An EMPLOYER discriminates by

- Refusing to interview, hire, or promote you;
- Denying you equal pay or privileges or conditions of employment due you;
- Discharging, demoting, or disciplining you.

An EMPLOYMENT AGENCY discriminates by

- Withholding full and equal services from you;
- Refusing to refer or place you.

A LABOR UNION discriminates by

- Denying you membership or training;
- Denying you equal treatment in referrals for work;
- Refusing to fairly represent you in a grievance.

HOW FEPC WORKS

When you file a charge with the Commission:

- Your charge is assigned to an investigator.
- The investigator will hold a conference with both you and the other party present. The purpose of the conference is to find out the facts of the case and attempt to reach a just settlement to which all parties can agree.
- If your case is not settled at the conference, the investigator will gather any additional evidence needed to reach a decision.
- If the investigation does not reveal evidence to support your charge, it will be dismissed.
- If the Commission does find substantial evidence to support your charge, it will notify you and the other party and again attempt to settle the case through conciliation.

SOME EXAMPLES OF EMPLOYMENT PRACTICES THAT THE COMMISSION HAS FOUND TO BE DISCRIMINATORY ARE:

- A black female filed a charge alleging that she was discriminatorily denied employment because she and her husband had been the subject of a wage deduction order and other family financial problems. The Commission agreed with the complainant because of case law establishing that an employer's reliance on credit problems as a bar to employment may have the effect of discriminating against minority groups much more frequently than non-minorities.

- A white male applied for a job as a factory assembler, but was rejected because he had been arrested previously. The man had not been convicted. The Commission found this to be a violation of the FEP Act which states that an employer cannot ask about an applicant's arrests.

- A female complainant filed charges alleging sex discrimination when she

FIGURE 2-2 (Continued)

FAIR EMPLOYMENT PRACTICES ARE REQUIRED BY LAW IN ILLINOIS*

It is also ILLEGAL for an EMPLOYER, EMPLOYMENT AGENCY, or LABOR UNION to treat you unfairly because:

- You have previously filed a charge of discrimination and/or
- You have openly opposed a practice which you believed was discriminatory and/or
- You have assisted, given testimony, or been a witness in a discrimination charge.

HOW FEPC WORKS

- If settlement proves impossible, the Commission will issue a formal complaint and there will be a public hearing at which both sides may be represented by counsel and have an opportunity to state their cases publicly with full protection of the law. The hearing will be before an Administrative Law Judge who, after studying all the evidence, will render a decision and recommend to the Commission an order resolving the case.

- The Commission will then review the Administrative Law Judge's decision and recommended order. The parties may file written pleadings and appear before the Commission to argue for or in opposition to the Administrative Law Judge's decision. The Commission will then reach a final decision in the case, which will be in writing and served upon all parties.

SOME EXAMPLES OF EMPLOYMENT PRACTICES THAT THE COMMISSION HAS FOUND TO BE DISCRIMINATORY ARE:

learned that the man who had previously held her job was paid more than she. After an investigation, the Commission found that the complainant had greater skills and qualifications than the man she replaced. Moreover, the complainant was paid less than other men performing the same duties. The employer could not give good reasons as to why this had happened and the Commission ordered back pay and salary equalization for the complainant.

- An employer refused to promote a minority male because he did not have a college degree. The man filed a complaint with the Commission charging that he was discriminated against because of his race. The Commission found that strict degree requirements have a discriminatory effect against minority persons, who tend to lack degrees in greater numbers than nonminorities, and the employer was

- If the final decision is in your favor, the Commission will order a remedy which will correct the wrong committed against you and prevent it from happening again. Typical remedies include: being hired for a job or promoted, receiving union membership, given referral by a union or employment agency, getting back pay or seniority, and an agreement by the other party to take whatever action is necessary to prevent discrimination.

- Orders issued by the Commission can be enforced in court.

not able to show that the degree requirement was necessary to perform the job well. It therefore sustained the complainant.

- A woman with epilepsy applied for an office job. Despite the fact that she was well qualified and provided a doctor's statement that her seizures were under control, the company did not hire her. The company stated that she might have a seizure and upset her co-workers. The woman was entitled to the job and the pay she lost while not holding the job.

*From "How to Exercise Your Rights under the Illinois Fair Employment Practices Act," (Springfield, Ill. Illinois Fair Employment Practices Commission, June, 1978).

tionally burden the individual already suffering from society's rejection and stigma. Figure 2–2 outlines the Illinois requirements.

In the left-hand column, we note that in Illinois prime violators of fair employment practices have been singled out for special attention. Notice that employment agencies and labor unions have been cited for unfair employment practices. Notice also how prohibited employment practices can occur. View each discrimination cited in the context of the ground rules.

If your employer fires you for failing to perform the minimum amount of work stipulated in your job description and for doing badly what is completed, you are not likely to have legal recourse. If your employer discharges you when you have done a superb job and several witnesses hear him say, "The only thing worse than having to hire women is having to hire handicapped old women and then promote them," you are likely to have a justified complaint.

Likewise, a charge could be made against an employer who refused to promote an employee because she was a woman, or because she was overweight and would be seen by the public if placed in the new position. Further, unfair treatment because a woman has stated her opposition to a practice that appeared illegal to her is illegal. She is entitled to inquire, "Why aren't there any saleswomen in the field?"

Finally, if you do file a complaint with an FEPC, it is illegal for your employer to treat you unfairly afterward. If he does, he may be in big trouble (with your help). On the other hand, as an employee, you are in the workplace to work, not to bait your employer.

The Action Sequence

Check Your Charge. If you are certain that your employment sex discrimination charge is valid and you want to work it out through testing the law, your first move is to call the nearest FEPC office in your state to check. Should you then wish to complain, make an appointment to file a charge, after inquiring how to do so. You must file within 180 days of the discriminatory action. The 180 days would begin on the day of the complaint or violation.

File quietly. You would go about filing your charge quietly, not revealing your plans to anyone at work. This is admittedly difficult. We all want support when we are about to do something scary, containing a large measure of the unknown. But consider that if somebody informs your employer, he will change a few of his ways temporarily, and your justified complaint is likely to be dismissed. The employer will have other ways of retaliating for what will be considered your disloyalty. So your best approach is your weapon of surprise; retain it. This sounds like battle strategy and it is.[9] You are battling for your livelihood and justice; your employer, with superior fire power, is battling for the status quo. The mediating force, once you get it started, is the FEPC.

Interview and investigation.   If your complaint falls within FEPC guidelines, the in-depth interview would take place. Your charge would then be given to an investigator, who would hold a conference with you and with your employer to achieve a satisfactory resolution of the charge. Ideally, all parties should be committed to work together to remove the unfair employment practice. If they are unable to cooperate, or if they demonstrate bad faith, the FEPC can issue orders that can be enforced in court.

Fight and stay strategy.   When a working woman has determined to see her justified complaint resolved, there is something more that she needs to know. "Tell her," said a friend who had been through it and emerged victorious, "Don't fight if you plan to leave." My friend won her case in 1974. She explained that if you start the furor and then quit, you leave the smouldering embers of bad feelings. These bad feelings will follow you the way flame travels down a fuse; meanwhile, they have negative effects on the women who remain and may become victims of unfair employment practices. "Furthermore, if you leave," she continued, "you don't get any reward. All you get is the inconvenience of having to look for another job or some time on unemployment compensation, and you may end up in a worse place than the one you were in." Her conclusion is obvious: Starting something you don't finish may hurt you.

My friend was indicating that determination to see the issue through signals development of a thick skin and some objectivity. These attributes frighten opponents and make your victory more likely. If you also know how to use your legal assets, you are likely to win, as she did. She merely made the motions, but she did not have to go to court or even beyond the conciliation conference. Her employer paid up handsomely; she received a promotion and a salary adjustment and continued to perform in her constructive, creative manner. She had, and used, the goods. That was her choice for action.

One must remember that employers want neither the adverse publicity nor to be taken into court on an unfair employment charge. Working women tend to underestimate the power they hold in that.

However, things have changed for working women. Currently, when an injured employee seeks expert advice (from an affirmative action officer or lawyer), she is asked, "What would it take to make you whole? What remedy are you seeking? What is the best thing for you to do next?" Such thinking has led to a completely different strategy for working women with unfair employment treatment complaints.

Fight-and-fly strategy. Your cost of staying and fighting employment discrimination may be too high. Your cost must be calculated in dollars, energy, stress, psychological welfare, and career alternatives. Sometimes the healthiest, most economical move is to cut your losses and leave. But that doesn't mean you must give up your complaint.

If you have been dismissed or nonpromoted (thus have lost your job), if you have offered to negotiate and your employers refuse, if you have been offered a demotion without cause, you would be sensible to depart. Either there is no place for you at the old stand, or you'd be miserable (and foolish) if you remained.

If you feel that the discriminatory action has given you a push toward a new career, take a chance on yourself—go after it. If you are almost brand new to the organization or are at entry level, consider a lateral move. And if your rank is so high that no other women are within several levels of yours, seriously consider a lateral move to a larger organization. In these situations, you can improve your career possibilities by initiating constructive action. Staying put, by contrast, will probably get you little other than grief-laden "security." If you do not trust your supervisors and any of the situations outlined is similar to yours, set a deadline date for farewells (do this mentally) and then begin to clean your desk. But you needn't forget about your employment discrimination complaint.

A partial example may be of interest. A thoroughly professional career woman accepted an executive position. She was delighted with it, dug in, and produced. By the second year, her boss had swamped her with trivia, which she goodnaturedly waded through. However, she gradually became aware that she had been set up as a token woman and to fail. The third year, nasty politics were clearly controlling her outcomes and those of her boss. Things came to a head too late for her to obtain an appropriate job in her field (which had a fixed hiring calendar). As a consolation prize, she was offered a new, low-status position that was totally unacceptable. Attempts at negotiating with her boss were fruitless. If you had been this working woman, what would you have done?

Her lawyers heard all of the details and advised her to consider a suit with hefty damages. "Paying money is what they understand. It makes them stop discriminating for a little while, which gives other women employees there a chance. And even if you don't win, they hate the publicity of being charged with sex discrimination by their highest-ranking woman. Besides, you don't even have to be there. You can go on with your career in the meantime."

The point is well taken. Sometimes the best course is to cut your losses, get a change of scene, be seen elsewhere, and avoid the bitterness and resentment that can poison even a saint who is a victim of employment and/or sex discrimination and then must stay and take it.

But whichever option is chosen—to stay or to leave—there is still another hurdle. It has to do with on-the-job confrontation tactics.

***What to Say* strategy.** Keep the game rules in mind. When an employee, a team member, must demonstrate to the world that the team doesn't play by the rules, team managers panic and do unpredictable things.[10] If you point out violations with the FEPC at your side, your employer may try additional unfair plays. There may be bribes and promises of promotions if you withdraw your complaint. A safe answer is, "Put it in writing." If they do, that's fine. Usually, their offer remains talk, so stand your ground. Sooner or later, the team manager will capitulate—agree to play by the rules and pay the penalties incurred for past errors—or will violate one more fair employment regulation, and you may have had your decision made to go to court.

CASE STUDY: THE EQUAL PAY ACT OF 1963

Most women who have gotten relief from unfair employment practices have fought against financial inequalities. Money is important, and men have gotten a disproportionate share of it. But before we study a federal law enacted to correct monetary inequalities in the workplace, let's review some related critical issues.

Among consequences of traditional ideas about the value of women's work are occupational sex segregation and large differences in earnings by sex.[11] Occupational segregation has pushed women into low-prestige, low-skilled, poorly compensated "women's" jobs. These are dead-end jobs not requiring additional skills and offering no mobility. Far less frequently routed into dead-end occupations, males are encouraged to seek challenging jobs; they tend to fill positions that offer opportunities dependent upon increased skills or that provide greater economic rewards as experience increases.

Sometimes women label their dead-end job "careers" in a misguided effort to gain equal compensation. Women also tend to rely upon overqualification in attempts to reach equal pay. Nevertheless, even when women have more education and experience than men doing the same job, they have still been paid less. If that happened to you, how did you feel?

While you recall your feelings, you might be interested to learn that an explanation given for unequal pay was that men felt threatened by the equal pay idea.[12] An index of this threat felt by males is found in women's wages. In the United States in 1978, women earned $0.57 for every $1.00 earned by men.[13] In 1978, working women's share of the work dollar was smaller than in earlier years when typical families had only a male breadwinner. These figures make a strong comment about how American society values women's work.[14] (See Figure 2–3.) However, there are laws designed to correct the value and wage differentials. The Equal Pay Act of 1963 (EPA) amended the FLSA so that men and women doing the same work must be paid equally. The EPA is unique in focusing solely on sex-based employment discrimination.[15] It was amended in 1972 and 1974 to extend its coverage. It specifically prohibits:

> Any discrimination* in wages (including overtime, sick and vacation pay) and fringe benefits (including health and life insurance, pension and other retirement benefits,** profit-sharing and bonus plans, credit union benefits) which is based on sex.[16]

> *Wage systems which result in unequal pay rates but are based on a merit system, a seniority system that measures earnings by the quality or quantity of production or any other factor than sex are not covered by the Act. (However, each of these systems must be applied equally to men and women.)

> **Employers are permitted to maintain fringe benefit policies which have a differential effect on persons because of their pay, if equal contributions are made for both groups.

Basic Provisions of the Equal Pay Act, Defined

The EPA requires that men and women performing equal work in the same establishment under similar conditions must receive the same pay if

FIGURE 2-3 "I agree, it's really outrageous . . . it's only 38 percent."
Paul Szep, *The Boston Globe*.

their jobs require equal skill, equal effort, and equal responsibility. A more precise definition of these terms is necessary.

First, the jobs need not be identical for comparison under EPA. Janitorial services furnished by men and cleaning services furnished by women in hospitals, schools, and business buildings can be compared in *any* building. Second, equal skill, equal effort, and equal responsibility are spelled out. Factors such as training, experience, education, and ability are evaluated as they apply to performance of a specific job to establish the equal skill qualification. To determine whether equal effort is expended for performance of a specific job, measurements of physical and mental exertion are made. Third, equal responsibility concerns the dependence of the employer upon the employee's performance and upon the importance of the job obligation. Equal responsibility, as defined, is one of the most subjective aspects of EPA.

All of the tests—equal work, equal skill, equal effort, and equal responsibility—have to be met for the equal pay standard to be applicable.[17] Cases have been tried involving janitors and cleaning women, saleswomen and salesmen in department stores, male and female press operators in a machine shop, librarians (female) and university faculty (mostly male), and clerical workers (female) and physical plant workers (male), among others. These examples indicate coverage scope.[18]

Are You Covered by EPA?

As a rule of thumb, if you are paid according to the minimum wage law, your employer is covered by EPA and therefore you are. So are employees of public and private educational institutions at all levels, regardless of whether the institution receives federal funds.[19] Thus, employees of pre-schools are included. Executives, administrators, professional employees, and salespeople were included by the 1972 extensions.

Some employees are exempt from EPA coverage. They include:

Military personnel; State and local elected public officials and their staffs; appointed policy-making officials; Employees of seasonal recreational centers; Switchboard employees of small telephone companies (less than 750 stations); Domestic workers who work less than 8 hours a week, or earn less than $50 during a three month period; Babysitters, part-time companions who work occasionally.[20]

Coverage thus includes all classifications and types of work.

As a working woman, you are probably covered by EPA. Supposing you had a complaint in 1977, what could you have done? Figure 2–4 gives some relief measures. If you had consulted them, and the Wage and Hour Division had concluded that you had been discriminated against, your chances of receiving a satisfactory judgment would have been high.

The Department of Labor's Wage and Hour Division, in its administration of EPA, had a small backlog of employee complaints, selected complaints for action carefully (those coinciding equals we described above are a hard test to pass), and in about 90 percent of them complainants were awarded back pay or wage increases or both voluntarily. In instances where there was no voluntary compliance, the division could sue in the complainant's behalf.

FIGURE 2–4 Getting Some Equal Pay Act Complaint Action

1. I could have telephoned, written to, or appeared at the closest office of:

   The Wage and Hour Division
   Department of Labor

   No special form was needed for my complaint.
2. I could have gotten someone else to complain in my behalf.
3. I could have had my complaint investigated within three months of the time I filed it.
4. My name would not have been revealed as the complainant.
5. I could have hired a lawyer and filed a suit against my employer. If I had won the suit, under the EPA, I could have been awarded attorney's fees by the court.

The distinction mentioned under FLSA between willful and nonwillful discrimination was retained under EPA. Employees would have three years to file for a complaint of willful discrimination and two years for a complaint of nonwillful discrimination. There would be no time limit on filing if an employer continued the sex-discriminatory wage policy that led to your complaint. Stiffer penalties to the willfully discriminating employer include more back pay from time of filing the complaint (three years for a willful violation of EPA, two years for nonwillful violations).

Finally, EPA requires employers to keep records and to grant the government access to these records. Thus, the employer can conceivably be required to divulge self-damaging information when an EPA complaint is filed. The employer is, in effect, forced to police the organization to root out EPA violations. Apparently, few employers have thought about these potential consequences of the EPA recordkeeping provisions. Paying workers in accord with the law emerges as an economical alternative to employment sex discrimination in wages.

Change in EPA Enforcement Agency

On July 1, 1979, the administration and enforcement of EPA was shifted from the Wage and Hour Division of the Department of Labor, where its record of achievements for women was unmatched, to the Equal Employment Opportunities Commission (EEOC). (See Chapter 3.) Admittedly, both the number of cases investigated and the number awaiting action under EPA as administered by the Wage and Hour Division had been small, and while favorable settlements were the rule, collection of back pay and other awards did not invariably take place.[21] Nevertheless, EPA under the Wage and Hour Division provided a refuge for individual working women who had sex-based discrimination problems. It may now be that individual working women whose complaints fall under EPA will have to go directly to a lawyer (rather than to a federal enforcement agency) and pursue justice through the courts. Enforcement of EPA may get lost under the new system administered by EEOC. A working woman trying to fight sex discrimination when she is paid less than the man at the next desk may have to rely more heavily on her wits and knowledge than she did before July 1, 1979.

A working woman wanting to end wage inequalities must understand how the legal establishment views the equal pay issue in the 1980s. Equal pay no longer is merely a matter of paying men and women the same hourly rate for the same work. Court tests have expanded and deepened the concept of equal pay; the EPA as stretched by legal interpretations and precedents now is concerned with highly complex cases.

Changes in the EPA are likewise related to the shift in compliance agency already alluded to. It is hoped that administration by the EEOC will enable still broader issues to be addressed, thereby eventually benefitting all working women.

CURRENT THRUSTS: PARRYING CHANGES

The pay equality issues of the 1980s—wage gap, comparable worth, pensions, and fringe benefits—represent new thrusts with respect to the Equal Pay Act. Changes in the composition of the workforce (women now outnumber men) and its qualifications (more women are highly qualified and all fields include some qualified women) since enactment of EPA have brought modifications in its interpretation. Removing sex-based discrimination from hourly wages is no longer the central issue. American women expect to devote major segments of their adulthood to the workplace; many of them are heads of households equally concerned with wages and: (1) job fairness and advancement, (2) planning decisions about pensions (how to obtain and manage them effectively), and (3) fringe benefits (how to learn about, become eligible for, and utilize them). Without information about how comparability of work is assessed, about how pensions and fringe benefits are accorded, working women are at a disadvantage. At the same time, the older wage inequality issue continues to require vigilance, monitoring, and elimination wherever instances surface.

So, in the 1980s, the EPA is attempting to provide equity across a larger landscape, one with a complex and varied terrain.

But no matter how complex, pay issues—what one is worth in the marketplace—and their relationship to gender are emotional dynamite. Don't be surprised if you overreact to the initial impact of documentation of pay inequity. Rage over injustice and unfairness is a normal response; digesting emotionally unpalatable information is a slow process demanding fortitude and great discipline. However, the ostrich pose is futile. Crudely put, refusal to face the problem and solve it—putting one's head in the sand—leaves the nether regions up in a highly vulnerable position. After problem recognition, you might reflect on how much productivity you've wasted through fury or depression. Then you are ready to start using your workplace energies more effectively.

The first thrust we examine is to promote equal pay for the same work regardless of the worker's sex.

The Wage Gap

The wage gap is the most obvious sign of pay discrimination based on sex. The definition of wage discrimination specifically prohibited such actions as (1) changing titles of jobs so that men can be paid more than women for the same work and (2) reduction of the higher (the man's) wage to the level of the lower (the woman's) wage. Such illegal, but common, practices contribute to continuation of wage discrimination and produce the wage gap. Figure 2–5 presents a wage gap example from the banking industry. Discrimination charges against Harris Bank were originally filed in 1974 and were updated in 1976.[22] Appearing slow to many working women, the legal deliberation has continued through 1980. Two noteworthy things occurred during the interval of deliberation. First, the Harris Bank made money from use of U.S. government funds on deposit there. Harris Bank lent those funds to businesses, earning interest on them. U.S. government funds are public funds; taxpayers contribute to them and the citizens own them. Yet few became indignant about permitting banks to profit from U.S. government funds while deliberation about violation of a federal law was in process. Second, should it be necessary for a group of working women to point out violations of EPA and to devote more than six years to litigation? Further, from the filing of charges against Harris Bank until settlement favoring the working women, men and women doing the same job received different pay. Harris Bank women were thus doubly penalized. They earned less than men doing the

FIGURE 2–5 The Harris Bank Case: Precedent for Equal Opportunity in Banking*

The multi-million dollar discrimination case against Harris Bank will finally be decided early in 1980. The formal hearing which was completed this fall was the culmination of a five-year campaign by Women Employed to achieve equal opportunity at Harris. The case will set a precedent for the entire banking industry.

THE FACTS OF THE CASE

The case involves discrimination in hiring, training, job placement, salary levels, and rates of promotion. It used to be a common practice at Harris to hire women with college degrees into clerical positions while they offered men with degrees access to training programs and career positions. Regardless of educational background, women were initially placed in less desirable jobs than men, and now find that they have not reached the position or salary that they would have attained without discrimination. Training programs were finally opened to women, but the training they received was inferior. Their assignments were mostly clerical, leaving them unqualified in the eyes of the bank for placement in better positions.

In general, women and minorities at Harris have remained in departments and job classifications that are lower paying and offer fewer opportunities for advancement than their white male counterparts have.

THE HISTORY AND STATUS OF THE CASE

In 1974, Women Employed began receiving complaints about these practices. With specific evidence of discrimination, Women Employed filed charges with the Treasury and Labor Departments in November, 1974. Since government enforcement action was virtually non-existent at that time, Women Employed had to conduct an extended pressure campaign to force the agencies to investigate the charges. Finally, in 1977, the government confirmed WE's findings and issued a formal administrative complaint alleging inadequate affirmative action by the bank. Since then, the government has demanded millions of dollars in back pay for the Harris employees who have suffered sex and race discrimination. The actual hearing on the complaint began last August in Washington. Women Employed participated throughout the process as a formal third party intervenor.

Since enforcement action began, Harris has refused to settle the case. Instead they spent over $1 million in legal fees to fight it. The bank filed numerous motions to prevent the facts from being presented in the hearing and to avoid compliance. All of the motions were denied. However, the bank has persisted in refusing to turn over to the court documents regarding their employment practices even though the judge has directly ordered the bank to do so.

THE HEARING

The case was presented in three phases. First, expert witnesses testified on the statistical evidence of discrimination at Harris. An extensive study of salary levels comparing men and women, minorities and non-minorities with comparable tenure, education, and experience revealed substantial income disparities. For the years 1974 through 1977, for example, women and minorities earned a total of approximately $12 million less than their white male counterparts.

In the second phase of the case, the government presented documentary evidence of discrimination and pinpointed specific practices such as separate interviewing, training, counseling processes, departments in the bank made "off limits" to women and minorities, and disparate salary administration practices. In the final stage of the hearing, Women Employed's witnesses, former and current Harris employees, testified about their individual cases of discrimination, citing unequal pay, inadequate training, and in some cases, years of denied promotions. The hearing concluded with final arguments on December 5, the last step before the judge issues his opinion.

THE SIGNIFICANCE OF THE CASE

The Harris case is the first in which the government has sought to bar a bank from serving as a depository for federal accounts on the basis of its discriminatory employment practices. It is the first time that the government has sought back wages for an affected class of bank employees. The final outcome will affect the entire industry.

The case will also set a precedent for future efforts to enforce federal anti-discrimination regulations. Because of this case, the government now has a statistical approach for identifying women and minorities owed back wages for past discrimination that could be applied to any employer.

The Wage Gap at Harris Bank

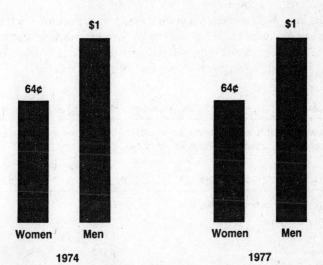

At the Harris Bank in 1974, women on the average earned 64¢ for every $1 earned by men. In 1977, the wage gap remained at 64¢.

*From *Women Employed NEWS* (Winter 1980), p. 3.

same work, and they fell further and further behind as inflation eroded the real value of their earnings.

Calculating the Wage Gap. When differences between the earnings of men and women are measured, two percentages are generally calculated. One might reveal the income of full-time, year-round women workers in major occupational groups during the year studied. The income column is compared with what men working in the same categories earned. Figure 2–6 gives the median earnings in 1969 for full-time, year-round workers by major occupational group.

You can see that male workers were much better paid than female workers in all occupational groups in 1969, five years after EPA went into effect. The largest wage differential—men earned more than twice as much as women—was found for sales workers. The smallest difference was found for professional and technical workers and for clerical workers, occupational groups in which men that year earned on the average 35 percent more than women doing substantially the same work. In 1969, relatively few women were in professional and technical fields, and very few men were in clerical work, further highlighting the financial effects of occupational segregation by sex.

The year 1969 was chosen as an index year to document a trend and to arouse your curiosity. What was the picture in your field last year? To find out, send a postcard requesting information about *Women Workers Today.* (The address is given at the end of this chapter).

FIGURE 2–6 1969 Wages of Full-time, Year-round Male and Female Workers*

Median wage or salary incomes of year-round, full-time women workers in selected major occupation groups in 1969 were as follows:

MAJOR OCCUPATION GROUP	INCOME	AS PERCENT OF MEN'S INCOME
Professional and technical workers	$7309	65
Nonfarm managers	6091	53
Clerical workers	5187	65
Operatives	4317	59
Sales workers	3704	41
Service workers (except private household)	3755	59

*From *Women Workers Today* (Washington, D.C.: U.S. Department of Labor, Employment Standards Administration, Women's Bureau, 1971), p. 6.

A second set of figures provides the average incomes for all male and female workers during several years. Women's annual earnings as a percentage of men's annual earnings are presented in Figure 2–7. The 1975–1977 figures reveal that economic conditions for working women have worsened. American women are receiving a smaller proportion of the wages men receive than used to be true. In addition, women workers as newcomers are let go first when the workforce shrinks. It has been difficult for women to achieve and maintain experiential equality with male coworkers, since they are laid off while men continue working. Meanwhile, layoffs keep women's paychecks smaller than those of men. These factors affect the realization of equal pay for equal work. They affect it negatively.

Realistic assessments lead one to predict that the wage gap will not be completely eliminated for many years. However, good faith employment practices could reduce it markedly. So could planning, goal setting, and monitoring of achievements. A modest proposal would reduce pay inequities a few percentage points annually for a few decades.

Ending the wage gap: shooting for a goal. Reasonable progress toward equal pay by the year 2000 posits a maximum differential of 20 percent across the board between male and female salaries. A 20 percent discrepancy would make allowance for a host of sex-discriminatory wage factors curable by time, effort, education, and litigation, plus the active participation of all Americans to rectify a practice that victimizes the entire nation. Even if that goal were reached, there still would be plenty of room for improvement.

Comparable Worth

The second thrust is to promote equal pay for work of comparable worth. Determining what comparable worth of work consists of is a thorny issue. Many civil rights attorneys think that comparable worth may lie beyond the scope of the EPA. We will examine the concept nevertheless.

To begin, here are some examples of pay differentials cited in articles focusing upon the comparable worth issue:[23]

1. Light truck driver making $100 a month more than senior legal stenographer
2. Automotive pool attendant making $139 a month more than key data operator

FIGURE 2–7 Comparison of Median Earnings of Year-Round, Full-Time Workers by Sex, 1955–1977*
(Persons 14 years of age and over)

| Year | MEDIAN EARNINGS | | EARNINGS GAP IN DOLLARS | WOMEN'S EARNINGS AS A PERCENT OF MEN'S |
	Women	Men		
1977	$8,618	$14,626	$6,008	58.9
1976	8,099	13,455	5,356	60.2
1975	7,504	12,758	5,254	58.8
1974	6,772	11,835	5,063	57.2
1973	6,335	11,186	4,851	56.6
1972	5,903	10,202	4,299	57.9
1971	5,593	9,399	3,806	59.5
1970	5,323	8,966	3,643	59.4
1969	4,977	8,227	3,250	60.5
1968	4,457	7,664	3,207	58.2
1967	4,150	7,182	3,032	57.8
1966	3,973	6,848	2,875	58.0
1965	3,823	6,375	2,552	60.0
1964	3,690	6,195	2,505	59.6
1963	3,561	5,978	2,417	59.6
1962	3,446	5,974	2,528	59.5
1961	3,351	5,644	2,293	59.4
1960	3,293	5,417	2,124	60.8
1959	3,193	5,209	2,016	61.3
1958	3,102	4,927	1,825	63.0
1957	3,008	4,713	1,705	63.8
1956	2,827	4,466	1,639	63.3
1955	2,719	4,252	1,533	63.9

For 1967–77, data include wage and salary income and earnings from self-employment; for 1955–66, data include wage and salary income only.

*From *The Earnings Gap between Men and Women* (Washington, D.C.: U.S. Department of Labor, Office of the Secretary, Women's Bureau, 1979), p. 6.

3. Custodian making $18 a month more than Library-Media Clerk II
4. Male department managers making 20 percent more monthly than female department managers with twice the number of years on the job

Each example contains violation of some EPA criterion; one violates them all. The EPA apparently lacks the breadth necessary to demonstrate in court that light truck driver (male) and senior legal stenographer (female) are jobs having comparable worth to society and thus should receive equal pay. One might argue that being a Library-Media Clerk II takes more skill, effort, and responsibility than being a custodian in the same workplace. The job announcement said, for custodian, "No requirements or specifications are given."[24] The Library-Media Clerk II job description was two paragraphs long. Arguing this case under the EPA, one might be tempted to ask more compensation for the Library-Media Clerk II than for the custodian. One might debate whether the custodian's job—to safeguard property having great value to society—entails a great degree of responsibility, but the skill and effort criteria could not be met at the level required for the Library-Media Clerk II position, which also involves a high degree of responsibility. These criteria—skill, effort, and responsibility—figure heavily in determining comparable worth.

Background on comparable worth.   Where women do not receive equal pay for jobs of comparable worth, three explanations predominate: (1) *Job segregation* slots workers in jobs by sex and creates job ghettos. Male jobs—in the construction ghetto, for instance—receive higher social value than female jobs in the childcare ghetto. Childcare workers lack upward mobility and opportunity for achievement of higher wages. (2) *Job devaluation* by sex results in devaluation of wages. Women's jobs are compensated on a lower scale than men's jobs. For example, clerical workers at the University of Massachusetts entered the 90 percent female office force at grade 3, while entry-level janitors (about 70 percent male) began at grade 7 with $1000 more per year.[25] Imagine running a university without clerical help. Would chaos occur without university janitors? (3) *Biased job evaluations* compound the problem.

Correctives are needed. Bias can enter when an employee is being evaluated, when the job itself is being evaluated, or both. The majority of supervisory personnel are male; therefore, correction of biased job evaluations would best be accomplished outside the workplace. First, jobs need to be evaluated; then performance in those jobs needs evaluation. Ideally, completed forms would be evaluated by independent raters pro-

FIGURE 2–8 The States and Comparable Worth Evaluations*

States involved[a]	Florida, Georgia, Idaho, Maine, Massachusetts, Minnesota, New Jersey, Pennsylvania, Washington, Wisconsin.
Criteria used to evaluate jobs	Knowledge, judgment, accountability, interpersonal skills, working conditions.
Process	Consulting firm does comparable worth study of all (or selected) state position classifications. Points are assigned on the basis of the criteria. Each position receives a score related to the amount of knowledge, judgment, and accountability the position requires. The other criteria are used by some states. Salary is computed for each position on the basis of the score it receives. Actual employees' salaries are compared with salaries derived by the evaluation. Salary readjustments generally take place.[b]
Results	Salary readjustments for men and women workers were found necessary. In Idaho, salaries of women working for the state rose an average of 16.2 percent; men's rose an average of 6.8 percent; secretarial salaries rose 20–30 percent. Some jobs were downgraded, but no incumbent's pay was cut. In Washington state, the gap of comparable worth was 20 percent, with men earning that much more than the evaluation indicated was justified. Implementing the salary readjustments in 1976 had a price tag of $55 million.

[a]Data on Washington state were drawn from "Women in the Workplace."
[b]Washington state had not implemented the salary readjustment because it was too costly; the other states had made readjustments.

Aids to Establishing Comparable Worth**

There are several possible approaches to establishing comparable worth for wages of women in traditional occupations. Those listed below are suggestions for study by groups interested in upgrading the status of women office workers. Each question could be the basis for studies and subsequent action and/or recommendations to legislative bodies.

1. Do college courses in personnel management include methods of job rating and job evaluation?

2. Can job-rating studies be obtained and used as a basis for improving women's wages?

3. Can such job ratings be incorporated into state government employment standards as has been done in some states (such as Idaho)?

4. Does the National Secretaries Association have material that could help in establishing a job rating for secretarial or clerical workers?

5. Do other organizations (Illinois Nurses Organization, for example) have similar material?

*From Carol Payne, "Successful Approaches for Improving Women's Employment" and "Women in the Workplace."

**From Nancy Winters, "Report on Status of Women Office Workers" (Chicago: Employment and Pensions Committee, Illinois Commission on the Status of Women, October 25, 1979).

vided with job descriptions and job performance data who knew neither the sex nor the name of the worker. Job titles providing clues to workers' sex should be suppressed.

Progress check on comparable worth. Has any progress been made? Yes, since the National Commission for Working Women Conference publicized the "Equal Pay for Work of Comparable Worth" slogan, the concept has been accepted as an idea.

People are taking it seriously. For instance, columnist Ellen Goodman suggests that ranking jobs according to their inherent worth might be more feasible than trying to reevaluate them all.[26] California law, in another elaboration of the concept, requires state employees to be paid wages comparable to workers in private or other public employment.[27] The national and some state governments are taking action on the concept, and court tests are in process. Meanwhile, working women's organizations are getting to the crux of the comparable worth issue; their objective is to change society's attitude toward the value of women's work.

Although wide pay-scale differences are still found between traditionally male and traditionally female jobs, the view that emphasizes objective value of work determinations is making progress. This comparable worth strategy has been adopted by at least ten state civil service systems, numerous local governments, and some corporations. Underlying the comparable worth strategy is the objective of compensating women fairly for the skills they have brought to the workplace.[28]

Maybe some of the suggestions in Figure 2–8 will help you begin working on the comparable worth problem. Or you might want to finish the chapter and then return to Figure 2–8 to see how it can help you.

The state comparable worth evaluations mentioned above and cited in Figure 2–8 are worth watching because they benefit most workers in classifications that have been undervalued. A fifth of the states have already undertaken these evaluations; others may be encouraged to follow suit. It may be possible to extend the classifications evaluated upward to include comparable worth at higher levels that have often been closed to women; it might provide a trail for women endeavoring to reach the upper portions of state civil service.

Unions have used the comparable worth concept in contract negotiations. Again, women workers have benefitted most from this procedure. Comparable worth was used by the International Brotherhood of Electrical Workers in a case against Westinghouse Electric Company in Fairmont, West Virginia.[29] The presiding judge dismissed the case, but its comparable worth aspect was settled favorably. As a result, 13 formerly female job classifications were increased a total of 25 labor grades, and 270 male and female employees received retroactive wage adjustments. The union is seeking similar settlements at other Westinghouse plants. Finally, the Third Court of Appeals will now hear comparable worth cases, and the union has filed an appeal based on comparable worth. Such cases build important legal precedents.

Laws, too, are beginning to incorporate the comparable worth concept. For instance, Section 311 (d)(2) of the Comprehensive Employment and Training Act Amendments of 1978 authorizes the Secretary of Labor to:

> investigate the extent to which job and wage classification systems undervalue certain skills and responsibilities on the basis of the sex of the persons who usually hold the positions.[30]

Likewise, studies are being done to determine the extent of the undervaluation of skills and responsibilities of women's jobs and the subsequent classifications and wages assigned to the performance of such work. This means that jobs traditionally held by women are being reevaluated in terms of what it takes—skill, effort, responsibility—to perform them.

These studies were given impetus by the 1970 work of Norma Briggs as the woman staff member of the Women in Wisconsin Apprenticeship.[31] That federally funded project wanted to train disadvantaged, unemployed women as day-care teachers but ran into snarls of red tape that made the project's objective impossible to achieve. One unexpected outcome was a research study documenting how women's jobs were undervalued in the Department of Labor's *Dictionary of Occupational Titles,* and the sex-discriminatory effect job devaluation had upon funding of projects designed to train women.[32] The allegations made by Briggs and widely publicized during International Women's Year have been acted upon. The *Dictionary of Occupational Titles* is being revised, while projects to help women enter vocations providing upward mobility have been funded.

Comparable worth: unfinished business. What remains to be done is to educate working women about how to accomplish both comparable worth job and wage classifications and their implementation.[33] One approach will be discussed in the next chapter in an evaluation of the relative merits of the EPA and Title VII of the Civil Rights Act of 1964 for achieving comparable worth.

Pensions and Fringe Benefits

The third thrust is to promote equal pensions and fringe benefits. We do not often focus upon this final EPA issue of equalities surrounding work.

Headlines a few years ago warned that equal pensions for all workers would cost millions. Despite differential life expectancies for men and women, we were warned that government regulations would require equal payments and equal pensions.

A landmark case. A case heard in the spring of 1978 before the Supreme Court was brought by women employees of the Los Angeles Water and Power Department.[34] These workers had paid almost 15 percent more of their salaries toward pensions than male coworkers earning the same amount. Supreme Court Justice John Paul Stevens, in his opinion for the majority, wrote that the Civil Rights Act referred to individuals and their protection, while actuarial tables on which pension payments—into funds and later to retired persons—are calculated, treat workers as classes rather than as individuals. Stevens noted that when employees are viewed and classified by race, sex, or religion, traditional assumptions about groups are promoted. Steven's view is interesting and ultimately fair.

However, lower courts had ruled in favor of the women employees, finding that there had been sex discrimination; back pay, retroactive from the onset of the unequal payments to January 1, 1975, when the practice ceased, was ordered. That lower court decision, a triumph for the concept of equal treatment and equal pay, for Title VII and for working women, was barred by the Supreme Court. It would have set a precedent considered too expensive for the nation's pension funds and employers.

But henceforth payments made to pension funds by employers must be equal for men and women earning the same amount. Thus, in the future, two workers who have the same salary history and length of service should receive the same pension when they retire, even if one worker is female and the other male. Some pension plans offer workers options or choices; alternatives chosen would affect the eventual payout, as would the age at which the retirement begins. But choices made, or risks voluntarily taken, are not the effects of sex discrimination.

Pensions, actuarial tables, and individual retirees. Pension contributions, like insurance premiums, are evaluated in terms of statistical tables of life expectancy. Actuaries determined that women outlived men;

therefore, women should pay larger pension contributions or premiums than men in order to receive equal benefits, or pay equal premiums or pension contributions and receive smaller benefits. Employers making employee pension contributions operated under the same rules. The small force of working women said and did little about this peculiar arithmetic. One peculiarity was that the outcomes for working women were based on life expectancy for *all* women. Nobody bothered to find out what the life expectancy for working women was, or whether they lived longer than men (virtually all of whom are in the workforce).

When women indisputably lived longer than men, on the average, this kind of thinking might have made a little sense. But not necessarily, because relatively few women worked outside the home, and the sex-based pension issue hardly ever arose since most working women did not receive pensions. Later, as the proportion of women working expanded rapidly, those covered by pension plans got either greater salary deductions or smaller pensions. Yet it has been observed that, as more women work, they begin to fall heir to the same ailments working men have always been prone to. Do working women really live longer than men? We don't know. Nor do we know how well actuarial tables predict for today's workers who are paying in for future benefits. In any case, actuarial tables must deal with people on the average while pensions and insurance are directly linked to individuals.

Shifting the pension risk. The matter boils down to who takes the risk. In the past, actuaries have successfully, certainly without malice or forethought, shifted the risk to women. Now some of the risk is being returned to the odds makers, the actuaries, and to employers and the public. This is another aspect of pension equality; all concerned share the risks.

Consider a woman who died before age 65, having paid more into her pension account than a male born the same year who lived to retire. Consider a woman who lived to age 80 in poverty after retirement. Surely these were risk equalizers. The joker was that they had not chosen the risk; it was chosen for them. The Supreme Court decision has furnished an important precedent, the critical import of which is that no individual should be required to assume an unfair or unequitable risk when planning for the future. The risk should be assumed in such a manner that major groups, standing to lose or gain from the outcomes, participate fairly. Today, employers, employees, pension plans, and the government share the burden; they pay their money and take their chances in the longevity sweepstakes.

Fringe benefit equality. The Supreme Court decision also deals with the question of equal compensation. When the employer contributes, pension plans are fringe benefits. Group insurance coverage for life and medical protection and other employment-related benefits such as discounts on purchases are fringes, too. The Department of Labor has proposed regulations that would make it illegal for employers to pay for employees to join private clubs with discriminatory membership policies. Such fringe benefit clubs can provide useful contacts that would be unavailable to coworkers excluded because of sex (or race or religion).

Employers calculate the cost of each employee's fringe benefits, expressing it as a percentage of salary or by reporting the total compensation for the year. Employers include government-mandated benefits such as social security payments or head taxes and voluntary contributions such as tuition payments or tuition reimbursement which depend upon employee initiative. These benefits are an important chunk of a worker's compensation, sometimes approaching 40 percent of the total, exclusive of bonuses. Few working women give this part of their compensation package much thought. Here is an example.

Fringe benefit word magic. An unhappy coworker once told me, "Oh, I can't leave; the fringe benefits are too good." What were those fringe benefits? Our pension, a state retirement system without employer contribution, only became vested—owned by the employee—after ten years of employment; employees who left before than got back their contributions plus 4.58 percent interest (a rate lower than savings bank interest). The group insurance consisted of a term policy worth twice one's salary. There was no social security coverage. There was an adequate health care plan having good dental benefits. "What do you mean, the fringe benefits are too good?" I asked. I had calculated that receipt of social security coverage plus an employer contribution to the pension plan equal to that mandated for employees would have added 14 percent to each worker's compensation. I concluded, "We aren't getting *any* fringe benefits we can take with us when we leave." Both of us had been complacent, penny wise and pound foolish. Meanwhile, by talking of wondrous benefits, our employer practiced word magic, not benevolence. I learned to examine the fringe benefits before accepting a new job.

Fringe benefits include extras: profit sharing, paid holidays, vacation, sick leave, and personal days. If the last three are related to length of service and level of employment, then the longer you stay the more time off you get, or the higher your rank the longer your vacation, or both. The federal government is becoming increasingly interested in fringe benefits; it would like to tax them. So far, that has been avoided. However, with the federal government and the Supreme Court watching fringe benefits, it certainly would be advisable for working women to do the same.

WAGING THE PAY EQUALITY BATTLE: PLAYING FIELD MANEUVERS

How can we use these facts? We now emphasize strategies for achieving equal wages, pay, and compensation. The remaining task is to provide practical aid. Some advice and some guidelines may be helpful in encouraging working women to persist until the desired result is realized.

Planning and Training for Action

A detailed checklist providing for legal rights and nonlitigious choices for action is given in Figure 2–9. Results won't be immediate, and it does take time to pull together all of the necessary information. Examine and become familiar with the checklist. The hints that follow expand on suggestions made in Figure 2–9, but the checklist and the chapter complement rather than duplicate each other.

Documenting differential wage patterns for male and female workers may be difficult. Simply looking at the amounts currently being paid to male and female same-level employees is insufficient. For instance, if the female is new to the job while the male isn't, the male salary tends to be higher. And things become more complex. On my new job, five males at the next lower level all earned more than I; all had been employed there for 20 years. It is a good question whether that salary arrangement represented sex discrimination. My second year, personnel changes had me earning more than two new people (one male, one female) at the next lower level. One cannot automatically conclude that all pay differentials result from sex discrimination.

Still, many pay differentials are sex discriminatory. If you suspect that, your best strategy may be to turn to the male coworker being paid

FIGURE 2–9 Choices for Action

CHECKLIST SUGGESTIONS FOR SEX-BASED EQUAL PAY ACT DISCRIMINATION RELIEF[a]

Topic	Documentation[b]
1. Title and wages	Job descriptions; yours and those for males. Male job descriptions may have different titles and same duties; male salary scale may be higher.
2. Skills	Inventory skills you use on the job according to those learned for and used only on job, those known before job, and those used on the job and for recreation or pleasure.
3. Duties performed	Record activities during several typical days; then make a list of duties performed. List the most important duties first, after organizing duties into categories. Estimate percentage of day devoted to each type of duty.
4. Effort	Mental effort and physical effort expended. How much energy, of what kinds, does your job take? Be honest.
5. Responsibility	What are you accountable for? Products, services, deadlines? List them. Are they really your responsibility or your superior's?
6. Compensation	Compute dollar value of all fringe benefits and add this amount to your annual salary. You may need to ask the personnel director for a list of all fringe benefits and the percentage value they have in your compensation package. Are you receiving what is due you? Could you, if you made the effort, use all of your fringes? What about male coworkers? How do their fringes and yours compare?
7. Experience in the organization	Did you train a male who was then promoted to a status higher than yours? More than one such male? Give narrative, with dates.
8. Insights into what pays off on this job	Who is getting the rewards? For what activities? List the people and their rewards and activities. Are there any apparent biases? Is it who you are rather than what you do that pays off?
9. Qualifications	Do women need higher qualifications than men to reach the same level? Can you document this and its effects on equal pay?

[a]Additional items dealing with hiring, promotion, or even whether you like the job (or field) can be added to the list. The list can be modified to account for situations covered by other regulations.
[b]Documentation includes evidence of sex-based violations of the EPA and evidence of your on-the-job performance and outcomes.

FIGURE 2-9 (Continued)

CONSTRUCTIVE, NONLITIGIOUS APPROACHES TO EQUAL PAY

Topic	Documentation
1. Rewrite your résumé.	After performing the inventory above, redo your résumé, emphasizing your job objective, and points documented in items 2, 3, 5, 7, and 9 above.
2. Do library job research.	Find several job titles that appeal to you and that mention points in your résumé. Assess yourself. What are the qualifications for those job titles? Do you possess them? What is lacking? How can you achieve it? Study those jobs that interest you. Finally, obtain the salary range and total compensation package, broken down into its component parts, for each job of interest. Weigh the alternatives. Decide what each appealing job would be worth to you. If you are a homebody and an appealing job involves half-time travel, a perfect match of other qualifications, plus an ideal compensation package would not make you and that job compatible.
3. Check with your personnel director.	What is likely to open up soon? How can you prepare to be considered as a serious applicant? You may need to ask this every few weeks.
4. Locate nearby employers.	Use the phone book. Call local companies that might be able to help you locate your ideal job. Get the name of a supervisor of your potential ideal job and make an appointment. Tell the supervisor you need help in generating a list of employers of people in the appealing job. Get names of others who can help you with information. Create a chain that will lead you to a job you want.
5. Do your homework.	Before each appointment for help and information, learn all you can about the organization. Let the person you see know that you know some good things about his or her workplace, as well as what it does.
6. Follow up the appointment.	Send a genuine note of thanks to the person you saw. Indicate that you appreciate the time that person spent helping you.
7. Ask for a raise at your current workplace.	If you have done all of the above, asking for a raise should not be overwhelming. Try it. You now know what you want to do, what your skills and experience are worth. Create a closer match between expectation and actuality.

more than you for doing the same job with the same qualifications and length of service in the position as yourself, or to the new worker with fewer qualifications who is paid much more, or to a worker in another department whose job requires the same skills, effort, and responsibility as yours but who is paid more. Transform such workers into allies. You may need to explain to such workers that under the EPA salaries can only be raised. No male coworker can lose money by sharing information about earnings.

A nonthreatening way to approach the topic of legal rights is to show your coworkers the Lawful Law Fool Quiz, Figure 1–4 in Chapter 1. Let them discover what they know about their legal rights. Money matters usually surface after the quiz since they appear in many items. If not, then broach the subject. Having created this opening, move within a week or so to gathering data. Your goal is to be accurate and perfectly objective. It will be a relief to find that you are not a victim of wage discrimination.

If the salary figures gathered indicate disparity, you could invite the male coworkers involved to join in your complaint. Male coworkers involved would be protected from employer retaliation for revealing salary information (workers are free to do this in any case, although employers dislike it) during the complaint investigation. Opposite-sex coworkers paid more than you make excellent co-complainants. What employer would expect that strategy? It is virtually unheard of for a victim and a victor to gang up against the establishment.

Modifying Game Rules

Another approach to achieving pay equality has to do with your ground rules, your description or operational contract. The job description should mirror what you actually do.

Wise working women update their job descriptions annually. This process requires collecting copies of similar job descriptions (with different titles, comparable duties) from personnel (or want ads or from the *Dictionary of Occupational Titles*) and by inquiring about other opportunities. Inquire about higher-level jobs open to someone having your skills. Persistence pays off; don't stop collecting with a fistful of traditionally women's job descriptions. Firmly insist upon information about other jobs utilizing your specific skills. Faithfully read the organization's newsletter and suggest titles to your personnel director.

After learning the titles and collecting job descriptions, study them. Compare each with your title and job description. Discuss your title and job description with your supervisor. Propose an appropriate title change. (It can take months to achieve; incidentally, many title changes are accompanied by larger paychecks.) Be sure to record and document by dated memo the request to meet with your supervisor, the actual meeting, and your thanks for it—whatever its outcome.

Professional Touches

Your plan might now hinge upon equal pay (and status) for jobs of comparable worth. At any hint of downgrading or demotion, innocently remark, "I thought we had a 'hold harmless guarantee' around here." Do not explain your remark. (A hold harmless guarantee means that even if a job's status is demoted, the incumbent's pay is not reduced.) Be advised that threats of demotion can be both unfair employment practice and sex discriminatory. The problem is that documentation cannot be hearsay; one needs witnesses. Everyone knows that violators of the laws are not going to provide witnesses if they can avoid it. But violators don't stop when they are ahead, and while what a supervisor says may not be evidence, what the supervisor does may be evidence of violation. If a supervisor threatens demotion, some sex-based wage discrimination will probably emerge.

Begin a log to detail the skill, effort, and responsibility your job requires. If different, detail the skill, effort, and responsibility you actually use in performing your job. Have this log available for discussion, comparison, and salary readjustments. The log is also handy for revising your résumé, a task sometimes hard to begin. Organize the log so that the major tasks and responsibilities are listed before less important ones. You then make your case with your employer and get your résumé in shape with the same effort. Figure 2–9 indicates one method of using the materials prepared, thus furnishing a script for legal rights action along with constructive nonlitigious approaches to equal pay.

After making a rough sketch for your résumé, put it away for a week or more. Then scrutinize it with the critical eye of a prospective employer. On the basis of the résumé, would you want to interview *you*? Correct any content and format flaws. When satisfied, type your rough draft; take it with you when you follow the ideas in Figure 2–9. When a local employer remarks that you have a good résumé, print it up. Remember two things: The résumé's function is to get you an interview. Work on your résumé at home, not in the workplace. Your efforts will benefit you; don't expect your employer to foot the bill.

Create a Cheering Section

You will need support. If you feel that you have a valid complaint, check with working women peers outside your workplace, preferably in a women's organization. If you do not belong to one, contact the National Commission on Working Women for leads to groups. (The address is given at the end of this chapter.) Being able to discuss strategy with other working women can be a saving grace, particularly of your sense of humor—an asset unwise to discount—which is every working woman's trusted ally.

Play Back and Evaluate Each Inning

Keep working on documentation until you have received a variety of reactions and some advice, and you have generated your plan of action. As it stands, you have two choices: You decide either to stay or to leave. Determine logically which course is best by looking at all of those dated documents amassed to determine first whether the legal rights you originally thought were being violated still apply. Maybe you have not focused on the appropriate legal right; maybe another game plan would be superior. Or maybe by having developed an organized approach and job confidence, you find yourself offered a promotion and decide to accept it. That would be the unexpected ending, the equivalent of real-life Alice in Wonderland.

More likely, you will spend a good deal of time finding your best solution to the equal pay issue. The search may be quite painful. It may make you wonder at times whether you deserve the unfair treatment you are receiving; that kind of self-pity is a luxury most of us can't afford. It is a great deal smarter to take for granted that you deserve fair treatment and fair pay. Make a clean start. The second performance is easier, smoother. You are becoming more professional; equal pay will come, and with it resolution of the comparable work, equable pension and fringe benefit issues.

When that happens, you'll be wiser, a workplace role model who knows the playing field maneuvers needed to wage the equal pay battle. You will have become a natural resource for working women, knowing that wage inequities can exist anywhere and being in a position to assist the unwary working woman. It is your turn to assist someone who stands where you used to be. Teach her the job world's makeup and send her on stage.

ADDITIONAL INFORMATION SOURCES

Useful organizations mentioned in the chapter:

Federally Employed Women
National Press Building, Suite 481
Washington, D.C. 20045

National Commission on Working Women
1121 Connecticut Avenue, N.W., Suite 400
Washington, D.C. 20036

To write for *Women Workers Today*:
Office of the Secretary
Women's Bureau
U.S. Department of Labor
Washington, D.C. 20210

For a free list of all federal agency Federal Women's Program Managers:
FWP
1900 E St., N.W., Rm. 7540, OPM
Washington, D.C. 20415

NOTES

1. Barbara Mayer Wertheimer, *We Were There: The Story of Working Women in America* (New York: Pantheon Books, 1977), p. 309. A plaque outside the building, now part of New York University, marks the site of the fire.

2. *Ibid.*, p. 315.

3. One reader remarked on the aptness of the analogy of the merit system to political patronage. She hadn't thought of that. If you find it where you work, beware.

4. For the often shocking story of women's treatment while working for the U.S. government, see Ross K. Baker, "Entry of Women into the Federal Job World—at a Price," *Smithsonian* 8, no. 4 (July 1977): 82–91.

5. See Susan D. Ross and Ann Barcher, *The Rights of Women: An American Civil Liberties Union Handbook* (New York: Bantam Books, 1983), pp. 308–355. States without Fair Employment Practices Commissions in 1973 were Arkansas, Florida, Georgia, Louisiana, North Carolina, North Dakota, South Carolina, Tennessee, and Texas. While North Dakota lacks an FEPC, it does have a statute prohibiting discrimination against women jockeys. As of July 1, 1980, the Illinois Human Rights Commission will hear and decide discrimination cases; this

commission will replace the Illinois FEPC. Other states may make similar modifications.

6. From "Brief History of FEPC," in *How to Exercise Your Rights under the Illinois Fair Employment Practices Act* (Springfield, Ill.: FEPC, 1978).

7. Ross, *The Rights of Women*, p. 82.

8. This hinged box was shaped like a woman; the inside was filled with the business ends of iron nails. A sinner was placed inside, and the halves were brought together. I have not discovered appropriate words to describe that masculine madness.

9. Betty Lehan Harrigan, *Games Mother Never Taught You* (New York: Warner Books, 1977), has excellent chapters on the world of work as a battlefield; chapters 2, 4, 12, and 13 provide a basic training course. Even if you think these games are silly, you owe it to yourself to know about them. Incidentally, this is a battlefield for power, not primarily for sex prizes.

10. Margaret Hennig and Anne Jardim, *The Managerial Woman* (Garden City, N.Y.: Anchor Press/Doubleday, 1977), should be read for instruction in the game mystique, which little boys learn automatically and women have to study. There are fine reflections on differences in attitude between men and women, which affect their working relationships and job success.

11. A conference on "The Implications of Occupational Segregation" was held at Wellesley College in 1975. Papers presented there may be found in Martha Blaxall and Barbara Reagan, eds., *Women and the Workplace: The Implications of Occupational Segregation* (Chicago: University of Chicago Press, 1976).

12. Louise Kapp Howe, *Pink Collar Workers: Inside the World of Women's Work* (New York: Avon, 1978). Howe cites a study of the *Dictionary of Occupational Titles* used by the U.S. government to classify occupations according to their value. Occupations involving child care and other nurturing functions (which are "women's occupations," sex-segregated occupations) receive the lowest rating used. See pp. 237–42.

13. Department of Labor figures from the Women's Bureau show that, in 1977, women employed full-time all year grossed $0.59 for every $1.00 fully employed men grossed; in 1976, the median woman's wage was $0.57 for every male dollar earned. Since 1961, differences in male and female wages have remained almost stable, but the wage differential per $1.00 grossed is *greater* than in 1955, when it was $0.36 rather than $0.41 (1977) or 0.43 (1978). See "The Earnings Gap Between Men and Women," (Washington, D.C.: Department of Labor, Women's Bureau, 1979) for details. *Higher Education and National Affairs* (Washington, D.C., November 9, 1979), p. 7, reported on an EEOC statement to the effect that job segregation is used to explain the wage gap. The EEOC contended that, de-

spite the enactment of major civil rights legislation since 1963, the earnings gap has increased. An article, "Salary Survey, 1980" in *Working Woman* 5, no. 2 (February 1980): 33, states that "nationally, women earn 62 percent of what men earn." Unfortunately, sources for the statement are not provided. Jennifer Fortenbaugh, in "Working Woman 4th Annual Salary Survey," *Working Woman* (January 1983): 65–68 corrects that. Fortenbaugh states, "Women continue to earn substantially less than men (59.2 percent of men's annual earnings)," p. 65. Data reported are from 1981, with sources; professional fields are covered.

14. The low rating accorded women's work in the *Dictionary of Occupational Titles* is .878; only .888 is lower. The original study, "Women's Work—Up from .878, Report on the DOT Research Project" (University of Wisconsin–Extension, Women's Education Resources, January 1975), led to a revision of the Dictionary (DOT) and a reevaluation of the jobs. The DOT rates several thousand occupations on the skill required in dealing with the categories of data, people, and things. Each category is rated on a scale extending from a high of 0 to a low of 8. Foster mothers, for instance, were rated .878; jobs with such low ratings could only receive four weeks of federal funding, creating a Catch–22 situation where helping women to become gainfully employed was the object.

15. Osta Underwood, "Legislation and Litigation: Impact on Working Women," p. 45 in Dorothy Jongeward and Dru Scott, eds., *Affirmative Action for Women* (Reading, Mass. Addison-Wesley, 1975).

16. " . . . *To Form a More Perfect Union. . .*" *Justice for American Women* (Washington, D.C.: National Commission on the Observance of International Women's Year, 1976), p. 349.

17. Phyllis A. Wallace, "Impact of Equal Employment Opportunity Laws," p. 125 in Juanita M. Kreps, ed., *Women and the American Economy : A Look to the 1980s.* (Englewood Cliffs, N.J.: Prentice-Hall, Inc., 1976). Wallace does not include equal work among the criteria required for a violation of the EPA. She lumps the other items by saying that the Wage and Hour Division's definition is "such that equal does not mean identical."

18. See Underwood, "Legislation and Litigation," p. 47; and "Equal Pay for Work of Comparable Value Contacts" (Washington, D.C.: Women's Bureau, U.S. Department of Labor, 1979).

19. If you are an educational institution employee, you may want to refer to this point when you read Chapter 5 on the education acts and allied legislation, which emphasizes protection for employees of educational institutions that receive federal funds.

20. Adapted from " . . . *To Form a More Perfect Union . . .,*" Note 4, p. 350.

21. Martha W. Griffiths, "Can We Still Afford Occupational Segregation? Some Remarks," p. 11 in Blaxall and Regan, eds., *Women and the Workplace,* points out that less than half of the back pay awarded to women on violations of the EPA has been paid.

22. Women Employed furnished information that there was a hearing in summer 1978, followed by final arguments in December 1979, but by June 1980 no decision had been reached.

23. Examples 1 and 2 from *California Women: A Bulletin from the California Commission on the Status of Women* (Sacramento, Calif: May/June 1978); example 3 from Women's Bureau, Department of Labor, August 1977; example 4 from *Chicago Sun-Times,* October 30, 1979, p. 25.

24. Women's Bureau, August 1977.

25. "Equal Pay for Work of Comparable Value Contacts," p. 2.

26. Ellen Goodman, "Beyond 'Equal Pay for Equal Work,'" *Chicago Sun-Times,* October 10, 1978, p. 35.

27. "Discrimination Charged against Clerical Workers," *California Women* (May–June 1978): 14.

28. Carol Payne, "Successful Approaches to Improving Women's Employment," *Women and Work* 6 (League of Women Voters Education Fund, 1979).

29. *Ibid.*

30. "Equal Pay for Work of Comparable Value Contacts," p. 2.

31. " . . . *To Form a More Perfect Union . . . ,*" pp. 65– 67.

'32. See note 14 above.

33. See Goodman, "Beyond 'Equal Pay' . . . ," and Margaret Moses, "Pay Equity: The Issue of the 80s," *aclu Women's Rights Report* 1, no. 4 (Winter 1979–80).

34. This is the so-called Manhart case, Los Angeles Dept. of Water and Power v. Manhart, 46 U.S.L.W. 437.

The Major Contest
civil rights legislation: impacts on women's equal employment opportunity

CHALLENGES IN COURT

Mindset

Knowing about laws and legal rights is important. But working women require something more. They need to learn how to use existing legislation to secure equal employment opportunities. That's what this chapter is about.

It focuses upon Title VII of the Civil Rights Act of 1964, which prohibits discrimination—including sex discrimination—in terms and conditions of employment. As the law was amended, its compliance agency, the Equal Employment Opportunity Commission (EEOC), was established. The EEOC has broad, important powers. How these powers are used to enforce the law should be of interest to all working women. You may recall from the last chapter that the EEOC now also is the compliance agency for the EPA, so the continuation of the comparable worth discussion appears here; suggestions for implementing action are given.

It would be inaccurate to leave readers with the impression that working women's occupational problems have been solved by Title VII and the EEOC. They haven't been; much remains to be done. Critical comments are furnished to highlight areas that require large improvements; successful strategies speak for themselves.

The main purpose of the Civil Rights Act of 1964 was to get federal legislation that prohibited discrimination onto the books. Although the discrimination that legislators wished to go on record *against* was racial, the act passed included color, religion, national origin, and, as an afterthought (Virginia Representative Smith's addition of) sex.[1] Thereby the federal government was challenging the age-old right of employers to negotiate with their employees without interference.

But that was not the end of Title VII's new wrinkles. Since sex discrimination was a violation of the new law except where a bona fide occupational qualification existed, most jobs (and careers) had to be opened to both sexes, or rather to qualified applicants regardless of sex.[2] Compliance with the Civil Rights Act thus requires shifts in practices and attitudes, for Title VII prohibits discrimination in terms and conditions of employment under a wide range of circumstances.

Bringing a New Role into Court

In 1969, in an unprecedented move, the National Organization for Women (NOW) in Pittsburgh filed a complaint with the local Commission on Human Relations against *The Pittsburgh Press*, which advertised jobs under such headings as "Male–Interest" and "Female–Interest." While *The Press* insisted its policy was not discriminatory, NOW persevered. In a second unusual action, a psychologist, Sandra L. Bem, was asked to testify at the complaint hearing. As preparation, Bem performed a study to determine the behavior of women applicants when confronted with sex-labeled job advertisements. Specifically, Bem asked, "Do sex-segregated want ads discourage women from considering those jobs which *The Pittsburgh Press* classifies as 'Male–Interest'?"[3] The disclaimer used by *The Press* on its want ad pages was prominently featured on every other page of the study's booklet.

Each subject (52 college women) was asked to state her preference on a scale ranging from +3, "definitely willing to apply for the job," to −3, "definitely unwilling to apply for the job," as she rated every ad, regardless of label. The women subjects were reluctant to apply for jobs described as "Male–Interest." Nor was anyone surprised to find that the "Male–Interest" column job titles and descriptions—from ads that had appeared in the *Press*—provided a wider range of opportunities. But it was surprising to find some classifications cross-listed—Bookkeepers, Executive Secretaries, Programmers, and Teachers—only four years after Title VII became effective, and one wondered whether the jobs were identical, or whether the titles disguised totally different jobs.

Certain occupations were only for women—Dietitian, Interior Decorator, Librarian, Registered Nurse, Social Worker, Cosmetics Supervisor Beginner, Stewardess, and Travel Reservationist.[4] These job titles tend to reflect traditional women's roles. The jobs listed for "Male–Interest" replace the (female) "Beginner" classification with "Trainee," a word implying possibility of rapid advancement. The male columns also listed "Manager" and "Director" along with enticing titles like Buyer, Commercial Artist, Pharmacist, Public Relations, Real Estate Sales, Reporters, and Writers. Bem convinced the judge.[5] Her comments provide food for thought:

> In responding to the complaint lodged against it, *The Pittsburgh Press* stated that "there are fundamental differences between men and women . . . [which] manifest themselves in job preferences." But psychological research reveals no fundamental sex differences that would be relevant to the world of work in a modern technological society like ours. In fact, if "fundamental" sex differences were truly to be adopted as the criterion for a "bona fide occupational qualification," then we can think of only two jobs for which all members of one sex or the other would be disqualified: sperm donor and wet nurse! Indeed, an anthropologist visiting

our culture would find it amusing that in the same society where the position of gynecologist is filled almost exclusively by men, modesty requires the position of lingerie salesperson to be filled by a woman.

Getting Women on the Team

One creative reaction to promote equal employment opportunity consists of storming the bastions: securing mass applications by qualified women for openings listed as male. A few of the top jobs offered are selected. Lots of qualified women seriously apply for them; if no women are interviewed, then affirmative inaction can be suspected. Should this good faith application move fail, it may be necessary to rehearse the new role. Counteroffers of legal action and subsequent followup may be required. Keep in mind that both strength and safety lie in numbers; women need to learn how to use both to reduce violations of the Civil Rights Act of 1964.

Check your local papers' presentations of job offerings. That will introduce you to local enforcement of Title VII provisions. There are wide regional differences in awareness of, adherence to, and attitudes about this federal provision.

All of us think in terms of what we were taught to expect and what feels natural to us, rather than what might be rational and sensible. Title VII is legal, rational, and sensible; our behavior may be anything but. We give ourselves away when someone announces that her children were delivered by a "woman obstetrician" or when another thanks us for compliments on her vest, saying, "My son made and designed it." A male kindergarten teacher or nurse, a woman pilot or urologist may give us pause. However, ingrained as sex stereotypes may be, they furnish facile, partial answers for slow Title VII implementation.

UPWARD MOBILITY:
A THEME AND VARIATIONS

Occupational Tokenism

Of course, it is hard to be the first telephone linewoman, or woman minister, or company vice-president. Nobody wants to be an occupational token.[6] One's perceptions can be distorted if one is the token—the only woman—in a large group. One may wonder whether one is crazy, or whether everyone else is; neither solution is terribly comforting.

An organization sincere about enforcing Title VII will rarely put a lone woman in a new role; at least two women will be placed at the same time and rank, and thorough orientation will be furnished, because new roles require undoing of old stereotypes of kind, degree, or rank. Needless to say, women in new roles present a threat to those comfortable with old ways. And those who feel threatened frequently react with hostility and opposition, or state with pride that they have placed the first woman at that level (or in that position) and then withdraw all support.

Junior Women and Senior Men

Major opposition to Title VII rallied around questions of seniority and promotion. It was soon realized that attempts either to redress past employment grievances of women and minorities or to achieve present equality would create problems from supporters of the status quo. Some, like the heavy imbiber, a guest at a women's organization meeting, might echo his hostile toast to "Women—once my superiors, now my equals." Employed males might feel threatened by being required to learn and to live with new ground rules: "I don't think I am going to be able to cope with a less competent and experienced woman having it ahead of me . . . . I'll fight it."[7] Women lived with that problem for decades. The Civil Rights Act gave white males an equal opportunity to share this slice of reality.

Few Equals

Yet, despite past experiences, working women felt both guilty and ambivalent about the promotion and seniority issue. Some expressed their feelings by quoting a late 1960s phrase: "To be equal to a man, a woman has to be twice as good." And even when they were twice as good, women had conflicts about promotion, fearing loss of femininity and popularity as they moved up in the workplace. Women even felt guilty about seniority once they had achieved a taste of it.

Reluctant Women

Another group—women who found themselves promoted from or trained out of comfortable niches—felt threatened. They rarely knew if their rise was the result of performance, talent, malleability and lack of troublemaking, or a consent decree or fear of one. Needless to say, no working woman wants to be promoted to fill a quota or to meet a management goal. In addition, when a long-deferred, deserved promotion is suddenly received, it can be extremely bewildering. To make matters worse, the forced promotion was often to a department about which the woman was ignorant and in which she knew no one. Instead of delight at her promotion, she suspected that she had been set up to fail.

Ambitious Women

The field of education furnishes another variant on upward mobility. It was all right for women to be elementary school teachers but not acceptable for women to be in positions of authority such as principal or superintendent. Female teachers never earn what male principals and superintendents do. The salary discrepancy cannot be erased by demonstrating that starting salaries today are the same for beginning males and females having equal training, when males are promoted from teaching to more lucrative positions in administration while women are encouraged to gain more training as classroom teachers.

Women Available for Moving Upward

Since enactment of Title VII, it has become clear that there are plenty of experienced, trained women available for high-level jobs. When dealing with working women having both years or decades of professional experience and the required credentials, we begin to see the importance of seniority. Our perceptions sharpen when we focus upon tangible rewards. Long, valuable, effective service should be worth something to employer and employee. Yet, among women with credentials and experience, few who have sought advancement reached the levels identified with seniority.

Obstacles to Upward Mobility

Since men have often objected to having women promoted and have blocked their mobility, many women workers remain in low-level positions. The seniority paradox becomes apparent when women who have worked long and well lack seniority, while male workers who put in the same years have seniority and may register loud protests when women request access to a fairer portion of the rewards.

In times of economic crisis, when jobs are scarce or when prices are rising fast, the seniority issue may be prominent, especially when the last hired, particularly in entry-level jobs, tend to be the first fired or discharged.[8] The last hired tend to be women and minority group members. This situation culminates in the seniority versus affirmative action issue involving conflicts between established seniority practices and procedures required by Title VII.[9] In several court cases, extant seniority provisions were upheld when the labor force was hired by nondiscriminatory practices, even though the labor force may end up predominantly white male because of cutbacks or layoffs. However, in one situation, where women applied for but were not hired until much later (thus had not achieved any seniority) and were all laid off during a cutback, they were paid for the time between their layoff and the later layoff date their seniority would have entitled them to if hired earlier. This is some progress, but it is an exception, a curiosity. Much remains to be done, or begun, for women continue to be employed in great numbers at the lower rungs of the occupational ladder and to remain there for far too long.

Fielding the Law

What does Title VII prohibit? How does it work in practice? How is it supposed to work?

As amended, Title VII of the Civil Rights Act of 1964 "prohibits discrimination in compensation, all terms, conditions and privileges of employment by employers, employment agencies, labor organizations, and joint labor management committees, because of an individual's race, color, religion, sex, or national origin." Small and large enterprises are affected by Title VII. Since 1973, any employer having 15 or more employees or any labor union having that many members comes under the provisions of the law.[10] Periodic "Guidelines" have further defined Title VII's scope, while amendments have made it more comprehensive.[11]

This law means that all Americans must be considered for hiring, promotions, and training according to their ability and job skills. Illegal non-job-related reasons for failure to hire include sex, national origin, race, color, and even popular beliefs. Title VII states that one cannot be denied a chance to prove one's ability on the job for such reasons. Furthermore, in one landmark case it was determined that the consequences of an employer's actions, rather than the employer's intentions, were what counted.[12] If what the employer *did* ended up by discriminating against the employment opportunities of a group that the Civil Rights Act protects, then the employer must prove that the action was necessary to the safe, businesslike conduct of the enterprise or take the consequences. Such consequences, under Title VII, are purposely expensive; often the complainant, or employee, is the prime beneficiary. Title VII's objective is to discourage discrimination by providing Jeffersonian equality of opportunity to all Americans.[13]

The equality of opportunity concept assumed that freedom was available for all individuals to use in pursuit of their objectives. Those who did not achieve had chosen not to use their freedom for self-enhancement. It was a simple notion from a different time, one in which the natural aristocracy resulting from equality of opportunity would be composed almost exclusively of white gentleman farmers—intellectuals like Jefferson.

The notion that followed was worse: Once rid of overt discrimination, individuals who had not used their opportunity would be free to do so. Then they would be responsible for their own fates.

According to this view, women ought not to complain about their lack of representation in American power centers. They should have used their opportunity and freedom, once they could manage their own property and jobs, vote, and earn equal pay.

Alas, there is no overnight solution to working women's problems implicit in contradictions between freedom and protection on the one hand, and between (overt and covert) discrimination and normative stereotypes on the other. Title VII legislated away contradictions between job freedom and job protection but has given rise to new contradictions requiring fair resolutions: seniority, health issues, wages and salary, back pay, fringe benefits, and referral, hiring, training, promotion, and discharge.

But civil rights legislation has not changed basic, subtle discrimination against women, nor was it intended to do so.[14] Norms—those societally accepted standards—and attitudes tend to victimize employed women. Men discriminate against women, while women use verbal aggression against one another, thereby doing considerable harm. Verbal aggression assures men that discriminatory behaviors toward women are acceptable; it reinforces those behaviors and tends to increase their frequency. Men further become convinced that women cannot cooperate, cannot defend or help one another. Men view women as unable to get their team or act together, so men don't want women players on their team. Tragically, women seeing high-status men discriminating against women workers feel they will never overcome sex discrimination, will never be able to use their full abilities in the workplace. To them it appears that nobody will stand up for individual working women. Title VII attempts to, but it does not always succeed. Examining Title VII enforcement structures and strategies yields some clues.

Makeup for Enforcement

Title VII of the Civil Rights Act of 1964, as amended, is enforced by the Equal Employment Opportunity Commission (EEOC). The EEOC is a five-member commission of presidential appointees empowered to appoint necessary staff and to pursue the activities the law requires, reporting:

> . . . at the close of each year . . . to . . . Congress and then to the President concerning the action it has taken . . . on the cause of and means of eliminating discrimination and [making] such recommendations for further legislation as may appear desirable.[15]

The EEOC can intervene in and initiate civil actions, provide expenses for witnesses, cooperate with other agencies, assist employers in achieving compliance, file charges, serve notice on employers, and assist the Attorney General in presenting litigation in which EEOC is involved before the Supreme Court. Procedural powers of the EEOC include the right to issue, amend, or withdraw regulations needed for carrying out its duties. Affirmative action plans and their implementation are within the EEOC mandate.

The EEOC set up its network of regional offices promptly in response to these broad powers. Then complaints flooded in. But no one had predicted the enormous response of working women when given the opportunity to file complaints of unequal employment treatment based on sex. Charges from the eighth EEOC report plainly indicate that working women felt they were receiving discriminatory treatment and wanted relief. (See Figure 3–1.) Judging from the complaints, sex discrimination was worst in apprenticeship situations, educational institutions, and state and local governments. Interestingly enough, while the overwhelming majority of sex discrimination complaints came from individual women rather than from groups, the EEOC decided early to strike a blow for justice in the big corporations. This approach rapidly had an impact but failed to recognize the problems of thousands of individual women laboring in small offices, businesses, schools, and the like. Thus, a contradiction arose between the Title VII promises of the EEOC and prosecution

FIGURE 3–1 Some Percentages from the EEOC Eighth Annual Report, 1974, Sex Discrimination Charges, 1973*

RESPONDENT			
	Female	Male	Total
Private employers	84.6	15.3	99.9
State and local government	90.3	9.6	99.9
Educational institutions	91.4	8.5	99.9
Apprenticeship committee	95.0	5.0	100.0
Employment agencies	56.3	43.6	99.9
Unions	82.9	17.0	99.9
Labor–management	89.2	10.8	100.0
Other multiple respondents	91.1	8.8	99.9

*Calculated from numerical data given in Eighth Annual Report, U.S. Equal Employment Opportunity Commission, Washington, D.C., 1974.

of cases offering relief mainly to employees of giant American business, industry, and government.

Working women like us saw flyers about employment discrimination, or used checklists similar to the one in Figure 3–2, and awoke to the painful realization that sex discrimination wasn't "out there"; it was happening to us.

In defense of the EEOC's approach, obviously landmark cases must be tried for the law to be clarified; there is a need for precedents, increasingly clear guides to prohibited and condoned action. At the same time, those working women who pin their hopes on Title VII have found the EEOC wanting. They think the EEOC should do something for them.

Such working women are grasping at straws. They know about the EEOC and are ready to unload their burden of sex discrimination and other unfair employment treatment. They want relief now. Yet, even with rapid enforcement, relief takes time to achieve. Figure 3–3 presents an outline of the process from the workplace to the EEOC. Nine and a half weeks have elapsed before one gets down to the EEOC regional office. By then one might have developed an ulcer . . .

Filing a complaint is not easy; it is stressful. Working women do not feel that the EEOC wants to help them. A friend of mine who tried unsuccessfully, because she did not speak legalese, was advised that she could consult either a service for a small fee or a lawyer who would charge more, before going to the EEOC office. She said:

FIGURE 3–2 Equal Employment Opportunity Minimal Checklist

1.	Are you now doing more than or different things from those you were hired to do, for the same pay?	Yes ___	No ___
2.	If you have applied for a promotion, was a male having less experience, less seniority, and less education given the job?	Yes ___	No ___
3.	Has it ever been suggested in any way that part of your job involves sexual services (or buying gifts for your superior's wife)?	Yes ___	No ___
4.	Are you continually expected to do more work or a higher quality of work than your male peers?	Yes ___	No ___
5.	Are you the only woman at your level in your organization?	Yes ___	No ___
6.	Do you receive the same fringe benefits as male employees?	Yes ___	No___
7.	Has the "carrot and the stick" game been played at your place of employment? (Have you been promised a better job verbally, worked hard for it, and then not gotten it?)	Yes ___	No ___

Why should we have to pay to get fair treatment on the job? After all, we do pay taxes and the EEOC is part of the government. EEOC should help us file our complaints right instead of fobbing it off on someone else. EEOC should be specially [sic] helpful to us wage earners who need it worst.

She apparently felt that working women can't get away with buck passing, and neither should the EEOC.

President Carter, in 1977, reorganized and streamlined the EEOC. Then the Equal Pay Act enforcement was transferred from the Wage and Hour Division of the Department of Labor to the EEOC. Yet, despite reorganization, the "new" EEOC seems unable to please anyone. Even its recent commissioner, Eleanor Holmes Norton, an activist in civil rights and a respected attorney, couldn't seem to make it work.

The American Civil Liberties Union *Women's Rights Report* described the procedures. The earlier EEOC procedure had complainants state and file their own charges. Such charges related to individual or classwide allegations of job sex discrimination. But the streamlined approach is rather different and has done away with most of the individual charges. In fact, complainants no longer file their own charges; they dictate their story to an EEOC intake worker (usually not a lawyer), who narrows the charge and often discourages the complainant. These proce-

FIGURE 3–3 So You Have a Complaint: Timetable

WHEN	WHO	WHAT	FOLLOW-UP
Day 1	Immediate supervisor	You have a problem and want to make an appointment.	Written memo, day after appointment.
Day 31	Immediate supervisor	If no action after one month.	Written reminder of discussion about problem.
Day 36	Personnel officer	Problem continues; need appointment to describe it and get professional advice—content of appointment: I sent you copies of two memos about my problem. How can we solve it diplomatically?	Written memo day after appointment; copy to immediate supervisor.
		If no action after one more month.	
Day 66	Personnel officer	This meeting is to let you know I filed a complaint with EEOC (or other appropriate agency) about this matter yesterday. Keep cool, stay on the job, report any harassment to the compliance agency immediately.	Copy of your complaint document after meeting to personnel officer and immediate supervisor.

dures violate the EEOC's own guidelines but not the directive to cut down the case backlog. The new system is known as "rapid charge processing." (Its result appears to be rapid charge discharging.)

This procedure contrasts with the old one in which patterns of discrimination were sought and individual complaints were systematically expanded to include entire classes of employees where patterns of discrimination were found. We learned that if an employee gets through the intake procedure, which in some regions must be done in person, and insists on filing her complaint, the EEOC will conduct an investigation. The investigation is like a Keystone Cops movie.

During the investigation, the deck is stacked against the employee once more. The EEOC telephones the company personnel office, records the company's story, and inquires about the possibility of a settlement. If settlement appears unlikely, then the complainant must agree to a conference conducted by an EEOC officer. The conference involves the complainant on one side and her boss, personnel officer, and company lawyer on the other.

Courts do not put plaintiffs through this kind of process. It might be funny if it weren't so serious. To a bystander it resembles a marvelous connivance to let the employer off absolutely free. The EEOC officer usually has problems, and the individual working woman complainant who truly needs help always has problems. It is not surprising, therefore, that the EEOC's chief under the Reagan administration, Clarence Thomas, has created yet another system, one that stresses litigation (rather than the assumption of settling all charges out of court) in job bias cases.[16]

None of these procedures favors individual working women who are victimized by job sex discrimination. In view of this, and to increase the possibility of action, if three women worked together to obtain relief through the EEOC, each could use the other two as witnesses. While gathering of documentation would be simplified; nothing will make it pleasant.

While you are trying to decide whether to run the gauntlet of the EEOC, some information about rarely publicized types of discriminatory acts might be of interest. These concern employment agencies and unions and general types of prohibited employment discrimination. The last sentence of Figure 3–4 is especially interesting. If one were not a working woman, one might be tempted to excuse what one publication called Washington's "backing and filling on the civil rights issue for the past eight years,"[17] (1967 to 1975) on the grounds of the shifts in the two party

FIGURE 3–4 Types of Discriminatory Acts*

Discrimination based on race, color, religion, sex, or national origin is unlawful.

For *employers,* with regard to:

- Classified advertising
- Testing
- Hiring or firing
- Different wages for equal work
- Transfer, promotion, layoff, and recall
- Use of company facilities
- Training and apprenticeship programs
- Fringe benefits such as life insurance, health insurance, retirement plans, disability leave, and pay
- Causing or attempting to cause a union to discriminate
- Other terms and conditions of employment

For *employment agencies,* with regard to:

- Classified advertising
- Testing
- Receiving, classifying, or referring applicants for employment

For *unions,* with regard to:

- Applications for membership
- Testing
- Segregation or classification of members
- Referrals for employment
- Training and apprenticeship programs.
- Fringe benefits, such as life insurance, health insurance, retirement plans, disability leave, and pay
- Overt discriminatory conduct, including causing or attempting to cause an employer to discriminate

It pays to check with the nearest EEOC district office when you have a question about job discrimination or terms or conditions of employment. Such requirements as a high school diploma or not having an arrest record may be discriminatory *unless they clearly relate to job performance.*

Employers are required by law to post in a conspicuous place a notice giving summaries of the law and information about the filing of charges.

*From *Know Your Rights: What You Should Know about Equal Employment Opportunity,* (Washington, D.C.: Equal Employment Opportunity Commission, 1977), p. 2.

system that affect all government installations having presidential appointees as chiefs. Nevertheless, the pendulum has continued to swing between huge backlogs and incredible enforcement delays and EEOC's apparent refusal to pursue violators with all the power at its command.[18]

By summer 1977 the backlog of complaint cases had reached 123,000.[19] This might appear to be a pattern of support of employment discrimination, but clearly the task has been vast.

President Carter's 1977 procedure cut the backlogs drastically. Yet one wonders whether other factors coming into play when an employee enters the unfamiliar legal, governmental setting to discuss painful events on her job, and her fears of retaliation for revealing them have not further reduced the backlog of cases.

Suppose you do attempt to get justice. Remember that if your complaint is not accepted, it is not added to the backlog at the EEOC. However, if your employer harasses you, or tries to fire you after you try to complain, you do have a second chance with EEOC. Then your complaint might be considered, and you won't be afraid to file the second time around. You might even turn into a complaint addict, like one work-seeking woman who wrote in *Equal Opportunity Forum* about some of the tactics workers and job seekers encounter, namely that complaint investigators may interpret EEOC guidelines loosely. As a woman job applicant, she reported that top-ranked finalists may all be male while less preferred finalists may all be female. If top males all refuse the job offer, the job description may be modified and the salary raised. Then a male finalist accepts. The woman applicant contended that the EEOC investigator then revised his candidate pool assessment to exclude top male candidates refusing the position. Thus, remaining finalists—the male who accepted and females who received no job offer—appeared to represent organizational adherence to affirmative action hiring practices.[20]

After working for a time, some women have job-related sex discrimination problems that they usually try to solve in-house; sometimes they are unsuccessful and file a complaint with the EEOC.

Let's suppose you have filed a complaint. If your complaint is accepted and investigated, be patient. Your employer must tolerate you until the matter has been resolved by conciliation, a court case, or a consent decree. While awaiting the outcome, your employer may try to convince all involved that you have a personality problem, not a justified complaint. Should that occur, while it would be futile to inquire how many males were thought to have a personality problem, do keep your eyes open. There may be other sex-discriminatory practices around needing to be changed.

We are ready to move from our examination of the EEOC's shortcomings to an appraisal of some of its strengths. The EEOC has long enjoyed a good reputation for issuing forward-thinking guidelines on sex discrimination.[21] *Guidelines on Discrimination because of Sex,* issued periodically, reflect the political tone of the administration in power.[22] Therefore, we predict increasingly conservative *Guidelines* will be issued under the Reagan administration.

If it were possible to achieve, we would recommend a balanced EEOC investigation procedure, one that includes a representative for the worker; anything less seems a mockery of justice.

Comparable Worth Revisited

Our previous discussion of comparable worth ended when the EPA merged with the EEOC on July 1, 1979. Now we pick up the tale again. In Glendale, Arizona, the EEOC requested an injunction from a federal judge to halt the allegedly illegal practice of paying women less than males doing the same work.[23] A large, nationwide department and catalogue store, Montgomery Ward, was charged with paying male department managers 20 percent more monthly than female department managers with twice the number of years on the job. A sizable number of Montgomery Ward employees are affected by the suit filed by the EEOC—Montgomery Ward employees in the United States number about 100,000. These employees are learning about the laws prohibiting sex discrimination in employment and about the concept of comparable worth.

A fall 1979 conference in Washington, D.C., featured Eleanor Holmes Norton, then commissioner of the EEOC, whose presence, prestige, and vehemence promoted the comparable worth concept. Norton provided examples of pay inequity by employers and commented on her own inability to believe that the women's jobs involved had intrinsically less value than the men's jobs with which they were compared.[24] One could infer that Norton did not believe that the law intended to sanction pay inequity or inequity in the value of men's and women's work.

Once responsibility for administering the EPA shifted from the Department of Labor to the EEOC, as Margaret Moses of the American Civil Liberties Union tells us, the issue for litigation became whether "Title VII's coverage of sex-based discrimination [is] much broader than that of the Equal Pay Act."[25]

Moses suggests a litigation strategy to bring pay equity matters under Title VII. (See Figure 3–5.) While steps given refer mainly to attorneys and the courts, working women can now request that Title VII be used in their cases. But they should first acquaint themselves with the latest developments regarding Title VII and the comparable worth issue. For instance, in August 1980, a decision by the Third U.S. Circuit Court of Appeals in Philadelphia agreed in a suit against Westinghouse Electric Corporation by five women workers that the federal Civil Rights Act allows women to claim equal pay for doing jobs comparable to those performed by men. Commissioner Norton hailed the decision as one of "historic dimensions because it applies Title 7 [sic] to the most pervasive form of discrimination remaining unaddressed by the statute."[26]

FIGURE 3–5 Litigation Strategy for Comparable Worth Cases*

1. Establish that Title VII applies to all sex-based wage and compensation charges.

    Advantages: Title VII is broader in its provisions than the EPA is. A precedent for trying cases under Title VII now exists. The strategy furnishes one basis for litigation of such charges.

2. Establish that Title VII is sufficiently broad to cover the comparable worth situation.

    Advantages: A legal precedent for comparable worth is now available in the Westinghouse Electric case. A law is available that all attorneys can use for similar cases.
    Additional precedents will develop and will strengthen the law.
    Additional decisions will strengthen the comparable worth concept.

3. The EEOC will provide some guidelines for job evaluation useful in developing standards of proof.

    Advantages: Courts need guidelines to determine whether wages have been depressed because of sex-biased job evaluations, devaluation of wages, or biased job evaluation.
    Guidelines assist lawyers and judges in court, assist employees out of court, and may deter employers from evasion of the issue of comparable worth.

*Adapted from Margaret Moses, "Pay Equity: The Issues of the 80s," *aclu Women's Rights Report* 1, no. 4 (Winter 1979–80): pp. 1, 7.

Having that precedent, working women can familiarize themselves with updated EEOC guidelines and can furnish documentation of comparable worth jobs through their organizations. Groups able to provide large-scale documentation of violations of comparable worth can hold hearings or offer to testify in favor of the concept. Working women can publicize the outcomes of such evaluations, can educate political candidates about the concept, and can support its promoters. Working women can both inform their employers about comparable worth and monitor progress. Finally, Moses reminds those organizations involved in the pay equity issue and attorneys handling comparable worth cases that maximizing prospects of success requires a network for cooperation and for exchanging information and strategy. Working women are the backbone of that network.

Player's Experience

Employed women are less interested in networks and guidelines than in their personal job progress. When EEOC reorganization took place, President Carter shared that interest. But he also determined that a major cause of ineffective enforcement of federal laws providing for equal job treatment for women was fragmentation of the civil rights machinery. Carter believed that simplifying and centralizing this machinery would improve its function.

Before Carter acted, 25 federal agencies were involved in equal employment law enforcement. The House Labor Committee Subcommittee on Equal Opportunities had reported that government efforts were disjointed, minimal, and almost ineffectual. Reorganization began after this report. The Carter plan selected the newly reorganized EEOC to administer many laws that had been enforced by various government agencies.

However, despite the newly simplified, centralized, understaffed, combined agency with its formal procedures, and its political need to demonstrate effectiveness, individual working women seeking help are again overlooked. While working women are involved or included in class action suits filed against giant corporations, the centralized structure is not sympathetic to the plight of those individual working women who have employment complaints related to sex discrimination. Centralized, simplified structures need big cases like the class action suits against American Telephone and Telegraph Company, Sears Roebuck, and Montgomery Ward. Such cases make the investigative or enforcement agency appear to be doing its job. It may be. But you rarely hear its praise from women working in two- and three-person offices, or as elementary school teachers or factory workers.

We undoubtedly needed test cases to broaden the enforcement of Title VII by the EEOC. Still, one yearns nostalgically for the EEOC's early years when individual women could file discrimination complaints and attack inconsistent practices that also denied freedom of job choice. Ross illustrates how "protective laws" ostensibly enacted for women's benefit really served the purposes of discrimination. Her example is Lorena Weeks, who worked for Southern Bell Telephone where she applied for promotion to switchman. She was not promoted because the company claimed that switchmen were required to lift 31-pound fire extinguishers and a Georgia law prohibited women from doing that. Somehow, the company forgot that her present, less well paid position required Weeks to lift a 35-pound typewriter. Weeks sued and after years of legal action won the job plus the compensation she would have earned as a switchman during the interval.[27] Though she filed alone, the Weeks findings are applicable to a group or class of women—those denied access to job opportunities because of "protective laws." The case was important; alas, today it more resembles muscle flexing than real action.

The recent EEOC attempts to weed out "weak" complaints from "strong" ones is reminiscent of an older division of jobs into "light" and "heavy" and "women's work" and "men's work." Title VII decreed such distinctions sex discriminatory. What is now needed relative to EEOC complaints is ameliorative action within a reasonable time span. One wonders what the human cost of EEOC failure to provide help is. It is probably incalculably high; to those refused legal redress and its attendant sanctions, we must add women who are unable to act in their own behalf and those who give up. All working women benefit or suffer as a consequence of the EEOC's effectiveness. We would do well to keep that in mind.

EEOC AS UMPIRE

The EEOC clarifies as well as enforces. However, Supreme Court decisions can run counter to the EEOC's hopes. *General Electric* v. *Gilbert* is an illustration. In that case, the court found no discrimination in G.E.'s practice of providing medical insurance benefits to men (for procedures including vasectomies and hair transplants) while denying medical insurance benefits to women employees disabled by pregnancy. The Supreme

Court considered the exclusion justified since pregnancy benefits were more related to "condition" than to "gender."[28] It was an incredible decision and one rejecting the EEOC guidelines that recommend inclusion of pregnancy-related disabilities in company insurance plans.

Happily, a 1978 amendment to the Civil Rights Act now prohibits sex discrimination based on pregnancy—a major victory. We include a picture for every working woman ever "disabled by" or suffering under the "temporary disability" of pregnancy. The cartoon becomes "funny" in light of the ban on pregnancy discrimination, but that does not detract from the subject's seriousness.

The Women's Bureau said:

> Overturning the adverse rulings, the new law specifically amends Title VII to define the terms "because of sex" and "on the basis of sex" to include because of or on the basis of pregnancy, childbirth, or related medical conditions. It requires women affected by pregnancy, childbirth or related medical conditions to be treated *the same* for all employment-related purposes, including receipt of benefits under fringe programs, *as other persons not so affected but similar in their ability or inability to work.*[29]

That, too, was a victory. So was the equal pension decision already discussed. Each victory strengthens the positive side of the equal employment opportunity ledger. Working women remain disappointed. They deserve strong enforcement of Title VII. As we assess the accomplishments under the EEOC and the job to be done, we have to admit it will be a long, arduous struggle to achieve equal employment opportunity for America's working women. How can we, as individual working women, speed the achievement of equal employment opportunity?

The Choices for Action (Figure 3–7) suggest methods for achieving favorable resolution of Title VII problems. A legal action route (A) is sketched for those having Title VII complaints and grievances. Women wanting to test the EEOC enforcement procedure directly might find the legal approach useful. Working women unlikely to go to court or to the EEOC may be helped by suggestions for improving Title VII effectiveness through increasing awareness of and bolstering enforcement of Title VII; they might find the other part of Figure 3–7 (B—Title VII, out of court) more helpful. Some working women may use the choices for action as a jumping-off place for their own strategies. More power to them!

Whatever your preference, the message is clear: Nourish and cherish Title VII, or it will wither on the vine and a later generation will need to replant where it once grew.

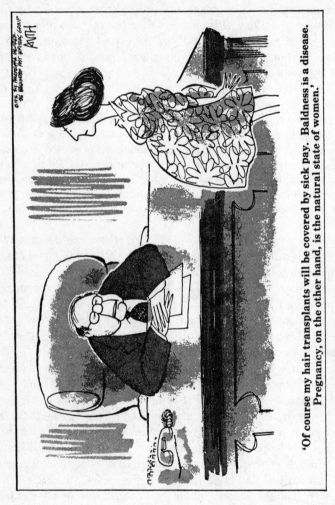

'Of course my hair transplants will be covered by sick pay. Baldness is a disease. Pregnancy, on the other hand, is the natural state of women.'

FIGURE 3-6 Tony Auth, *The Philadelphia Inquirer*.

FIGURE 3-7 Choices for Action: Title VII and Individual Working Women

A. *The Legal Action Route*

   I. Building a Class
       1. Organizing working women in small enterprises
       2. Sharing grievances and complaints
       3. Defining the class
       4. Filing a class action suit with the EEOC

   II. Finding Suitable Casting Models
       1. Finding cases that have been successful
       2. Finding approaches to Title VII that have worked recently
       3. Fitting your case into a model

   III. Planning Courses of Action
       1. Determining size of the class needed
       2. Gathering data and documents
       3. Filing the complaint of class action

   IV. The Legal Action
       1. Deciding on legal representation
       2. Monitoring the action
       3. Publicizing the outcome
       4. Taking further steps

B. *Title VII Out of Court*

   I. Bolstering Enforcement of Title VII
       1. Reading current materials about Title VII actions
       2. Discussing these materials objectively with coworkers
       3. Supporting elected officials whose actions support Title VII

   II. Increasing Awareness of Title VII
       1. Asking for and setting up lunchtime workshop at work on Title VII
       2. Rating your organization on Title VII compliance*
       3. Listing what Title VII enforcement could do for you

   III. Getting Results for Title VII
       1. Joining the nonpartisan League of Women Voters and working on Title VII with other members
       2. Planning a course of implementation of Title VII which you can put into action now
       3. Selecting one result you expect to achieve (be specific; give yourself a deadline date for achieving your result)

*The procedures outlined in Chapter 4 can be modified for this purpose.

ADDITIONAL INFORMATION SOURCES

If you are a federal employee or an applicant for federal employment and think you've been discriminated against, contact the equal employment opportunity director of the agency involved for information about filing complaints, your appeals rights, and the limits for filing an appeal. Two compliance agencies that may be of help to you are:

> Office of Appeals and Review
> Equal Employment Opportunity Commission
> Washington, D.C. 20419

> Merit Systems Protection Board
> Washington, D.C. 20419

If you think you have been discriminated against by an apprenticeship program:

> Bureau of Apprenticeship and Training
> Employment and Training Administration
> U.S. Department of Labor
> Washington, D.C. 20213

If you think you have been discriminated against in employment by a law enforcement agency:

> Office of Civil Rights Compliance
> Law Enforcement Assistance Administration
> U.S. Department of Justice
> Washington, D.C. 20531

If you have complained to another agency about employment discrimination and you feel that your complaint has not been properly handled:

> Office of Interagency Coordination
> Equal Employment Opportunity Commission
> Washington, D.C. 20506

For violations of the following, the address of the compliance agency is below the law or regulation:

Title VII of the Civil Rights Act of 1964
Equal Employment Opportunity Commission
2401 E Street, N.W.
Washington, D.C. 20506
(or regional EEOC office)

Equal Pay Act of 1963
EEOC, as above.

Title IX of the Education Amendments of 1972
Office for Civil Rights
Department of Education
Washington, D.C. 20201

Executive Order 11246 (applies to contractors on federal funds)
Office for Civil Rights
Department of Education
Washington, D.C. 20201

or

Office for Federal Contract Compliance Programs
Employment Standards Administration
Department of Labor
Washington, D.C. 20210

Also see the information about compliance agencies given in the chapters relating to each of the legal provisions. Since addresses change, do check, wherever possible, before sending information. This avoids delays.

NOTES

1. See Caroline Bird, *Born Female* (New York: Pocket Books, 1969), for a stunning account of the events in Congress, in Chapter I, "Ladies' Day in the House." There, on p. 7, Representative Edith Green opposed the amendment because she felt that Negro women had suffered much more discrimination than she had. However, Shirley Chisholm took the other view, and in an often quoted remark stated that she had suffered far more discrimination as a woman than as a black. Edward N. Bomsey, "What Management Is Doing about Women in the Workforce," in Mildred E. Katzell and William C. Byham, eds., *Women in the Workforce: Confrontation with Change* (New York: Behavioral Publications, 1972), whose legal expertise lay in the field of equal employment opportunity, in 1972 stated that by the time President Johnson signed the Civil Rights Act of

1964, women's groups were not yet planning the women's rights confrontations and demonstrations seen a few years later, p. 57.

2. There are few bona fide occupational qualifications. Two most often cited apparently originated with Bem and appear on p. 70 in a quotation from her study of sex-segregated job ads. Karen DeCrow, *Sexist Justice* (New York: Vintage, 1974), Chapters 5 and 6, cites the landmark cases and gives perceptive analyses of the crucial issues.

3. Sandra L. Bem and Daryl J. Bem, "Sex-Segregated Want Ads: Do They Discourage Female Job Applicants?" in J. Herbert Hamsher and Harold Sigall, *Psychology and Social Issues* (New York: Macmillan, 1973), pp. 261–65.

4. Margaret Hennig and Anne Jardim, *The Managerial Woman* (Garden City, N.Y.: Anchor Press/Doubleday, 1977), p. 66, exclude from consideration of women who have "made it in the man's world" those in the women's field of cosmetics. It is assumed that "women's fields" are easier terrains for women to conquer; little evidence exists to support such a conclusion. The case in Florida of *Diaz* v. *Pan American World Airlines, Inc.*, adds androgynous balance. Diaz, male, wanted to be a steward. A psychologist's testimony—this time in favor of Pan Am's female-only stewardesses policy—was sought. The lower court allowed the discriminatory hiring. Diaz lost, appealed, and had the earlier decision reversed. See De Crow, *Sexist Justice*, pp. 97 and 100–101.

5. Bem, "Sex-Segregated Want Ads," p. 264.

6. Solomon Asch, *Social Psychology* (Englewood Cliffs, N.J.: Prentice-Hall, 1952). Asch, in Chapter 16, pp. 450–501, described experiments illustrating what happens to judgment and perception when everyone else insisted that the subject was wrong. We have suggested application of the findings of these experiments to the situation of the occupational token.

7. Hennig and Jardim, *The Managerial Woman*, p. 191.

8. See Chapter 2 on the wage gap.

9. Phyllis A. Wallace, "Impact of Equal Employment Opportunity Laws," in Juanita M. Kreps, ed., *Women and the American Economy: A Look to the 1980s* (Englewood Cliffs, N.J.: Prentice-Hall, Inc., 1976), pp. 143–48; also see Susan D. Ross and Ann Barcher, *The Rights of Women: An American Civil Liberties Handbook*, Revised (New York: Bantam Books, 1983), pp. 31–32. The authors point out that seniority remains a determinant of job stability and advancement, but that court decisions have forced modifications in seniority systems that can benefit working women. Ross points out that the new rules can aid working women who can demonstrate that their assignment to poorly paid departments was based upon sex-discriminatory practices. In such cases, women workers may utilize seniority rights to attempt mobility into more lucrative positions in higher-paying segments of the company.

10. Dorothy Jongeward and Dru Scott, *Affirmative Action for Women* (Reading, Mass.: Addison-Wesley, 1975), p. 52.

11. The "Ban against Pregnancy Discrimination" (Washington, D.C.: U.S. Department of Labor, Women's Bureau, March 1979) makes sex discrimination based on pregnancy, childbirth, or related medical conditions illegal.

12. Wallace, "Impact of Equal Employment Opportunity Laws," p. 124. The case was *Griggs* v. *Duke Power Company*, March 1971.

13. William H. Chafe, "Looking Backward in Order to Look Forward: Women, Work and Social Values in America," in Kreps, ed., *Women and the American Economy*, pp. 26–30, presents a discussion of "The Issue of Equality."

14. One form of this is that all working women—regardless of race, creed, nationality, or national origin—have two jobs, one inside and one outside the home. This is a universal example of normative stereotyping intimately related to concepts of "woman's place." Working men, by equally well-known contrast, have one job.

15. "The Equal Employment Opportunity Act of 1972" (Washington, D.C.: Subcommittee on Labor of the Committee on Labor and Public Welfare, U.S. Senate, March 1972), p. 7.

16. "What's Wrong with the New EEOC?" *aclu Women's Rights Report* 1, no. 2 (Summer 1979): 1. Also see Joann S. Lublin, "EEOC Alters Stance to Stress Litigation in Job-Bias Cases," *The Wall Street Journal*, October 28, 1983, p. 2.

17. *Business Week*, July 25, 1977, p. 116, describes the reorganization of the EEOC with the advent of a new Democratic administration.

18. " . . . *To Form a More Perfect Union* . . . " *Justice for American Women* (Washington, D.C.: National Commission on the Observance of International Women's Year, 1976); some sex discrimination cases filed in 1970 had not been processed by 1976 when the IWY report was published, p. 49.

19. *Business Week*, July 25, 1977, p. 116.

20. Kay Sandra, "Affirmative Action Addict Kicks the Habit . . . Almost," *Equal Opportunity Forum*, October 1980, p. 38.

21. " . . . *To Form a More Perfect Union* . . . " When a question arose between two civil rights agencies regarding an employment standard, the IWY recommended adherence to the EEOC guidelines, p. 48.

22. Wallace, "Impact of Equal Opportunity Laws," pp. 128–29. *Guidelines on Discrimination Because of Sex* was released by the EEOC in December 1965, August 1969, and April 1972, and was awaited in 1978. *Guidelines on Sexual Harassment* appeared April 11, 1980.

23. "U.S. Charges Ward's Pays Women Less," *Chicago Sun-Times*, October 13, 1979, p. 25.

24. "Women Lose Ground at Pay Window," *Chicago Sun-Times*, *October 30, 1979, p. 26*.

25. *Margaret Moses, "Pay Equity: The Issue of the 80s," aclu Women's Rights Report* 1, no. 4 (Winter 1979–80): 1.

26. "Victory for Women," *The antiochian*, October 1980, p. 1.

27. Ross and Barcher, *The Rights of Women*, p. 29.

28. *Clearinghouse International Newsletter* 3, no. 5 (May 1978): 1.

29. "Ban against Pregnancy Discrimination," p. 1.

My wife works so I can go to school; she also takes a course. The place is a real mess. One night I pointed to some dust under the sofa and she said, "Oink, oink."

Male college student, 1971

Being Your Own Referee
an affirmative action rating plan

WHAT'S A GOOD
AFFIRMATIVE ACTION PROGRAM?

Mindset

It would be insane to expect an employer to let you—a mere employee—
see the organization's affirmative action plan; the organization is not required to prove to the general public that it has an affirmative action plan.
But that need not stop you. This chapter offers some ideas about what you
can do.

First, there are three steps:

1. You can learn what affirmative action is and how it is supposed to work.
2. Then you can assess the affirmative action situation where you work.
3. You can bring violations to the attention of the compliance agency.

You will learn in this chapter that penalties to the organization are stiff
ones.[1] But government compliance agencies are not looking for things to
investigate. They feel they have enough to occupy them.

Meanwhile, working women seeking affirmative action usually are
not lawyers and may forget that legal problems connected with affirmative
action are extremely complex. There are, however, plenty of nonlegal
considerations. One thorny nonlegal point is that the behavioral difficulty
of changing long ingrained habits and attitudes is often mentioned. Despite that, it is in the interest of both sides—employees and
management—to work for full affirmative action. Affirmative action
makes for good business, big profits, contented employees, and social
prestige. We still have far to go before we can say we've truly given democracy a chance.[2] That's what affirmative action in the workplace is all
about—democracy in action.

SHEDDING THE LOSER ROLE

When I first experienced workplace sex discrimination, I denied it. Then
I became paralyzed by rage. Rage was followed by the feeling that I could
do something crazy, perhaps even violent, to those who had caused such
great and unwarranted pain. The acutely distressing stabs subsided gradually. I was left with no defense, no rebuttal; no one had ever given any

clue to improvements in performance that might make me eligible for promotion. There had never been anything but praise for my work.

Failing to receive the overdue promotion, I left, ironically for a far superior position. In time I was able to acknowledge that I had been discriminated against as a working woman.

A few years after that, a management vacancy occurred where I then worked. A petition was circulated demanding that the vacancy be filled by a woman, apparently a specific in-house woman. Where I worked, 20 percent of the top jobs (two) were filled by women; adding another would have put the organization on the side of the angels (28 percent or more women) regarding affirmative action.

So, why did I object to that petition? First, the notion that any employee might be selected primarily for gender rather than qualifications was offensive; it would have been delightful had the successful candidate also been a woman. Second, because many qualified women could have applied for the position, that petition made it appear that there were no qualified women around. Affirmative action is supposed to redress past wrongs, not to perpetuate them. Failure to consider qualified working women for promotion and failure to consider working women as qualified for advancement are attempts to make a mockery of affirmative action.

Other tactics are used to simulate support of affirmative action. One scheme simply shifted an organization's payroll schedule. Clerical employees received weekly paychecks; employees in higher positions were paid twice a month. To signify compliance with affirmative action some job titles were changed and all employees were paid every two weeks. No tasks or wages changed. It is not affirmative action to move from violation of one law to violation of another. Yet, when this curious maneuver was reported to several women, each of them credited a different company with it. Few suggested that the practice was wrong.

Physical and Mental Training:
Affirmative Action Awareness Muscles

Our purpose is to share information about sex discrimination and affirmative action. We are not going to focus on quotas, goals, or percentages. Those are quantitative approaches, often applied internally. We prefer to present a qualitative way of examining affirmative action—from the outside.

The aim is to generate a practical approach to affirmative action for working women. We'll start with a little workout, a warm-up, and some stretching exercises to strengthen your affirmative action awareness muscles. These muscles are controlled by the brain, though arousing them may take some doing. Unlike many other muscles, these can be exercised during the entire workday with healthful effects. Gradual working up to that level is suggested; one does not jump into mental calisthenics. These exercises require no special equipment and may be performed while sitting and observing, even while working. Reading is another route to development of affirmative action muscles and a broader background.

Here are two sample problems for you to practice on. The first makes you a manager:

> Assume that you are responsible for staffing a new branch factory employing 1000 women and 2000 men. Your branch is independent of the parent company with regard to staffing and attendant policies. What would be the five most important things you could do to ensure that affirmative action became a fact in your factory? (*Hint*: as a manager, you are not on the scene to cause trouble or to violate the law.)

The second problem offers other challenges:

> You are a consultant to management. There has been a complaint about a department's treatment of women. Your job is to provide a plan so that women are treated in accordance with the law. Your plan, or program, becomes operative in 30 days. You must give detailed examples of the violations and back them up by stating which parts of which laws are being violated. Management wants two different remediation strategies for each violation. (*Hint*: People are peculiar, and tact helps, but compliance must be provided for.)

You might spend a little time now tackling these sample problems. You already have ideas about fair employment practices, equal pay, and civil rights legislation. If you work for an educational institution, you might want to look at Chapter 5 first. Later there will be some responses working women presented to the first problem.

Here's some basic training to help you. Affirmative action requires that the applicant pool for a position mirror either the population distribution in the region or the available labor pool.[3] If the applicant pool contains only white clerical workers, something is wrong; if all are of the same sex, that's even worse. Second, after the applicant pool is complete, the best qualified applicant, regardless of sex, ethnic group, and so on, must be offered the job. This two-stage procedure is fundamental to the affirmative action process. Employer and employee are expected to demonstrate good faith during the hiring process; not all do. Employers who violate the spirit of affirmative action probably are likely to violate the letter of the law.

The idea of affirmative action may be resisted as contrary to a deeply rooted American principle: that equality of opportunity, defined as equal access to education, is crucial. Since colonial days, Americans have assumed that equality of educational opportunity would make democracy perfect. But nobody ever expected equality of outcomes or rewards.

Belief in equal educational opportunity was so strong that Andrew Carnegie, a self-made millionaire who endowed libraries and foundations, seriously proposed a law that would have made each citizen's assets revert to the state at death. Carnegie's notion was to give all individuals an equal start in the race, not to "predetermine outcome of the race by proportions or access to goals."[4] In fact, our public educational system was established in such a way that large numbers of Americans came close to having an equal start in the race.

But neither equality of opportunity nor equality of education got women to the starting line. Nor were women viewed as victims of discrimination until late in the equalitarian struggle; affirmative action for women arrived on the employment scene much later.

Today, in fields representing technological developments, openness of the race and availability of jobs may permit women to start on an equal footing with male workers. Still, working women must exercise their affirmative action awareness muscles to ensure that equality of job entry is matched by equal pay.[5] Furthermore, entry-level jobs providing affirmative action bases for women often require specialized training. Potential employers need not provide such training; applicants must be prepared to work.

Technical, as differentiated from technological, fields include several whose workforce is almost all women. The allied health fields—medical laboratory technician, dental hygienist—come to mind.[6] Risks involved in unisex employment fields include the familiar stereotypes. If a field is predominantly female, it can't be important; therefore, it commands low prestige and receives low pay. Advancement may be extremely slow. Another risk is being isolated from mainstream activity because the communications networks and corridors of power are controlled by men. Finally, when women succeed in a unisex employment field, retribution from men may be swift and destructive; the replacement of female midwives by male obstetricians is one example. It is to everyone's advantage to have both men and women employed in all fields.

Affirmative action is intended to increase women's (and minority) participation in the workforce. Two affirmative action targets—job entry and access to advancement—must be recognized. We have been discussing job entry. Approaching it requires having accurate, current information so that hitting the job bull's eye occurs before all of the job arrows (and one's confidence) are shot. Recent data revealed that only 1.7 percent of the 255,000 apprentices being trained in the United States were women. These women were found in less than half (44 percent) of the 450 apprentice trades listed by the Department of Labor.[7] When apprentices complete their lengthy, intensive training, they are prepared for jobs with futures. They apply for jobs like this:

> *Wanted*: Engineering technician. Technical education and/or experience required. Good starting salary. Excellent opportunities for advancement.[8]

Do you know a woman who would qualify? Or are your women friends either underqualified or overqualified? Do you know a man who could qualify? Is there something wrong with the replies to such acid tests? Why don't women train to enter the engineering technologies? Probably because they know little or nothing about them. When will large numbers of women prepare for, apply for, and obtain positions in fields where opportunity exists?

Perhaps it will happen when a match is provided among (1) interest and ability, (2) training, and (3) availability of jobs. Little progress has been made in considering the individual's interest and ability before training. Women have not done themselves a favor by selecting an occupation mainly because it pays well or because a lot of women are in it. It is wise to consider personal values; one owes it to oneself to choose a suitable, satisfying occupation.

Entry-level (and dead-end) jobs are plentiful for women today—with periodic raises but no new challenges. Increased responsibility often turns into more of the same—more accounts, more files—and is the result of longevity of the organization, not increased capacity of the woman worker.

The second target of affirmative action is equal access to higher-level employment opportunity. Progress has been slower and resistance stronger than for job entry. Apparently, many males feel that while it is now all right to have women around the workplace, having women manage anything remains almost unthinkable. Meanwhile, the inaccurate refrain of "no qualified women applicants" continues to be heard. Promotion of qualified women, currently available in fields ranging from astronaut to zoologist, has been slow; women's fine workplace records tend to be forgotten when merit, promotion, and training are due.

We'll stop here and get back to the sample problems. You may have enough hints and information to make a trial run with real world-of-work difficulties. The sample problems asked some hard questions, which working women, myself among them, tried to answer. It was one way of exercising our flabby affirmative action awareness muscles.

AA—FIVE POINTS

Almost all of the working women who did the sample problems stressed management's commitment to affirmative action:

> The important thing is to remember that in order to comply, recruitment and selection must be done in a way that reflects the company's commitment to its AA program and gets the desired results.
>
> My attitude . . . is that affirmative action plans are only as good as management's commitment to them. I continue to see very subtly covered up cases of discrimination within the business world. However, I hope that in time, affirmative action plans and other nondiscrimination efforts will allow me to fulfill my potential in the business world through a system of hiring and promotion that is equitable.

Let's look closely at this and other important aspects of affirmative action.

Active Management Support

Point 1: Active support by top-level management is fundamental to a successful affirmative action program. A climate of support contrasts vividly with "trying to make a good impression." The former reflects positively upon the organization's integrity and its management. The latter may contribute to suspension of trust. It is risky to work for an untrustworthy outfit; we feel this as strongly when we desperately need employment as when we want to improve our workforce position. It is unlikely that any minority people are found in bona fide management positions in organizations only trying to make a good impression. It dawned on me that large firms hiring hundreds of women that had no on-site personnel officer usually also lacked an affirmative action program on-site. Technically, such organizations were complying with the law because they had personnel officers and an affirmative action plan at the main office, although most of the employees worked elsewhere. One organization promoted a few women to "office manager"; the women convinced themselves that they had entered the ranks of management. This was not the case. Should you have doubts about your organization or one you apply to, keep in mind that top management's position on affirmative action can be assessed by observation. "By their deeds shall you know them."

The supportive climate components of affirmative action include providing an equal chance in the race, then objectively rewarding for demonstrated performance—what management *does*. Smooth organizational functioning and mouthing of correct sentiments is not enough. Management must demonstrate dedication to providing fair treatment at the entry level and opportunity to advance, even to the management level. The ideal supportive climate provided by management would include unruffled calm when government personnel visit on-site for compliance checks with affirmative action requirements, or when an employee files a claim.[9] A clear contrast with this attitude is:

> The feds were in again this week. They said we weren't meeting our quotas of broads, niggers, and you know who else. I spend so damned much time on body counts, I can't get my work done.[10]

A supportive climate is not totally altruistic. It would exploit the good business, good public relations potential in truly affirmative action. Achieving that climate would probably require reeducation of top management nationwide. The goal would be a representative organizational team capable of communicating and cooperating to get the job at hand done. That won't happen very fast.[11]

The dynamics have to be understood, among them awareness that it takes a heap of followers to produce a leader. Management cannot manage without workers willing to be supervised. The mass of workers can exert massive pressure, like an earthquake, upon the small, thin layers at the top. Management can minimize tremors and trauma and can gain worker support by becoming responsive to workers' views and representative of the composition of the workforce. Affirmative action is about that, too.

Hopeful signs that top managers are becoming willing to tackle those problems in new ways would be found in management's acknowledgment that a problem exists. This would be followed by awareness that management is part of the problem and must take constructive, corrective action and become part of the solution. For example, recently the affirmative action officer of an organization reported to top management that while one unit now contained both minority and women entry-level managers, another unit was totally lacking these important role models. The president responded that continued improvement was a task of the entire management team and that he expected results soon. Reinforcing this view, a working woman/student in her role as management consultant (in our second sample problem), wrote:

> This plan needs total support from management to be effective. I feel that the best way to begin this program is for management to meet to review the material to give them a better understanding of what discrimination is and how we can deal with it.

We tend to forget that managers may be so busy managing that they get out of synch with their society, and that managers both rely on experts and delegate tasks and responsibilities. Finally, a supportive climate for affirmative action furnished by top-level management may be something top-level managers do not understand because they have never experienced it.[12]

Hiring Practices

Point 2: A good affirmative action program utilizes objective hiring practices. Employing an elementary school teacher because she has shapely legs is as stupid as choosing the surgeon with the best address. Alas, much of today's hiring is hardly more sophisticated. Among the remedies are attention to (1) job counseling, (2) the elimination of dead-end jobs, and (3) the creation of real career paths for women. Another suggestion is that all advertising and posting of job openings, all circulation of job descriptions, and collection of applicant résumés and other applicant pool information be done by the personnel manager and personnel staff.

The advantages of such a system are not widely recognized; they were not cited by many of the working women who responded to the first sample problem. Here are some major advantages of locating objective hiring practices within a personnel unit whose manager reports to the organization's chief executive officer on a regular basis:

1. Preliminary screening of candidates saves supervisors time in staffing their sections.

2. Adequate candidate pools can be achieved, while competitive salaries and qualifications are maintained.

3. Personnel is aware of employee interests, talents, and experience as well as job classifications, thus can function as a clearinghouse for internal and external job applicants.

4. The supportive climate for affirmative action can be encouraged, documented, and publicized.

5. Top management involvement in the structure of the total workforce aids in supporting and enforcing affirmative action or in placing responsibility for any lack of success.

Achievement of these five advantages when objective hiring practices are utilized permits the personnel unit to mediate when differences arise between management and workers related to job conditions. The personnel unit may also mediate between managers of different levels. Personnel units may represent organizations by performing governmentally imposed affirmative action tasks such as documentation of applicant pool composition, instructions to search committees, or submission of workforce composition statistics.

In an ideal affirmative action situation, the personnel unit's basic function is facilitation; in providing service and objectivity, it seeks to place the right person in the right job at the right time. How are personnel functions carried out in your workplace? Consider how well the criteria of objectivity and service are being met. Are issues or personalities central in personnel disputes? Does personnel encourage or discourage cooperation between management and workers? Lastly, is your personnel unit committed to affirmative action?

It may seem very radical to ask yourself these questions. But if you do not come to grips with them, who will? You have the right (and responsibility) to evaluate your top management and personnel unit. Assess them on two levels at least: How well do they meet affirmative action mandates, and how consistent are the organization's stated affirmative action policies and actual implementation? You may want to defer your judgment on the consistency issue until you have read the next section.

Training and Promotion

Point 3: Affirmative action is encouraged through open training and promotion at all levels. This third logical step in our good affirmative action program flows from the first two. If top management provides a supportive climate permitting personnel to furnish service and objectivity in its areas of responsibility, it then follows that training and promotion will be open. Employees wanting, and ready for, advancement will be seriously considered as candidates when vacancies occur.

Open training and promotion do not exist nationwide today; there are both subtle and irrational obstacles. But there has been progress. Job entry is relatively open today, even for women, and is dependent upon the demand for workers. Unfortunately, access to training and promotion is less advanced than access to job entry.

Training availability can outrun possibility of promotion. Thousands of women have learned this after completing courses or programs designed to lead to vocational challenges or interesting careers. When an employer encourages women to prepare for better positions—for example, by offering tuition benefits—disappointment grows geometrically when promotion does not follow training. Disappointment is doubled when the training has been occupationally oriented and the working woman cannot use her new skills. She may become bitter as she finds herself ever more overqualified. She is twice frustrated—by being overqualified and by having been fooled into taking more unbeneficial training. Employers unwittingly aggravate this situation by subsidizing only vocationally related training.

Working women could inquire about the prospects for promotion before taking training. If the outlook were bleak, they could ask about tuition benefits for nonoccupational or cognate courses. Working women could explain the benefits of a policy of enriching workers' lives and experience through education, even where no immediate economic outcome would result. This aspect of affirmative action is rarely considered.

It is important to offer employees beneficial training, since no affirmative action program can guarantee automatic promotion after training. An obvious fact is that the further up the occupational ladder a worker goes, the less additional space is available.

For these reasons, one free benefit all employers could provide is to give potential trainees the straight scoop—even when it demands that employees rethink training options. Such a procedure—giving the facts first, treating the working woman as an adult—could mean that personnel might suggest that she cut her losses, go elsewhere into another line of work in order to maximize later gains where real opportunity exists. The final decision rests with the working woman; giving her sound information about prospects is a critical aspect of open training and promotion.

By contrast, affirmative action programs should not coerce any worker into more training and responsibility than she wants. We cannot afford to forget that each working woman is an individual. Oversights resulting from thinking about women in general do violence to another fundamental affirmative action premise: that the worker be expected to make choices about her occupational role. We need to reaffirm that there is nothing wrong with liking one's job and deciding to stay put until we want to make a change.

Some women are good at their jobs, find them adequately demanding and adequately status-y. A truly affirmative action program would include in its goals that of determining by objective means which employees were content where they were. Such assessments would naturally be updated regularly so that shifts would be incorporated into the affirmative action program. An ideal program would offer on-the-job or job-associated refresher training for contented working women wishing to continue doing a first-rate job. Providing updating in no way implies reduction in the amount and kinds of training needed for promotion. Both types of training must be included in the affirmative action program. Updating is to keep employees current in their areas of expertise; training related to promotion is more obviously affirmative since it offers the potential of organizational action to redress past wrongs. Correction of past wrongs is close to the purpose of affirmative action, which was to equalize opportunities and to provide a route whereby those rarely given a chance to rise to the top could begin the journey upward.

Discussions with women in management and with working women students preparing for management positions have sensitized us to the wide range values women consider in setting their career goals. Women tend to have groups of interests in different locations. Workplace, home, and campus are examples. Women value these focal places highly, and they add another factor: people, the social side of life. The variety is dizzying and absorbs energy. All women realize this, and some women choose not to attempt top-level management positions. Unfortunately, women who do make a conscious choice, either to start climbing or not to, find little workplace support, less in affirmative action programs.

Program Responsibility

Point 4: Delegating responsibility for the affirmative action program to a knowledgeable, skilled, dedicated, capable officer is essential. The person responsible for managing and implementing the program has a complicated task. A perfect candidate would be an intelligent, warm, business-like, tactful woman or minority group member who understood and could explain to management such complex issues as (1) why some talented women workers refuse to be promoted; (2) why offering women training when there will be no vacancies in the career track for them after training weakens morale, is diametrically opposed to the spirit of affirmative action, and does not make the organization look good; and (3) that qualified, motivated women deserve serious consideration for and promotion to the management positions for which they apply. The affirmative action officer's most difficult explanatory task would be to increase understanding among male top-level managers of the ways in which upwardly mobile working women construe support from their supervisors. Management-level women with whom we have talked about this cite it as the major obstacle they face in their careers. It has many forms: not letting the woman know what decisions have been made or what policies are now in force, providing her office with furniture designed for a male giant (or, conversely, identical to that of her secretary), not providing equal access to the boss, and so on. Each organization tends to have different support areas that need analysis and shoring up. Here change can only come from the top male managers, but the affirmative action officer can provide the impetus to that change.

The affirmative action officer would have to understand and explain to workers such complex issues as (1) why the composition of the management team is so unrepresentative of the workforce and how this is to be remedied, (2) how to present organizationwide workers' issues to management, and, sometimes, (3) why their support of affirmative action is important.

When issues arise in which workers and management disagree, the affirmative action officer remains neutral—neither part of management nor of the rank and file—and objective, so that any decisions made may be effective, be binding, and uphold the law. To achieve this, it is imperative that the affirmative action officer's judgment is trusted by all. Meanwhile, such an officer's main duty is to make sure that management and rank and file know what the law is and are kept aware of its changes. The total organization also needs to be informed of how company policy and workforce composition reflect the organization's compliance.

Where affirmative action program responsibility is being effectively handled, the three conditions—active management support, objective hiring practices, and training and promotions—are being met.

The affirmative action officer must be careful to avoid blurting. An affirmative action officer I heard about announced to a large group of "grieving" in-house candidates, "Yup, you've got a case, and I guarantee one of you will get the job." In fact, they did not have a case. The internal candidates were all women; thus, there was no sex discrimination. Besides, a woman had been offered the position. Male candidates, all external to the organization, lacked the required skills and were not interviewed. There were interview irregularities such as telling one in-house candidate, "You know what the job is, and we know what you can do." While a rude, unskilled interviewer is not automatically sex discriminatory, by blurting the affirmative action officer provoked dissension. The situation was compounded when complaints about the procedure reached the president's office, where the inevitable explosion occurred, followed by a full investigation.

The affirmative action officer apparently had not done the necessary homework, did not know the law, and made a snap judgment; thus, he was unable to function as a mediator, a conciliator, a buffer. Much ill will was generated.

Where the affirmative action officer keeps up with the law, investigates complaints thoroughly before commenting on them, and arranges for conciliation and needed remediation, affirmative action increases. Where the affirmative action officer can communicate effectively with management, personnel, rank and file, unions, attorneys, and compliance agencies, good will and progressive actions are a happy outcome.

In sum, the affirmative action officer's job is a compound of paralegal, psychological, and personnel skills. Frequently challenged, the incumbent often feels besieged. Yet, the affirmative action officer's job has a great potential for positive impact. Goals and quotas stated in the affirmative action plan are far less important than continuous workplace progress.

Goals and Quotas

Point 5: Setting affirmative action goals means setting your sights at a certain level of improvement. Few organizations meet their goals. Organizations opposing affirmative action talk about "quotas," and they say nasty things. *Quotas* is a dirty word not supposed to be used in conjunction with affirmative action programs because it implies that a fixed number of persons of some kind must be found, hired, or trained. *Goals* is a clean word in this context.

Numerical categorization of workers was supposed to ensure that positive action would take place. It is easier to count things as a measure of progress than to assess progress in other ways, but enumeration led to excesses such as counting a nonwhite woman worker twice (once as nonwhite, once as female). While such double counting is illegal, it is true that organizations want to look good whatever that achievement involves. There are multiple forms to fill as documentation of meeting organizational affirmative action goals. But people who fill out the forms usually know little about who gets hired. Few employees and managers see the forms that are filed. However, the entire organization can see the composition of its workforce.

Employees know immediately when a woman moves into management, when one joins management from outside, or when a highly placed woman leaves and is replaced by one or two more expensive men. When new women managers arrive, working women realize that affirmative action is taking place. When back-sliding occurs—a man or men hired to replace a woman—employees wonder about their organization. Women employees may wonder whether their organization has been violating the law all along.

Working women often hear that there were no qualified women applicants for various positions. They also hear, "We couldn't get a woman engineer (mathematician, computer scientist, executive) because they cost too much. Women in those fields are scarcer than hen's teeth. They write their own ticket." Yet these same organizations may discourage their female employees from getting training to qualify them for such jobs. Or they may refuse to bend their salary scales to permit hiring women where none had been before, or they feel forced to hire an occupational token (hoping she won't last long).

If your organization avoids these transparent behaviors, it probably does positive things, too. It may offer affirmative action awareness training during the general employment orientation, or inform employees about the workforce composition annually or semiannually. It may require job description updates once a year and use them to find likely in-house candidates for training and promotion. Or it may require employees to detail new skills so that job upgrading can proceed. Truly affirmative-action-oriented organizations will circulate their competitors' job offerings.

We've touched upon an array of positive and negative aspects of the workplace related to affirmative action. The five points—management support, hiring practices, training and promotion, program responsibility, and goals and quotas—should serve as a guide for the final section. It is now your turn to apply the concepts, to exercise your affirmative action awareness muscles in the real world.

Rate Your Organization

It is not an easy task to gather ideas and the information you need to rate your organization. Take your time, and be fair. Although your primary interest is the quality of affirmative action at your workplace, quantifying results provides an overall rating and pinpoints areas in which your organization strongly and weakly supports affirmative action.

If you assign double points to management support and hiring practices, one and one-half points to training and promotion, and one point each to program responsibility and goals and quotas, you should have a rough measure of your organization's commitment to affirmative action. A perfect score is 7.5; it is extremely doubtful that any organization has earned that score.

As you evaluate, first listen to what top management says; then observe what it does. Make a list of positive affirmative action taken. Make a list of negative, or anti–affirmative action taken. What's left? Is it superior, average, or poor evidence of active top management support for affirmative action? Superior? Then assign 2 points and move to the next topic. Average? Assign 1 point. Poor? Assign 0.5 points or 0 points and move on. When tackling hiring practices, consult an organization directory or, if unavailable, the organization telephone directory. Count the number of directors, count the number of women directors, and finally compute the percentage of women directors. Are there any women at a higher level? How many? What are their job titles? Check Chapter 1 to review what staff and line jobs indicate, for these have direct bearing upon affirmative action. If no women in your organization are in line positions, subtract 0.5 from the score you assigned to hiring practices.

Divide training and promotion into segments that apply where you work. Perhaps training (0.5) and promotion (0.5) and coercion versus career counseling (0.5) would fit. Program responsibility depends upon the affirmative action officer; rate that person as excellent (1.0), good (0.75), fair (0.50), poor (0.25), or totally ineffective (0) in performance of the affirmative action officer's duties. Use the categories suggested earlier, or specify your own.

Goals must be evaluated by achievements. Focus mainly upon working women, but if none has been hired in management or nontraditional positions recently, include minority-group men in your evaluation.

An overall score of 7.0 is excellent; it might also mean that you have been more generous and loyal than accurate. An overall score of less than 3.0 ought to make you wonder about the affirmative action program at your workplace and whether it is the best place for you to pursue your worklife.

WORKING WOMEN WINNERS

Now go back to our second sample problem. Pretend your organization is being described. Have violations occurred there in the past year? What kinds? Title VII of the Civil Rights Act of 1964 (Chapter 3)? Equal Pay Act of 1963 (Chapter 2)? Title IX of the Education Act (Chapter 5)? What can be done about them? This exercise is intended to strengthen your affirmative action awareness muscles and your confidence. You could do the exercise right now. To help you, should you—or another working woman—need it, a list of compliance agencies for employers covered by affirmative action requirements is now provided, where you will also find a useful directory.

You might be a little bewildered by the title of this section on affirmative action. The puzzle is solved by learning what the exercise has to teach. Part of the lesson is that winners have constructive solutions to the problems they wrestle. After reading the sample problem carefully, you'll note that it asked you to find violations of working women's legal rights and alternatives for correcting the violations. These alternatives are limited only by your creativity within obvious workplace constraints. When you have finished with the problem, you'll be part of the solution. You'll be on your way.

ADDITIONAL INFORMATION SOURCES

Two additional helpful items are intended for employers and for employees. Getting copies of what employers are expected to do rounds out the picture, but you ought to know what you can do as well:

Request *Guidelines on Equal Employment Opportunity* from:

Equal Employment Opportunity Commission
Office of Voluntary Programs
1800 G Street NW
Washington, D.C., 20506
(or the Regional Office serving your area)

Request *Know Your Rights: What You Should Know about Equal Employment Opportunity* from:

Equal Employment Opportunity Commission
2401 E Street NW
Washington, D.C., 20506

Finally, check your library for the wording of the Equal Employment Opportunity Act of 1972 and amendments.

You might like to write for a single (free) copy of "A Compilation of Federal Laws and Executive Orders for Nondiscrimination and Equal Opportunity Programs" from:

U.S. General Accounting Office
Distribution Section, Room 1518
441 G Street, N.W.
Washington, D.C. 20548

For a useful directory, *Women Helping Women: A State by State Directory of Services*, 1981:

Women's Action Alliance
370 Lexington Avenue
New York, N.Y. 10017

NOTES

1. The American Telephone and Telegraph Company case, in which a consent decree was obtained in 1973, is an excellent illustration of how costly noncompliance with affirmative action can be. AT&T was fined millions of dollars in employee damages and was ordered to promote and train a large number of women and minority group workers. Thus, progress was enforced. It is doubtful whether the company became a staunch supporter of affirmative action as a result.

2. While researching this book, I learned of a large contribution by the Coors Beer Company to a foundation that was actively working against equality for

women. Coors was banned from our house. If, say, 25 percent of the wives of Colorado beer drinkers had done likewise and told the press why, Coors would have listened. If you don't like what a company is doing and you can substantiate the company's action, boycott. The boycott is a useful legal tool. A hurt in the purse is a serious comment.

3. If the organization is located in an area having 30 percent Caucasian, 30 percent black, 30 percent Asian, and 10 percent other racial groups, the applicant pool must either resemble this distribution, or it can be calculated with reference to the job classification and the distribution of workers in that classification. However, where gross deficits exist, training of workers is sometimes required. Women have sometimes been the beneficiaries.

4. Seymor Martin Lipsett, "Equity of Access to Education, with Special Reference to Racial and Minority Groups," talk presented at Northwestern University, Evanston, Ill., July 12, 1978. Lipsett noted important shifts in American society, which indicated that changes have taken place in access patterns: (1) where *Fortune 500* top management is educated today, (2) the approximately equal percentage of black and white youths in college as documented for the first time by the U.S. Census, (3) the War on Poverty. Lipsett suggests that further changes are needed in resource allocation to make equality of educational access a reality.

5. Lauren DeVuyst, "Educating for Underemployment? A Comparison of Female and Male Respondents of Student Follow-up Studies," paper presented to American Educational Research Association, Special Interest Group for Junior/ Community College Research, Northcentral Region, Springfield, Ill., July 13, 1978. A professional audience hearing this paper, which documented sex discrimination for equally trained graduates of a vocational program, sat in silence when it was suggested that these acts were violations of the Equal Pay Act of 1963. Apparently, these educators, from public postsecondary institutions, were ignorant about this 15-year-old federal law.

6. We have been told that research has repeatedly demonstrated that women do a better job of cleaning and filling teeth than men do. In Ohio, paradentals—dental workers—were licensed for a time. They did a booming business (and charged less than dentists) because they were good at their work. Pressure from dentists (mainly male) had the licensing rescinded by the legislature.

7. Louise McCants, "Comment: Breaking the Barriers: Women in the Technologies," *Community College Review* 5, no. 4 (Spring 1978): 4–10.

8. Susan K. Grady and Bill J. Frye, "The Female As Technician," *Community College Review* 5, no. 4 (Spring 1978): 11–16.

9. A quotation immediately preceding Chapter 2 indicated that segments of the federal government—for example, the U.S. Senate—could initiate a bit of affirmative action.

10. Paraphrase of comments made by a top management official in a nationwide transportation company.

11. During World War II, it was naively expected that integrated assembly lines would lead to integration outside the workplace and after the national emergency was over. Unfortunately, there was only workplace cooperation. Integrated military units responded similarly. The persons involved in both situations did not possess high status; they "suffered" integration. Military officers and managers, as groups, were overwhelmingly white and male; they rarely associated with the lower echelons. There may be an affirmative action lesson for management in this.

12. American organizations have devoted little time and effort toward the development and exploration of cooperative methods of getting work accomplished. Signs from Europe and from Asia indicate that this is the wave of the future. Women could play a creative role in the "productivity through people" principle praised in management books such as *In Search of Excellence* by Thomas J. Peters and Robert H. Waterman, Jr. (New York: Harper and Row, 1982).

Equality is not when a female Einstein gets promoted to assistant professor; equality is when a female schlemiel moves ahead as fast as a male schlemiel.

EWALD B. NYQUIST, New York
State Commissioner of Education,
1975.

I'd taught; I'd published; I'd done lots of valuable fieldwork. But all this experience is not seen as valuable because I am a female. If a man doesn't follow the standard academic path he's "bringing rich noncampus experience to the job"—in a woman, it's "lack of focus."

Forty-six-year-old assistant professor,
as quoted by Mary Crawford in *Ms.*,
November 1978, p. 61.

Prisoner's Base
the education amendments and working women

EDUCATIONAL GAMES AND ROLES

Mindset

Education is pervasive and crucial; the nation's fate may depend upon it. Although this chapter deals mainly with women employees of educational institutions at all levels and with governmental and industrial employees whose positions involve education or training, women not currently working in such settings can benefit from learning what their education-related rights are. Knowledge about educational legislation is extremely important during these times when changing technological and economic conditions make it likely that most working women will encounter minor or major career shifts every decade. Many of these changes will involve education or training—that means putting women in the student role. And more than a few women find themselves suddenly thrust into employment as educators or trainers.

Anecdotal material is presented about how it used to be and currently is for females in the American educational system. When you finish the chapter, you'll be acutely aware of how important it is for women to take an active, major role in rehumanizing the American educational system. Every working woman who has had an educational—or, since most of us, including men, are products of our educational system, an occupational—experience that did not aid her to utilize the greatest share of her potential will want to assure that American education improves.

This chapter describes educational legislation and then outlines what has happened to women working in education since the laws went into effect. The section on educational sex discrimination cases is unpleasant reading, but it is part of the background you need. Finally, the educational map of America is summed up, giving you an opportunity to compare your experience with what you've just read. The choices for action may motivate you to constructive activity that will improve America's educational map.

"Prisoner's Base" is a game children used to play. The prisoners were herded together inside a circle. They gained freedom by escaping when their guards weren't watching, or they were rescued by teammates.

One could view women as prisoners and education as the liberating agent. No agent is infallible; sometimes the liberator failed, and not all prisoners were liberated. Sometimes the rescuers got caught, or some prisoners heroically distracted the guards and their teammates were freed.

How has education functioned to liberate you? Have you sacrificed so that another could have a fuller life, a better career? Whatever your answer, as a working woman you are not alone. Nor are you alone as a woman working in education; others share your hopes and your frustrations.

A little earlier we used the Prisoner's Base scenario with education as the heroine, the nurturing agent of liberation. There is a better heroine—you, the working woman who makes education her tool, using it to help determine her choices, changes, challenges. When the script is thus transformed, you gain some control over your options, and Prisoner's Base retreats to a game of childhood; the chapter's first analogy becomes a cautionary tale.

The transformation requires hard work, including the shedding of counterproductive beliefs, attitudes, and stereotyped ideas. Perhaps this is most difficult to do when one is a woman working in education. One reason is that the long tradition of women working in education—in the less prestigious and in the unisex jobs—skews our perceptions, so we fail to see anything wrong with it. Furthermore, it is extremely difficult to be objective about one's workplace if one likes the work and feels it is constructive and important.

Education is important, but when it comes to careers in education women generally have accepted walk-on parts, leaving the star billing to the men. We could do with more American educational heroines.

When women working in education sift career outcomes by asking themselves questions—why teach instead of lead? type instead of administer educational budgets? counsel and guide rather than council, legislate, or negotiate?—beliefs, attitudes, and stereotypes begin to crumble. Other questions follow: Have my actions been based upon irrational beliefs, unfair pressure and persuasion, rather than factual information? Am I an elementary school teacher (or assistant professor of home economics or secretarial science) because I have a vocation (a "calling")?

If you feel that gender generalizations (and falsehoods) were a major determinant of your current workforce position, you can choose to use education to forge a new future through learning new parts or improving your use of the work environment. You may be about to formulate new job strategies, make important personal decisions, and update your perceptions and participation. If so, you are eager to discover how the laws can assist you, how alternatives and information presented can encourage your action.

Getting Bit Parts

Madie Frees, a working woman educated during the Depression, shared thoughts about why girls' high grades in school do not produce workplace success. The issue is complex: "It isn't what you know, but how you know it," said Frees.

She noted that girls who excell are rewarded in school for such behavior; they soon believe that education and success are related, and they enjoy learning. These females don't understand that rewarded school behaviors predict marketplace failure. "Even in education?" I asked. She nodded. Girls get good school grades for not rocking the boat, for following directions in a nonthinking, noncritical way. As women, they need to realize that marketplace rewards are related to originality, accomplishment, dynamism, leadership, risk taking, and other actions governed by norms not explicitly taught to girls. She added that strategies for getting ahead may be learned by analyzing the behaviors that successful people use as well as those unsuccessful people display.

Frees, who recently had thought a lot about careers, pinpointed events in her awakening. "Rebellious" attitudes went back to an elementary school teacher who, having been carefully packaged, carefully packaged the girls who came through her assembly line:

> Miss Ostrander, my fifth grade art teacher, had us outline a large egg with the point toward the bottom of the paper. She had us do a large penmanship exercise across the top third, then a smaller one across the bottom third; then we turned the paper and made lines down the middle. Eventually, we made eyes near the first penmanship exercise, a mouth near the second, and a nose between. We were told how to make hair and a neck. Miss Ostrander asked, "Who likes her face enough to show it to the class?" Seven of us stood up. Miss Ostrander, swift as the wind, put a number on each paper. Mine said 73—a bad grade. I was furious; I had been tricked. And for 30 years I thought I was wrong, that my face was rotten. Maybe my picture, which differed from Miss Ostrander's perfection by a hopeless 27 percent, had a touch of creativity. Who knows now? I reacted by being hurt and by disliking Miss Ostrander and art. I should have kept on liking my picture. Now I wish I had framed it.

If Frees is right that schools teach pupils to doubt their native good judgment and replace it with social prescription, then self-confidence would suffer. Being educated is not enough; each of us requires courage and the confidence that we can meet adult challenges.

A worse influence on growing girls, whether in schools or in homes, masks a control device causing distress equal to the social processing. Again Frees felt her experience was typical, though she can hardly believe it today:

> Girls traditionally went to high school and studied what they would (including typing, cooking, and boys), while boys learned a trade or prepared for college. High school girls learned that it was a man's world and that they had no educational future. They had been conned, and many of them realized it without being able to fight for their lives. Expectations and stereotypes were so deeply ingrained that girls could usually be dissuaded from their heartfelt yearnings by mention of "nice girls don't . . . " All girls wanted to be nice girls; they wanted that more than knowledge, skills, satisfaction, more even than sanity; that's what their real education consisted of.

"Nice girls" had been educated not to question. While "nice girls" grew up to be ladies, increasing numbers became less and less "nice" as they matured. These girls grew up to be women who thought and acted.

They thought of careers besides people-centered elementary school teaching, nursing, and social work. Subject-centered college teaching became a possible vocational choice for super-dedicated intellectual women. Admittedly, few women felt equal to concurrent tasks of career, marriage, and motherhood. Jessie Bernard, who successfully combined these occupations during the 1940s, wrote a book called *Academic Women*. She described the species and paid particular attention to its then tiny subset: married academic women. These married academic women were different from Bernard in salient respects. Their academic roles were secondary to their wifely or motherly roles, and they only performed academic tasks when their families consented. By contrast, Bernard had a doctorate, did academic work when she chose, and managed to get out of the devastating "fringe benefit status."

The fringe benefit status competed with the professional status.[1] It represents a differentiation in level of commitment to work. Married women (and mothers) were viewed as professionally, intellectually, and socially on the fringe of the hallowed academic groves. Married women were fringes in another sense; they were assets for colleges that were near their homes or that employed their husbands. When employed, it usually was on a part-time, last minute basis. These women were thought to accept such conditions because they were so anxious to work. No one believed they had to work. Instead, an institution offering them paltry opportunities did them a favor. Working faculty wives received none of the fringe benefits their professional-status, tenure-track colleagues took for granted and would not work without.

College and university administrators often preferred hiring a married man, expecting him to bring a "two-fer" along. The translation "two for the price of one" is a derogatory reference to what academic married women were believed to be worth. But many academic women needed work because their husbands were poorly paid. Under such conditions, few academic women maintained their self-esteem, felt adequate as teachers, or were producing scholars. Obviously, the "two-fer" brush used to tar married women academics infected the careers of the single scholars, too.

I was a "two-fer" for two horrible years. Eventually, I found another college job. To be a "one-fer"—hired on my own merits—meant commuting 66 miles a day to work. Though it was fine for me as a young academic, wife, and mother, the superwoman routine eliminated ideas of further training and advancement. Older women (as I now am) would be unlikely to have stamina enough for the multiple demands of full-time college teaching, commuting, mothering, and wifing. Academic men have never been expected to perform simultaneously on so many fronts.

Happily, flexible solutions became available beginning in the 1960s. Academic women never again need to be fringe benefit status "two-fers" (or basket cases). We have the laws, basic equipment, to help women in academe. Playing in academic settings without knowledge about the laws is foolish and unnecessary, and may be injurious.

EQUIPMENT FOR THE GAME: EDUCATIONAL AMENDMENTS AND THE REST OF THE TEAM

Rules and Realities[2]

Pieces of legal equipment particularly helpful to working women employed by educational institutions are:

1. The Equal Pay Act of 1963, as amended by the Education Amendements of 1972.
2. Title VII of the Civil Rights Act of 1964, as amended by the Equal Employment Opportunity Act of 1972.

3. Executive Order 11246, as amended by 11375.

4. Title VII (Section 799A) and Title VIII (Section 845) of the Public Health Service Act, as amended by the Comprehensive Health Manpower Act and the Nurse Training Amendments Act of 1971.

5. Title IX of the Education Amendments of 1972, as amended by the Bayh Amendment of 1974 and the Education Amendments of 1976, as well as the Women's Educational Equity Act of the Education Amendments of 1974.

The provisions of the above apply to public and private colleges and universities, preschools, and elementary and secondary schools—in short, to the entire educational establishment with few exceptions.

Education, the Equal Pay Act, and Title VII of the Civil Rights Act.

The Equal Pay Act of 1963 (EPA) and Title VII of the Civil Rights Act of 1964 received detailed treatment in Chapters 2 and 3, respectively. As amended, the EPA applies to women employees because it includes all fringe benefits offered to male employees. If women employees are barred from or not offered access to classes, while male employees are encouraged to participate in them, sex discrimination could be charged. Thus, the Education Amendments significantly extended coverage of the EPA. Since June 1972, all educational employees—including executive, administrative, and professional employees of higher education institutions, including those working in preschools, private nursery schools, and kindergartens—are covered, even if the institution receives no federal funding.[3] Employees of preschools, nurseries, and kindergartens are invariably women.

Title VII of the Civil Rights Act of 1964 contains similar educational benefit provisions specifying that training cannot be offered to males only, whether offered at educational institutions or business sites by personnel of educational institutions. If training is not available to employees on an equal opportunity basis, then discrimination may be charged. This provision is important because women are often denied advancement on the grounds that they lack training. Training used to be denied, too, thus creating a vicious circle of occupational lockstep.

Education and Executive Order 11246.

The executive order (EO) is a prerogative of the president. Successive presidents may amend it. EO 11246, as amended by 11375, became effective in October 1968. It required that federal contracts include contractors' pledges of nondiscrimination against employees and applicants. Contractors also had to pledge to take affirmative action to ensure that no employee or applicant received sex-discriminatory treatment.

There is a subtle difference between the requirements of the EO and other legislation we've discussed. It can be illustrated by the contrast between "I never meant to hurt you" and "I meant not to hurt you." This difference in intention is too often overlooked. The executive order means not to hurt working women and underlines this by requiring positive action, filing of affirmative action plans, and providing for financial penalties. EO has teeth that can be used to strengthen implementation of other legislation passed because working women and minorities are not to be hurt.

Contractors were told that they could not discriminate on the basis of sex, race, color, religion, and national origin. These were inadequate, taboo grounds for denying an individual employment. The affirmative action regulation required contractors to make positive efforts to overcome past unfairness in employment, upgrading, demotion, transfer, recruitment (including advertising), layoff, termination, pay and other compensation (which could include educational opportunities), and selection for training and apprenticeship. All employees at all institutions having federal contracts of $10,000 or more are covered by EO 11246 as amended.

The critical aspect of the affirmative action order for working women wishing to enter traditionally male, highly skilled, well-paid fields is the apprenticeship provision. Heretofore, those women lacked the supervised, hands-on experience required for licensing and governed by entrance to apprenticeship programs. Plumbing and electrical expertise are examples. Today, women denied access to their chosen opportunity because of lack of apprenticeship have recourse under EO 11246 as amended. Women students in the technologies will appreciate this. What it potentially does is to solve the age-old dilemma of, "I can't get a job because I don't have experience, and nobody will hire me so that I can get experience." Apprenticeship is supervised experience.

Since voluntary compliance proved undependable, the EO was expanded:

As of January 19, 1973, all covered educational institutions, both public and private, were required to have *written* affirmative action plans.

"Federal Laws and Regulations Concerning Sex
Discrimination in Educational Institutions," Project
on the Status and Education of Women, June 1977, footnote 9.

Vocational and occupational programs in educational institutions had to provide written plans detailing their efforts to open their doors to women and others formerly excluded. But there are not enough government investigators to conduct the periodic reviews allowed; perhaps too few for performing the mandatory reviews required when contracts exceeding $1 million are awarded. Then, too, there's a giant step from a written affirmative action program to enforcement of affirmative action. Thus, the problem seems to be essentially one of citizen vigilance rather than of government investigation. The EO was not intended to have such an outcome. Nor is it alone among the educational acts in producing unexpected effects; other acts have had different, unintended significance.

Health Training Acts. Here we'll illustrate the need for a specific educational act and its strong enforcement. The Health Training Acts (consisting of Titles VII and VIII of the Public Health Service Acts, as amended by the Comprehensive Health Manpower Act and the Nurse Training Amendments of 1971) were intended to permit more women access to medical and allied health training. They have successfully increased participation by women in these fields. But working women continue to be subject to cruel choices. One such, found in some industries, is the choice between their jobs and their reproductive organs.[4]

It is our belief that strong enforcement of educational legislation such as the Health Training Acts would ultimately produce representative numbers of women trained as physicians and surgeons and thus would serve to eliminate inhumane excesses. One example should suffice.

Joan Bertin, staff counsel for the American Civil Liberties Union Women's Rights Project, presented her findings at a New York University Law School symposium. Bertin cited a pattern of workplace sex discrimination where hazardous substances are used and where "protective" policies have been adopted. Applying protective medical policies where women work with dangerous chemicals in formerly male jobs adds stereotyping to inconsistency, illogic, inequality, and sex discrimination.

Extensive research provides evidence that hazardous substances in the workplace have negative effects on the physical health and reproductive capabilities of American workers. However, when chemicals have these effects on male workers' health and reproductive capacity, the chemicals are removed.

Where "women's jobs"—Bertin cites the cosmetics industry— involve hazardous substances, nothing is done; but where women are doing traditionally male jobs, they face the choice between discharge and sterilization. The thinking may be that women are always pregnant, while men need corporate-level protection from assault to their sexual organs. The thinking ought to be that hazardous working conditions and substances (illegal under the Occupational Safety and Health Act—OSHA) affect not only female workers' reproductive organs but all workers' entire bodies. Such thinking ought to govern the actions of the medical establishment. Maybe it will one day when women physicians achieve sufficient influence to challenge the practices of medical education, medical associations, and corporate medicine.[5] At that time the Public Health Service Acts will have fulfilled their total promise.

Today, the nondiscrimination provision of the Health Training Acts affects specific educational institutions when they apply for and receive grants, loan guarantees, subsidies, or contracts from the federal government. These institutions are prohibited from sex discrimination in admissions, and their employees working directly with applicants to, or students in, such programs are protected from sex discrimination. (Such institutions train physicians, dentists, osteopaths, veterinarians, optometrists, podiatrists, public and allied health professionals, and nurses.)

The Public Health Service Acts' primary concerns with opening doors and improving the national health care services are gradually being answered. Virtually all American educational institutions that furnish health services instruction receive federal funds; therefore, the acts are enabling legislation for a large group of goal-directed women students. While there is no guarantee that a particular applicant will be accepted, qualified women can no longer be excluded because of their sex. The legislation has provided a powerful tool, one that working women in educational institutions covered by these acts could well study.

Title IX.

No person in the United States, shall on the basis of sex, be excluded from participation in, be denied the benefits of, or be subjected to discrimination under any education program or activity receiving federal financial assistance.

Title IX of the Education Amendments of 1972.

The prohibition against sex discrimination covers employment and recruitment (consideration and selection) for full- and part-time jobs. Hiring preference, even at one-sex institutions, is prohibited if it serves to perpetuate sex discrimination. The following additional matters are treated by Title IX:

. . . compensation; consideration for an award of tenure; application of nepotism policies; job assignments, classifications, and structure; granting and return from leaves of absence; leave to care for children or dependents; selection and financial support for training and for professional meetings; selection for tuition assistance and for sabbaticals and leaves of absence to pursue training; and employer-sponsored acitivities, including social or recreational programs. Recipients are prohibited from applying any policy based upon whether an applicant or employee is the head of a household or participating in pension or retirement plans that establish different optional or compulsory retirement ages based on sex or that otherwise discriminate in benefits on the basis of sex. Recipients are to treat pregnancy disabilities as other temporary disabilities are treated. In cases where the recipient does not maintain a leave policy, or a pregnant employee has insufficient leave, the recipient is to grant a reasonable leave, without pay, and reinstatement.

"Brief Highlights of Major Federal Laws and Order on Sex Discrimination in Employment," (Washington, D.C.; U.S. Department of Labor, Women's Bureau, August 1978), p. 6.

Title IX is important to women who work in educational institutions and in noneducational organizations operating federally funded educational programs, as classified staff, faculty, or administrators. As an educational administrator invited to address a professional meeting, I requested and received approval for travel funds. My supervisor was replaced before the meeting but after the program had been printed. The new supervisor decided to rescind the travel funds. No male administrator had ever experienced that, and it appeared that my sex was the major cause for the fund withdrawal. I went and participated; one does not renege upon a professional commitment. It was very expensive.

Had I realized that Title IX offered potential recourse, I could have filed a complaint. Had the supervisor realized the extent of Title IX coverage, he might have thought twice about taking such apparently sex-discriminatory action. (See Figure 5–1.)

Captains of School Teams

White males tend to be top administrators at educational institutions except preschools and kindergartens. In colleges and universities, women sometimes administer "women's fields" (as heads of art, language, nursing, and home economics departments, or as nurturing deans of students); women are rarely budget officers, vice-presidents, or grantspersons.[6] Few people know that Title IX specifically covers treat-

FIGURE 5–1 Compliance with Title IX*

DATE OF EFFECTIVENESS	ACTIVITY
July 1, 1973	Admissions provision: forbids sex discrimination in admissions.
July 21, 1975	Title IX becomes effective.
	All school systems, all educational institutions must file HEW Form 639 assuring compliance with Title IX and HEW implementation regulation.
	An institutional employee responsible for Title IX must be appointed.
	An institutional complaint or grievance procedure for Title IX should have been published and should be available to students and employees.
	Notification to all concerned parties of intent to comply with Title IX and its essence should have been made.
July 21, 1976	Plans for remediation as indicated by the institutional self-evaluation should be completed and on file.
	Remediation should have been accomplished.
	All institutions should be in compliance.
Who is covered by Title IX?	Students and parents
	Employees
	All bargaining units
	Fringe benefit plans

*Adapted from *Monitoring Title IX* (Washington, D.C.: AAUW, January 1977), p. 8; "Federal Laws and Regulations Concerning Sex Discrimination in Educational Institutions" (Washington, D.C.: Project on the Status and Education of Women, 1977); "Everything You Need to Know about Title IX" (Washington, D.C.: American Federation of Teachers, AFL–CIO, 1976)

ment of educational administrators; therefore, Title IX provisions intended to reinforce those of the Equal Pay Act, Title VII of the Civil Rights Act, EO 11246, and the Public Health Service Acts have frequently been ignored.

Since Title IX became effective, workplace progress for women administrators in education has been slow. Meanwhile, sizable pools of experienced, successful women are ready for upward mobility in most educational fields.

Nevertheless, there are exemplars in the educational token economy. They may be represented by presidents of major research universities (Lorene Rogers, a chemist, now retired from the University of

Texas at Austin; Hanna H. Gray, a historian, at the University of Chicago) and chancellors of state universities (Barbara S. Uehling, an experimental psychologist, of the University of Missouri; Barbara W. Newell of the University of Florida; and Ann Reynolds of the California State Universities).[7] There are women college presidents, provosts, and deans. However, there are not as many as would be expected when women students outnumber men students nationwide and when women academics have been working in higher education for more than 50 years.

Gradually, though, women should rise to greater administrative heights in larger numbers. A growing number of women are department chairs; chairing a department is a first step in higher education administration. Concomitantly, more women are studying for advanced degrees in educational administration.

Women are learning how to get to the top of the heap. One, a part-time parochial school teacher, began doctoral studies and then did a dissertation that impressed her advisor. A new Ph.D., she became a public school principal. Now she's assistant superintendent of a suburban school system. Bright and visible, she volunteers for whatever may help her get ahead; she may surface next as a full professor in a graduate department of education. If she decides on academe, she will soon be a department chair.

Too few women in educational administration have been as fortunate, sometimes because they misunderstand the important distinction between staff and line positions. Staff positions, particularly in education, tend to lead nowhere. Line positions provide an avenue for upward mobility. Figure 5–2 suggests line positions from student to educational institution president and beyond. Endeavoring educational administrators may have to serve in different capacities in different institutions. In using Figure 5–2, remember that there are fewer slots as one ascends the heights, and that while every aspirant will not reach the top, more women ought to. Obviously, Figure 5–2 can be modified for application to other administrative roles in education.

Not every educational employee aspires to presidencies and superintendencies, but women in education deserve assurance that their professional activity within the educational establishment is being fairly rewarded. Data on educational rewards are our next topic.

Earnings, Tenure, Promotion

Few women college faculty members earn what male college faculty members do. A release from the National Center for Education Statistics

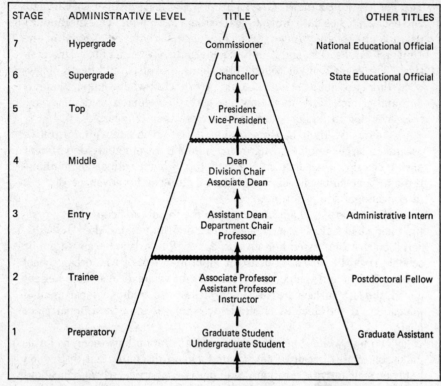

STAGE	ADMINISTRATIVE LEVEL	TITLE	OTHER TITLES
7	Hypergrade	Commissioner	National Educational Official
6	Supergrade	Chancellor	State Educational Official
5	Top	President / Vice-President	
4	Middle	Dean / Division Chair / Associate Dean	
3	Entry	Assistant Dean / Department Chair / Professor	Administrative Intern
2	Trainee	Associate Professor / Assistant Professor / Instructor	Postdoctoral Fellow
1	Preparatory	Graduate Student / Undergraduate Student	Graduate Assistant

FIGURE 5-2 Progression to College President and Beyond.

based on data from 2242 institutions indicates that women lagged in earnings and job stability in the 1979–80 academic year.[8] On 12-month contracts, women's average salary reported was \$19,816 while men's was \$27,039.[9] For all teaching ranks, disregarding sex, the average salary was \$25,283. This pertains even though entry-level salaries are equal for male and female faculty. Women faculty are concentrated in the lower ranks, in fields paying lower salaries, and in institutions of lesser prestige paying lower salaries, thus the discrepancies.

In addition, figures on full-time instructional faculty reveal that, despite new hires, women represent a smaller proportion of higher education faculties than they did in 1939.[10] Hiring is usually at the lower ranks with advancement within the institution, but since the higher education enterprise is currently under fire—high budgets and low enrollments are prime targets—and since the lower teaching ranks offer least job security, the future for women faculty members is not bright.

Women working as teachers and administrators in elementary and high schools face other advancement hurdles, which may be further complicated by another suprastructure: the teachers' union. Unions tend to polarize the ins and the outs. A side effect is that unions remove potential support by women teachers (the union ins) from women administrators (the union outs) who are ineligible for union membership. Job and union conditions combine to make adversaries of potential allies, thus creating negative career effects for women teachers and administrators who can be persuaded to disagree on personalities rather than upon issues. However, some unions have made efforts to deal with Title IX issues.[11] Issue-oriented overtures permit cooperation. Women teachers and administrators, for example, share a concern over child care and after-school care of children whose parents work.

Another issue related to Title IX, which may appear unimportant at first glance, concerns prohibition of sex stereotypes and sex bias in instructional materials. The Education Amendments of 1974 included the Women's Educational Equity Act (WEEA), which provided funds for developing unbiased materials and programs plus training in their use. Many educators believe that learners' self-esteem and self-confidence are influenced by the texts used; many recent research studies support this view. Some states have made sex-biased and sex-stereotyped instructional materials illegal.[12]

In addition to teachers and administrators, educational institutions employ many women to do tasks required by all organizations—typing, filing, and retrieving. These women, least likely to know about Title IX and other potentially beneficial provisions, are also least likely to use available opportunities to improve their workday status. Still, they have significant coverage under Title IX.

Despite impressive coverage available under these regulations, EOs, and acts, education's working women have not gained as much as was expected. Before blaming the women for these poor results, let's look at penalties for noncompliance, at the role of harassment, and finally at some rules we can write.

Penalties, Locker Rooms, and Relief Stations

Football teams huddle to plan winning plays. Women working in education could form an enormous group, or huddle, capable of producing constructive organizational action on local or national levels (the long-sighted view). But it seems that working women are most concerned with events at their workplace, with their locker room possibilities (the short-sighted view).

What could or would you do if you were a victim of sex discrimination in the educational institution where you worked? Encapsulated earlier were my experience and reactions to educational employment sex discrimination. Back then few women could have helped; fewer still cared or dared to.

If there had been a solid support group, I might have stayed despite documented violations of Title IX. But instances of academic women who fought sex discrimination with dismal results kept turning up. So did the often-repeated advice that remaining and complaining (even when justified) would get me a troublemaker label. No troops helped me battle for academic equity. I soon retreated to the ladies' room, put on a new face, and flew the coop. In retrospect it appears to have been a Chicken Little action.

Unfortunate side effects appeared. I felt rotten about not being promoted after being led to expect promotion; however, a kind of convoluted reasoning compounded my anguish and disbelief. I couldn't be correct in blaming sex discrimination for my lack of promotion. There must be something wrong with me, not with the college. Therefore, never thinking of seeking help from friends at other colleges, I felt ashamed, disgraced, and alone.

Today, no woman working in education has to suffer anger and disappointment alone. She can find or create a huddle to help plan short-term action and to provide support before she takes things out on herself. Ranking women in educational organizations are usually willing to listen and to offer tactics, encouragement, and sometimes mediation. Such women have usually experienced similar unfairness; they know what other women go through.

If there are no other women in your educational organization, you might either join or start a support group for the longer term and for noncrisis situations. A woman working in education is foolish to limit her choices to "put up and shut up" or "get out." That much has changed for the better.

Where the educational institution is legally at fault, its decision can be reversed. Educational institutions employ affirmative action officers to help them avoid this possibility and to assure their compliance with the laws and regulations as well as to provide "relief." These professionals can be good sources of information about the function of the laws and regulations.

The local labor or professional organization is another relief station, one that includes primary and secondary educational institutions. Labor union and educational institution agreements are not permitted to conflict with sex discrimination provisions of either the EO or federal legislation, and labor unions must follow the same rules as educational employers. The professional organizations can assist in achieving enforcement of the EO and federal legislation.

The American Association of University Professors (AAUP), active on local and national levels, maintains Committees A (on Academic Freedom and Tenure) and W (on Women) and has prepared a Higher Education Salary Evaluation Kit.[13] Carol S. Stern's "On Processing Complaints of Discrimination on the Basis of Sex," an AAUP publication, cites three types of evidence of sex discrimination usable in legal action.[14] They are (1) direct evidence of sex discrimination, which includes discriminatory criteria and tasks, and sexist remarks such as those heard from search committee members about what they will do if a woman is hired or granted tenure. Even candidates sometimes make sex-discriminatory remarks during the interview process. For instance, if a deanship candidate said, "Women are getting higher salaries than the engineers, I mean the males," unequal application of standards would be indicated. Other typical examples are: (2) males with lower educational and experiential qualifications being promoted, and (3) procedural deficiencies such as failure to notify women faculty about reappointment and termination and provisions for due process. Stern's article provides insights into when general patterns of sex discrimination at an institution of higher education should be brought to the attention of the national AAUP even though no individual complaint has been made.[15] Obviously, AAUP remedies, including conducting of investigations, are applied on campuses having chapters, while labor unions handle complaints in settings where they are the bargaining agents.

Solutions to bona fide sex discrimination complaints can be worked out between complainant and institution with assistance from the affirmative action officer, Title IX representative, or personnel director. During settlement negotiations, both sides are flexible. The complainant might waive her right to sue, while the institution might agree to change its illegal practice, make amends, and provide tangible assurance that sex discrimination will not recur.

All sex discrimination complaints have unique aspects—a good reason for attempting local settlement. Besides, the legal precedents may not fit your case. Further, judges tend to defer to educational administrators when sex discrimination questions arise in educational institutions, and often the educational administrators are unclear about the law. As a complainant, you have a better chance of informing educators about the laws than of teaching a judge educational administration. Moreover, the odds of achieving a binding settlement improve when conditions and decisions are written down. Our advice is to act on the scene and spell out the script. State exactly what the institution has promised to stop doing. Have all parties sign. Date the agreement.

Local resolution of a sex discrimination complaint may not be simple. You may follow your institution's entire procedure and find yourself a player in a waiting game. You wait. Nothing happens. People make appointments with you and then cancel or "forget" them. The idea is to tire you or get you to drop your sex discrimination complaint. Employers know endless variations of the waiting game.

Don't let it throw you. If your institution's procedures prove ineffective or if the sex discrimination continues, consider outside remedies. If you decide on legal advice, seek an expert in higher education law; the nearest graduate education department can supply names of experts, including the university's affirmative action officer, who may be able to suggest lawyers expert in sex discrimination matters.

If you want a lawyer, you also want to preserve an element of surprise. Do not let your employer know you have finally consulted one. On the other hand, you might decide to file a complaint directly. If you can afford it, do get expert legal representation.

Sex discrimination complaints are filed according to the law (or EO) violated. Violations of the EO are filed with a different agency from violations of Title IX. Figure 5–3 indicates which agencies accept educational institution sex discrimination complaints.

Employers who simultaneously and intentionally violate several provisions are more likely to have the scales of justice bang on their heads than are the employers whose single violations are accidental. Whether your employer will be notified about your complaint depends upon the federal law involved and the compliance agency that administers it. The EEOC generally notifies institutions of complaints that have been received, while the Office of Civil Rights (OCR) notifies the institution before it investigates.

While awaiting your next act, you might spend the intermission examining another swatch of sex discrimination fabric, which applies to all federal laws and regulations governing educational institutions. We call it the Harass Tweed.

FIGURE 5–3 Compliance Agencies Enforcing Federal Laws and Executive Orders Regulating Educational Institutions

THE MEASURES	COMPLIANCE AGENCIES
Title IX (Ed. Amend. 1972) Public Health Service Act Executive Order 11246	Office of Civil Rights Department of Education Health, Education, and Welfare Washington, D.C. 20201 *or* Regional HEW Office
Executive Order 11246	Office of Federal Contract Compliance Programs Employment Standards Administration Department of Labor Washington, D.C. 20210
Title VII (Civil Rights Act of 1964) Equal Pay Act	Equal Employment Opportunity Commission Washington, D.C. 20506 *or* Regional EEOC Office

The Harass Tweed

My dictionary says that "to harass" means to "exhaust, tire, fatigue." Harassment can take many forms, including employment harassment. Employment harassment has defined stages and tactics beginning after filing of an employee's complaint (of sex discrimination, sexual harassment, etc.). After a complaint, the harassment provision theoretically prevents both dismissal and further discrimination by the educational employer, so harassment goes underground and becomes covert. Its primary intention is to render the complainant incapable of job performance so that she quits or can legally be dismissed. An employee can increase the likelihood of protection legally due her by documenting any discriminatory actions, including reprisals against her, occurring after the complaint was filed.

No working woman expects employment harassment. Chances are she will be slow to recognize its manifestations, which are part of a concerted pattern of subtle, illegal, employer-initiated action. Such action draws heavily on tactics children viciously use: scapegoating, temper tantrums, rumors, gossip, social isolation, and public humiliation. But, in employment harassment, grown men, trained administrators, experts in the best management procedures, mete out carefully contrived managerial actions that never appear sex discriminatory.

Some examples: The employee's job may suddenly shrink as former responsibilities are removed. This is the amputation approach, implying, "You aren't competent, so we've reduced the job to your level." Or job duties may increase tremendously, as if to say, "We'll teach you who's running this place and your place in it," representing the stepfather approach. The employee finds that her formerly polite, friendly supervisor now pointedly ignores her—in fact, never addresses her. She is being "frozen out." In an epidemic version, nobody talks to her; she gets the "quick-freeze" treatment, a follow-the-administrator approach. She may be bombarded with incredible rumors about herself; she may be made a public example of ineffectiveness.

Clever sex discriminators can manipulate these tactics to rid themselves of several employees at once or can use them sequentially on a single employee. Such disruptions and pressures successfully increase job performance difficulties. The working woman thus victimized may voluntarily resign. She could pursue her complaint, but bewilderment, discouragement, and searching for a new job make this unlikely. If she drops her complaint, her former employer wins twice. He is free to continue discriminatory behaviors and is rid of the thorn in his side. Rare women who pursue the case after leaving the job are also disadvantaged; mediators are unwilling to believe the complaints of former employees. Such a woman is perceived as a quitter, unable to take it; meanwhile, her former employer, scot free, may feel justified, right to have gotten rid of a bad risk. Thus, any woman filing a complaint is in for a rough time. She'd better expect it and be prepared to fight for her rights.

Were the fabric of the harassment provision well woven and enforceable, it might remedy the feeling of being unraveled reported by working women who have made a sex discrimination complaint. Perhaps because women in education are verbal, or because educational organizations are worse workplaces, there are large numbers of such reports.

American jurisprudence, which regards the accused as innocent until proven guilty where sex discrimination is concerned, requires the victim to assume the burden of proof. Furthermore, where complaints of educational sex discrimination have been accepted by the compliance agency, the victim must demonstrate that violations have continued before action is taken to stop employment harassment. Meanwhile, the regulations offer blanket protection to women who help coworkers or compliance agencies in sex discrimination complaints, and to potential participants and applicants for employment who have complained. These protections are impossible to provide, but they sound so good.

We've seen that employment harassment does not happen by coincidence. If you've filed a complaint and experienced something like what was described, you are being harassed. The time is ripe for consideration of administering a dose of "elementary" education to your institution.

Writing a Few Rules of Your Own

"Two can play that game," was an adage in my family. What sayings can guide you and remind you to keep on target during this game's many innings?

As you generously share experience, letting sex-discriminating, harassing oppressors feel what you have felt, you resemble a good doctor. While prescribing medicine, you retain your virtue. Should a medical side effect appear, it will make the bad, sick guys highly visible.[16]

Unexpected endings—the paper caper and the representative campaign are provided as models. They may inspire you to new heights. Dispense the doses as you think of superior medicines.

The paper caper. Like "Hares and Hounds," the game in which one team (hares) drops real and false trails of shredded paper while the other (hounds) tries to outsmart and capture them, you can use the local press to illuminate sex discriminators at educational institutions.

Hares and Hounds requires some library homework. Read the local paper, noting stories about your educational institution and the writer's byline. After discreetly discovering whether the reporter is a political patsy, you may decide to contact the reporter. Reporters are motivated by hot stories. You've got one.

Your challenge includes avoiding libel, slander, and unprovable allegations while building an impression of administrative incompetence at your educational institution (but only if warranted). Scrupulously avoid mention of sex discrimination, grievances, or personal injustice—using them makes you a suspect person with a chip on her shoulder. Your role is that of a public-spirited citizen and a sweet young thing or grandmotherly and warm. Your chosen role is part of the game plan. For instance:

> How can they offer Data Processing to 500 students when all the keypunch machines were taken away before the semester began? What's left are ten terminals for those 500 students. But they say that somewhere there's a slush fund. How many terminals do you think $500,000 would buy?

Well, this person I know, she wouldn't want me to give her name, well, she worked there a whole year without signing her contract. She was having some legal disagreement with them; her lawyer said, "Don't sign." Nobody noticed it. She wasn't a secretary, either; she made 18 grand. Do they know what's going on?

You get the idea. These "innocent" news stories will make the board of trustees (or school board) cringe and act. If they don't, then work on the bigger challenge of replacing the Board.

The representative campaign.   Photocopy your evidence, attach a brief letter telling that you wanted to share these materials, and then send a copy to every elected local official—the board of trustees (or the school board), the state representatives, and the state senators—concerned with your educational institution. Address each one by name and title. This cure is best for public institutions and must be done shortly after you leave the job. A copy of the materials can be slipped to your friendly local reporter.

As a public-spirited citizen informing elected officials about events in their domain, you must sign your name. Therefore, you must have sound evidence, which you may be asked to produce. Check with a lawyer before using this strategy. Make sure there is sufficient support for your statements. Never go beyond the evidence.

Don't worry unduly. That you have any evidence rarely occurs to the sex discriminators and harassers at your educational institution. Sex discriminators generally are unaware of your mental capacity. If they perceived you as a thinking, feeling member of their species, they would act differently.

It can be documented that sex discrimination in educational institutions is widespread. We turn now to Pandora's envelope—a collection of random newspaper clippings detailing instances in American higher education gathered during a three-year period.

FOUL BALL: EDUCATIONAL
SEX DISCRIMINATION CASES

A few years back there weren't many sex discrimination cases in educational institutions, yet my friends working in education knew of many violations. I was amazed to find cases everywhere, having never imagined that sex discrimination existed in educational institutions nationwide. It was difficult to write about. One doesn't like to think one's bad experience is common. But women are still "at risk" in educational settings.

What's at Risk?

When the federal regulations and EO appeared, they were widely regarded as unnecessary or premature. It was thought that, given time, things would have righted themselves. Alas, things have not remedied themselves, even with federal government intervention. Women working in education, the regulations, and the belief women working in education have in the laws could all be considered at risk.

Actors in workplace dramas define "at risk" another way. Males heading the educational establishment fear that enforcement of the regulations and EO brings traditional views and job security into jeopardy. By contrast, women working in education fear losses should the regulations and EOs, which raised their expectations, go unenforced. They realistically fear that doors to upward mobility and professional advancement will continue to slam in their faces, resulting in more job stagnation and segregation. While male job security is not at risk, the other concerns may be justified. It depends on where one works.

To Enforce or Not to Enforce

Women working in American education tested the effectiveness of federal regulations, EOs, and their constitutional rights. Challenges came from students, faculty, administrators, organizations, and nonteaching educational workers. Pandora's envelope of clippings yielded over 90 examples of alleged violations from 36 states.

The federal regulations and EOs cover virtually every instructional institution in the nation (and some overseas installations, too), and all of the regulations apply to programs receiving federal funding. Thus, banning sex discrimination in education is an often-stated government policy.

During the Carter years, however, government agencies other than Health, Education, and Welfare were spending approximately $9.6 billion a year at educational institutions while ignoring Title IX sanctions, including regulation, or orders of termination of present funding and eligibility for future funding.[17] Enforcement of the sex discrimination ban could have been promoted for far less money.

The National Advisory Council on Women's Educational Programs, which reported on the Title IX enforcement efforts of federal agencies, felt forced to conclude that the agencies had not lived up to nor acknowledged their responsibilities related to Title IX. Part of the fault lies in the fact that no federal agency was assigned primary responsibility for enforcing the law. Nor was coordination of compliance efforts among the agencies assigned to any of them. Of course, an agency supporting the regulations could have assumed leadership in the enforcement efforts. None did—quite the contrary. The major findings of the study are given in Figure 5–4.

Federal agencies, such as the Departments of Agriculture, Defense, Justice, State, and Treasury, as well as the National Science Foundation and the Veterans Administration, were unaware that their educational programs come under Title IX. Such other agencies as the Departments of Commerce, Energy, and Labor were not sure which of their educational programs were covered. Therefore, accurate data on women in a variety of government-assisted educational programs were never collected. Thus, we lack information on women's treatment in these programs. Think about it. When you do something good, don't you tend to let people know about it? If you do something not quite up to snuff you lie low.

FIGURE 5–4 Major Findings in the Study of Title IX Activity by Federal Agencies Other than Health, Education, and Welfare*

1. Of the agencies having education/training programs subject only to Title IX, none has published Title IX regulations although the law is more than five years old.

2. Of the agencies with double coverage of their programs, most were unaware of the applicability of Title IX or of the need for intragovernmental coordination of standards and enforcement. There are no Title IX "delegation agreements" between agencies, (A "delegation agreement" is a means of intragovernmental coordination whereby one agency delegates its enforcement duties to another agency but retains legal responsibility for ensuring nondiscrimination in its programs.)

3. There is no lead agency designated by Executive Order to coordinate enforcement of Title IX and other sex discrimination provisions. This is a major reason why Title IX has not been enforced by those agencies subject to Title IX. The other agencies—subject to both Title IX and other sex discrimination provisions—have failed to focus specific attention on Title IX enforcement.

*From Nancy J. Balles, *The Unenforced Law: Title IX Activity by Federal Agencies Other than HEW* (Washington, D.C.: National Advisory Council on Women's Educational Programs, 1978), p. 7.

The Unenforced Law documents heavy charges and lets the government know that women are watching.[18] Some recommendations for corrections of violations of Title IX provisions by government agencies are made. The president appoints the National Advisory Council on Women's Educational Programs. Its function, as authorized by the Women's Educational Equity Act (WEEA) is to advise federal officials about matters relating to extending educational equity for women and girls.

Perhaps, as sociologist Bernice R. Sandler, who worked on the Title IX study, suggests, few people paid much attention to the National Advisory Council on Women's Educational Programs and to WEEA because many federal government officials do not view sex discrimination as real discrimination, and therefore make little effort to enforce such laws as Title IX. When the federal government agencies do not inform themselves about and do not obey federal laws, how can ordinary employees be expected to comply?

How did lots of ordinary women citizens, many of whom worked in education, hear about Title IX? How did we learn that when the report appeared, Title IX complaints became epidemic?

Scope and Cases

The outline map (on which Pandora's Envelope clippings have been located, see Figure 5–5) illustrates widespread distribution of Title IX and other sex discrimination in education complaints that had been referred to courts or enforcement agencies. When neither the government nor the nation's educational establishment upholds the law, then the one teaches chaos and corruption while the other nurtures disillusion and despair. Sex discrimination in education, despite laws forbidding it, calls for strong antidotes. These cases and complaints representing the orderly final attempts to make the system responsive and responsible are warning signals of a desperate battle. That so many women working in education are fighting for their legal rights emphasizes the seriousness of governmental failure to enforce anti-sex-discrimination regulations and the pervasiveness of working women's belief in education's power to achieve social change.

Figure 5–6 samples alleged violations brought to enforcement agencies. Among them are complaints by medical students claiming dismissal for personal appearance and hygiene plus interpersonal inability, denial of promotion and tenure by women faculty members, salary and

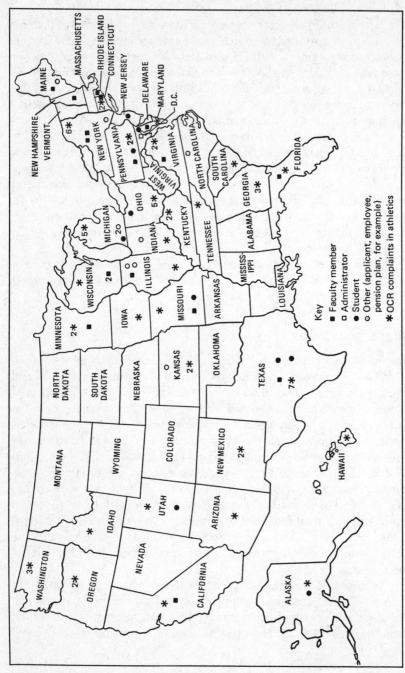

FIGURE 5-5 Pandora's Envelope of Sex Discrimination Complaints and Suits.

Key
- ■ Faculty member
- □ Administrator
- ● Student
- ○ Other (applicant, employee, pension plan, for example)
- ✱ OCR complaints in athletics

FIGURE 5-6 Representative Examples of Sex Discrimination Complaints in Higher Education*

STUDENTS AND FORMER STUDENTS[19]

Plaintiffs	Defendants	Charge	Action
Pamela Price	Yale University	Low course grade because of refusal to grant male professor sexual favors.	Price sued Yale under Title IX. Judge dismissed case for lack of evidence.
Geraldine C. Cannon, R.N., medical school applicant	University of Chicago and Northwestern University	Policies of the schools against admitting older applicants to medical school constitute sex-discriminatory action.	Cannon filed a complaint with HEW, which did not act on it; then she went to court. Supreme Court ruled that individuals have the right to file suit against educational institutions to enforce Title IX.
Charlotte Horowitz	University of Missouri Medical School, Kansas City	Sexist and antisemitic prejudices; prevention of graduation prevents acceptance of job contingent upon graduation.	Sued university in U.S. district court in 1973. Lost sex discrimination and antisemitism aspects, but court upheld stigmatism by dismissal, employment allegation, and says due process hearing required by Fourteenth Amendment was not given. Case was accepted by Supreme Court, but Horowitz lost.
Purdie	University of Utah	Fifty-one-year-old female denied admission to graduate program in Educational Psychology because of age.	Documents indicated she exceeded admission qualifications. District court dismissed action; she appealed to Supreme Court of Utah and won on equal protection clause and Utah State Constitution.
Sally B. Frank	Princeton University	Three all-male eating clubs discriminate against her because of her sex.	Filed complaint with New Jersey division of civil rights. No decision; question of jurisdiction.

FIGURE 5–6 (Continued)

FACULTY[20]

Plaintiffs	Defendants	Charge	Action
Connie Rae Kunda	Muhlenberg College	Physical Education instructor denied tenure; dismissed because she lacks terminal degree. She is given two years to get M.A. and does.	Court of appeals ruled that Kunda was discriminated against under Title VII of the Civil Rights Act barring job bias. Court ruled reinstatement, back pay, promotion to Assistant Professor.
Christine M. Sweeney	Keene State College	Not promoted although qualified, while men with similar credentials were promoted.	Circuit court of appeals ruled in favor of Sweeney.
Female faculty	Colby College	Pension plan discriminates against women despite equal payments. Women receive lower monthly retirement on grounds of longevity.	Supreme Court in Spring 1978 ruled that unequal premium payments were discriminatory. Supreme Court did not rule on unequal benefits. Case has been sent back for a full hearing, after a federal district court ruled against EEOC in 1977 and the court of appeals overruled the district court.
Doris Johnson	University of District of Columbia	Fired when an academic program was retrenched; not reinstated when an appropriate job opened up.	District of Columbia Labor Relations Board ordered rehiring and back pay of $20,000.
Janet Berry	University of Texas, Austin	Discrimination with regard to salary on basis of sex.	HEW ruled that the university had discriminated against Berry and could lose $40 million of federal contracts. University did not accept ruling but would take steps to ensure eligibility for federal funding.
Margaret T. Cussler	University of Maryland	Sex discrimination in promotion, salary, and other benefits in Sociology Department.	Case tried under Title VII of the Civil Rights Act and a Reconstruction Era civil rights act. Cussler lost her case.

ADMINISTRATION[21]

Dr. Ann Martin	Office of Education	Violation of agreement reached following investigation of sex discrimination charges made by Martin.	Martin filed suit to end reprisals against her and $25,000 damages.
Department of Health, Education, and Welfare	Hillsdale College	Refusal to sign compliance with Title IX.	HEW Appeals Board ruled Title IX violation even though no federal funds were received. Hillsdale participated in guaranteed student loan program, thus was covered by Title IX. Decision reversed earlier ruling by HEW administrative judge.

CLASSIFIED EMPLOYEES[22]

Female employees	Central Piedmont Community College	Were doing and did administrative work, received neither administrative salary nor title, and were not promoted according to job responsibility.	Suit filed in 1976. College found guilty of sex bias against Elizabeth Evans and four other women. Judge ordered back pay. College appealed.

OTHER[23]

Stanley Gundry	Moody Bible Institute	Wife's views expressed in her book, Women Be Free, led to his dismissal.	No information.

*Sources used for this table included: *The Chronicle of Higher Education* (issues of April 25, 1977; September 25, 1978; January 8, 1979; January 29, 1979; May 21, 1979; July 16, 1979; October 9, 1979; November 26, 1979; and March 3, 1980); *Higher Education and National Affairs*, April 22, 1977; *Federal Times*, May 20, 1978; *Phi Delta Kappan*, May 1978 and November 1979; *Equal Opportunity in Higher Education*, September 25, 1978.

job title complaints by women employees, and complaints by women administrators about being prevented from performing their jobs. In education, in America, these foul balls are left on the sidelines unless a player decides to run with hers.

SUMMING UP THE
EDUCATIONAL MAP OF AMERICA

The educational map of America is smudgy and gritty. Boundaries are less those of state than of gender lines. For whatever their positions, women in educational institutions get the same kind of treatment—treatment that is not based upon objective performance evaluations. Rather, the treatment appears to be emotional, irrational, illogical, and frequently inimical to the nation's interests. One is forced to conclude that the women just take it. Maybe just taking it is one reason why discrimination against women in educational institutions continues.

Nevertheless, unsung heroines are fighting back. Each case may represent thousands of undocumentable instances of sex discrimination, and possibly hundreds in which the victim is planning strategy, seeking help, registering a complaint, about to sue, or already in court. These alleged violations occurring after the federal regulations became effective underscore the magnitude of the incomplete task.

Federal funds can be terminated from any educational program or activity if it is found that they "are infected by a discriminatory environment" that requires "remedial action to overcome the effects of previous discrimination based on sex which has been found or identified in a federally assisted education program or activity."[24]

The document quoted above furnishes the rules and regulations for Title IX. Alas (like most of us women), the laws are beautiful, strong, and, at least occupationally, unfulfilled.

Among major explanations given for the ineffectiveness of strong laws and regulations to end sex discrimination in education are: that it takes time to interpret and apply the laws, slow processing and lack of investigators to enforce the laws, and bureaucratic indecision.

A consistent program to explain Title IX and other regulations to working women is needed. Women's groups nationwide could make it happen.[25] Without such involvement we cannot clean up the educational face of our land so we can be justly proud of it.

Choices for Action

How have your experiences led you to view the educational map of America? If you are employed by an educational institution or are planning to enter one, you might find choices for action worth thinking about. They are presented in a simple checklist in Figure 5–7. We strongly advise you to study and use it.

The checklist first provides an opportunity to determine which legal provisions apply to your educational institution or organization (section A). Next, some general Prisoner's Base problems are suggested (section B). There are so many others that you may want to create your own list. The checklist serves mainly as a warm-up for you; carry a pad and pen so you can jot down gender-related instances when they occur. Here is a sample: The male interviewer asked the female applicant if she would like some tea or coffee while waiting since the interviews were running late. When she accepted, instead of getting her a cup of prepared coffee, he directed his secretary to do it. You may never need these jottings, but if you don't have them you may well regret it. If you find your mind is a blank, you may want to review Chapter 4 along with the assessment you made of your employer's affirmative action attitude.

The checklist moves to assessment of the extent of sex discrimination (section C). This is the "misery loves miserable company" segment. If you are not alone, if you can document extensive discriminatory practice and you wish to do something about it, you may want to consider the possible strategies in section D or to generate some of your own. Some useful sources of additional information are listed at the end of the chapter. You might wish to contact some of them.

All of this takes time, effort, commitment, and decision making on your part, and may produce painful answers. You may be dismayed to discover that the world isn't out to get you and that your own attitude is not wholly affirmative. You may discover that opportunities have slipped away because you were too timid to grab them. Or you may find out that your educational institution holds beliefs and values so contrary to yours that continuing to work there is hardly your best choice for action. Finally, you may receive irrefutable confirmation of your worst fears.

Whatever the outcome, you will have embarked upon a continuing education, one that will stand you in good stead, that will help make the American educational map what it should be and American education the liberating force we all expected it to be. Your choices for action include commitment to that goal.

FIGURE 5–7 Choices for Action Checklist

A. *Legal Provisions Covering Your Educational Institution or Educational Employer*

	Yes	No	Don't Know
1. Equal Pay Act of 1963, as amended	____	____	____
2. Title VII of the Civil Rights Act, as amended	____	____	____
3. Executive Order 11246, as amended	____	____	____
4. Public Health Acts	____	____	____
5. Title IX of the Education Amendments, as amended	____	____	____

B. *Prisoner's Base Problems*

	Yes	No	Don't Know
1. Denial of opportunity to apply for or be accepted for			
a. admission	____	____	____
b. classes	____	____	____
c. programs	____	____	____
d. training	____	____	____
e. apprenticeship	____	____	____
f. employment	____	____	____
g. promotion or tenure	____	____	____
h. transfer	____	____	____
2. Failure to provide equal			
a. salary	____	____	____
b. benefits (insurance, pensions)	____	____	____
c. physical safety	____	____	____
d. vacations, leaves, sabbaticals	____	____	____
e. access to supervisor	____	____	____
f. workload	____	____	____
g. treatment	____	____	____
3. Harrassment: sexual or employment	____	____	____

C. *Extent of discriminatory employment practice*

	Yes	No	Don't Know
1. Against others in my employment category	____	____	____
2. Against workers in other categories			
a. women student workers	____	____	____
b. women faculty	____	____	____
c. women administrators	____	____	____

	Yes	No	Don't Know
d. women classified employees	___	___	___
e. nonwhite males	___	___	___
f. white males	___	___	___

	How many	% of women in unit	in inst.
3. Quantitative data			
a. Number and percentage of affected women coworkers	___	___	___

4.Specific nature of discrimination cited by coworkers. (Make a list.)

D. Possible Strategies

1. Organize for action.
2. Collect documented violations of A.1–5.
3. Analyze violations by categories B.1–2.
4. Compare violation instances as in C.1–3. to determine strongest issues, gain widest support from coworkers. Calculate C. 4.
5. Determine whether a women's organization, professional union, lawyer or legal organization, or governmental agency is most likely to achieve the remedy sought. File complaint with the correct compliance agency according to that agency's guidelines.
6. Or, decide to harass back and have some fun with the game as a learning experience.
7. Now, set your time limit on these activities. If no result is achieved within (one, two, three) years, I will (file suit, change jobs, etc.).
8. What I am going to start doing now to help others:
   a. information dissemination
   b. legal enforcement
   c. political pressure
   d. other

ADDITIONAL INFORMATION SOURCES

Among the organizations you might find helpful in relation to Title IX is SPRINT, an information and advice service of WEAL for women employed in athletics whose jobs are threatened:

SPRINT
805 15th Street, N.W.
Washington, D.C. 20005
(800) 424-5162

The project on the Status and Education of Women at the Association of American Colleges has up-to-date information on federal requirements in postsecondary institutions:

The Project on the Status and Education of Women
1818 R Street, N.W.
Washington, D.C. 20009
(202) 387-1300

The National Advisory Council on Women's Educational Programs sponsored *The Unenforced Law: Title IX Activity by Federal Agencies Other Than HEW* and may be contacted for information:

The National Advisory Council on Women's Educational Programs
1832 M Street, N.W., #821
Washington, D.C. 20036

Vocational Education Act addresses:

California Women
California Commission on the Status of Women
926 J Street, Room 1506
Sacramento, CA 95814
(916) 445-3173

Lawyers Committee for Civil Rights under the Law
The Federal Education Project
733 15th Street, N.W., Suite 520
Washington, D.C. 20005
(202) 628-6700

Project ACT
Women's Enterprises of Boston
739 Boylston Street
Boston, MA 02116
(617) 266-2243

NOTES

1. Jessie Bernard, *Academic Women* (New York: Meridan/New American Library, 1974), pp. 100–101 and 215.

2. This section utilized materials provided by the U.S. Department of Labor, the American Federation of Teachers, the Association of American Colleges, the American Association of University Women, and educational newspapers.

3. Dorothy Jongeward and Dru Scott, *Affirmative Action for Women* (Reading Mass.: Addison-Wesley, 1975), p. 43.

4. "Interpretive Guidelines on Employment Discrimination and Reproductive Hazards," *Federal Register*, February 1, 1980, pp. 7514–7517, interprets "the relationship between employment discrimination and the application of employer/contractor policies, practices and plans regarding reproductive hazards" (7514). The Occupational Safety and Health Act's (OSHA) role is to be that of consultation and coordination with EEOC and OFCCP (Office of Federal Contract Compliance Programs). The guidelines reaffirm goals of Title VII of the Civil Rights Act and EO 11246 but go further. Federal agencies given that responsibility are to assure hazard-free workplaces, sex discrimination is prohibited where reproductive hazards are found, and nondiscriminatory policy—and protective procedures—are required to be instituted. Joan E. Bertin, "New Wrongs for Working Women," *aclu Women's Rights Report* II, no. 2 (Fall 1980): 1,9, expands on this issue and discusses compliance from the women's rights aspect. Benton R. Schlender, in "Sterilization Is Main Issue in OSHA Suits," *The Wall Street Journal*, December 9, 1980, p. 29, states that American Cyanamid and Gulf Resources and Chemical Corporation's Bunker Hill units have been taken to court over their "fetus protection policies"—a nasty euphemism that masks the companies' real policies. The Labor Department unit charges that women employees have to make the choice between their jobs and "having themselves sterilized." Eleven female employees were "sterilized to retain employment." The Gulf Resources chairman asked whether freedom of choice meant that women employees should be allowed to work where there was a known health hazard. The companies further befogged the issue of health, safety, and illegality by insisting that it "must be decided as a sex discrimination issue under civil rights or labor law." A federal administrative judge agreed with this unexpected maneuver and threw out OSHA's citation against American Cyanamid in July 1980. Meanwhile, the OSHA lawyer, in referring to the corporate sterilization policy, commented that it was so bizarre that it must "be a violation of something."

5. See Diana Scully, *Men Who Control Women's Health: The Mis-education of Obstetricians and Gynecologists* (New York: Houghton-Mifflin, Co. 1980); and, for the general view of women's medical care, see Susan Schiefelbein, "The Female Patient: Heeded? Hustled? Healed?" *Saturday Review*, March 29, 1980, pp. 12–16. Paula Span, "A New Era for Feminist Health Clinics," *New York Times*

Magazine, November 23, 1980, pp. 108–16, reports that some male physicians are hearing the message. Span quotes one: "It's an anti-medical profession attitude: 'They're out to get you, sterilize you . . . ' ", p. 110. The male obstetrician/gynecologist quoted was opposed to the feminist health clinics, but he was aware of why they have multiplied nationwide.

6. "Women in the World: A Ford Foundation Position Paper" (New York: Ford Foundation, November 1980) states, "In the U.S., 19 out of 20 first-year college students attend schools where the top two administrators are male," p. 21. Also see Patricia Sexton, *Women in Education* (Bloomington, Ind.: Phi Delta Kappa, 1976), pp. 57–58, for insight into male domination of school decision making, which perpetuates inequities, sex stereotypes, and continued male educational leadership. Judith M. Gappa and Barbara S. Uehling, in *Women in Academe: Steps to Greater Equality* (Washington, D.C.: American Association for Higher Education, 1979), observed similar influences relative to women administrators in higher education. They found women administrators in positions that reinforce feminine stereotypes such as student counseling and service-related, rather than academic administrative, positions.

7. Sue Hubbell, "Barbara Uehling, of the University of Missouri," *Working Woman*, November 1980, pp. 86–92.

8. "Women Faculty Still Lag in Salary and Tenure for the 1979–80 Academic Year" (Washington, D.C.: U.S. Department of Health, Education, and Welfare, Education Division, National Center for Education Statistics 80–342, 1980).

9. *Ibid.*, Tables 3 and 2.

10. J. Victor Baldridge, David V. Curtis, and others, *Policy Making and Effective Leadership* (San Francisco: Jossey-Bass, 1978). See p. 177 for documentation of trends. Also see Elayn Bernay, "Affirmative Inaction," *Ms.* 7, no. 5 (November 1978): 87–90; and Mary Crawford, "Climbing the Ivy-Covered Walls," *Ms.* 7, no. 5 (November 1978): 61–64 and 91–94, for further corroboration. An editorial by Philip H. Abelson, "Women in Academia," *Science*, January 14, 1972, while overly optimistic about women's success with the legal apparatus for fighting sex discrimination, foreshadows the decline of the proportion of women on academic faculties.

11. "Everything You Need to Know about Title IX" (Washington, D.C.: American Federation of Teachers, AFL–CIO, 1976) contains a useful compliance assessment questionnaire and suggested contractual provisions, including childcare programs for children of working parents, which may be used in collective bargaining.

12. California is one. For results of the National Sex Equity Demonstration Project funded under WEEA, see Rita Bornstein, "Ambiguity As Opportunity and Constraint: Evolution of a Federal Sex Equity Education Program," presented at

American Educational Research Association Convention, New York, N.Y. March 1982.

13. For information, write to American Association of University Professors, Washington, D.C., about Scott, "Higher Education Salary Evaluation Kit: A Recommended Method for Flagging Women and Minority Persons for Whom There Is Apparent Salary Inequity and a Comparison of Results and Costs of Several Suggested Methods" (1977).

14. Carol S. Stern and others, "On Processing Complaints of Discrimination on the Basis of Sex," *AAUP Bulletin*, August 1977, pp. 233–34.

15. *Ibid.*, p. 236.

16. Doing this demands that you have demonstrable sex discrimination complaints, federal law violations and witnesses to them, or documents from your antagonists. Signed documents are best; initialed ones will do.

17. Nancy J. Balles, *The Unenforced Law: Title IX Activity by Federal Agencies Other Than HEW* (Washington, D.C.: National Advisory Council on Women's Educational Programs, 1978), p. 6.

18. *Ibid.* The entire document should be read and digested.

19. For information on these student examples see: *The Chronicle of Higher Education*, July 16, 1979 and November 2, 1983; *The Chronicle of Higher Education*, October 4, 1978 and May 21, 1979 for Cannon; and for another case, Lillie Walker v. George Washington University *Higher Education and National Affairs*, May 20, 1977. Among Horowitz references are: William A. Kaplin, *The Law of Higher Education* (San Francisco: Jossey-Bass, 1978), pp. 244-47; Thomas J. Flygare, "Schools and the Law—The Horowitz Case: No Hearing Required for 'Academic' Dismissals," *Phi Delta Kappan*, May 1978, pp. 626–27; *Higher Education and National Affairs*, April 22, 1977, p. 1; *The Chronicle of Higher Education*, April 25, 1977.

20. For information on the Johnson and Colby cases, see *The Chronicle of Higher Education*, January 8, 1979. The same publication, January 29, 1979 provides information on Berry, while an earlier issue, April 25, 1977 deals with the Cussler suit. Sweeney is found in *The Chronicle* on January 28, 1980. See the same publication, October 4, 1978 for a Supreme Court ruling in a faculty pay bias class action case, and January 22, 1979 for an individual sex bias suit.

21. "Office of Education Is Sued by Its Top Ranking Woman," *Federal Times*, May 20, 1979.

22. Classified employees at Central Piedmont Community College alleged that they trained successive male administrators for 7 years. The males became their

supervisors. The women filed a class action (Elizabeth Evans v. Central Piedmont Community College, North Carolina, 1976) and won a pyrrhic victory. The judge "tentatively" awarded back pay but left the settlement up to the college administration.

23. *The Chronicle of Higher Education,* October 9, 1979.

24. "Nondiscrimination on Basis of Sex," part II, *Federal Register* 40, no. 108 (June 4, 1975).

25. Higher Education and National Affairs, April 29, 1977. Women's groups such as PEER and Women's Equity Action League (WEAL) have long been working for enforcement. WEAL sued HEW in 1977, alleging that the department had not enforced Title IX. In 1979, WEAL and other groups requested that HEW officials be held in contempt of court unless they processed sex bias complaints. WEAL charged the 1977 agreement with OCR was being violated.

The loan department receptionist said I had to be a bank customer for at least six months to qualify for a bank loan; then the secretary told me the bank's minimum time for loans was seven years as a customer. I politely asked who could give me information on the bank's other loan policies. The secretary said everyone was busy and this was not a very good day.

Working woman/student researcher, 1978.

Getting It in Your Pocket
the Federal Equal Credit Opportunity Act

CREDIT AND RELATED CONCERNS

Mindset

Chapter 6 deals with obtaining money. The emphasis is on how to present yourself accurately as a good credit risk. We focus on what creditors look for, what borrowers expect, and how the federal laws mediate between creditors and borrowers. Legal protections that working women have related to money, such as the Equal Credit Opportunity Law, are discussed.

Checklists are furnished to help the working woman as potential borrower. Some role playing to make the first approach to a creditor easier is outlined. So is some hardheaded, realistic thinking. When you finish the chapter, you'll know that money grows in banks (and related institutions), not on trees. You'll have a better idea of how to harvest some and a notion of what the crop will cost. You'll also be aware of what resources you currently own that may assist you in borrowing money.

Your own name as an asset—or perhaps as a liability—as a working woman seeking credit is dealt with; so is what you can do as a married woman, working or not, to assure that you have a credit history. Insights into how to check up on your credit file are also given. These may turn out to be worth all the time you invest in reading the chapter.

Inflation has made it necessary for all women to learn where they stand in the American money market. You may never have needed to get money quickly to buy a house, pay educational or medical expenses, have emergency repairs done, or take advantage of an unexpected opportunity. These things may await you tomorrow. Even if all of your needs have been provided for so far, one day you may require a lender's services.

"Credit" means "he or she believes." Credit is related to believability. Women as a group (married women, in particular) still do not have much fiscal credibility. They do not get their fair share of credit. We want to help change that. The first step is understanding why American women have problems obtaining money.

Cultural patterns in this country have promoted the idea that males handle money, produce money, and provide for the economic needs of women and children. Immigrant groups coming to this country in the huge late nineteenth and early twentieth century influx followed different patterns but the same assumptions. What really happened was that Orthodox Jewish women controlled and often generated the funds while their husbands pursued their more important religious studies. Among the Italian and Irish groups, especially in urban centers, only women found jobs (in factories or as maids). They were hired because they cost far less than male labor. Thousands of these women supported their families as best they could. Sensitive to prevailing customs, the working women were so modest about their achievements that even today we perpetuate the myth of the male breadwinner. That myth permitted women and children to be seen as neither wanting money nor needing to know anything about it—a convenient fiction. Changed views about money and credit, however, are inescapable today.

Women now are proud of their financial success, especially when they are so-called self-made women. Merv Griffin began a show with the announcement that he had a surprise for his audience: eight millionaires would talk to them. The curtains opened on eight women. One, a madam, told her girls to buy real estate and had followed her own advice with obvious success. Another woman had founded two businesses, the second of which catered to women who, like herself, had lost a breast to cancer. A different kind of example is the growing number of young women who are currently MBA candidates. A third example can be drawn from the increasing percentage of women who work full-time.

It takes money to make money. One way to get money is to establish credit. American women have only recently begun to explore that aspect of marketplace life. And they have not had an easy time getting credit. But while American women may have difficulty getting the credit due them, they are well aware that credit is useful. American women could manage their financial resources better if they were wiser in the ways of credit. This chapter aims to supply a foundation for wisdom about credit.

The Credit Equation: C = L + B + G

The credit equation traditionally has two parts: the lender and the borrower (L+B). Each part plays a different role in the flow and creation of money. We will view these elements separately so that we can see how credit functions, where snags may arise, and what we can do to remove them. We are, moreover, adding a new element—government (G)—to the credit equation.

If everything went as smoothly in financial transactions as it is supposed to in love, we would not need this third element in the credit equation. Love can have a bumpy course, but in my experience it is simple compared to money. Stated concisely, the government has had to take an active role to assure all citizens equal opportunity to exercise their borrowing power. Legislation has been enacted to assist those who were not receiving fair treatment from those who controlled the money.

Women are among the potential beneficiaries of this government intervention. Obviously, women are more likely to benefit from legislation if they know about it, what it does, and how to ensure enforcement. Therefore, a major aspect of increasing wisdom about money and credit has to do with knowing what the law provides. Increasing money wisdom also concerns what the borrower needs to know and do to be "credible," "creditworthy," "a good credit risk." Women need to know, too, what the lender might do.

The lender. Lenders are not like you and me. For one thing, they have money. For another, lenders, usually banks, have different objectives from ours. Lenders exist to make money by providing money for a fee. Everyone knows that, yet when seeking the lender's assets and assistance, many women forget the lender's viewpoint.

Lenders must minimize the risk of losing their money. Lenders must maximize the probability of making money. Thus, lenders look for believable borrowers, good credit risks. There is nothing personal about that. Financial institutions must practice prudent lending or go bankrupt. If you have savings, you should want your bank to be cautious, because the money lent may be partly yours. Besides, the interest credited to your savings account is part of what your bank earned by lending your savings to someone. So, you have probably been a lender, although you may not have thought of yourself that way.

The borrower. It used to be said that the customer is always right. But customers who are borrowers (seekers) or debtors (successful seekers) can find themselves in the wrong. Misunderstandings and emotions are connected with money matters, leading to the conclusion that money is usually a symptom rather than a cause.

In one misunderstanding, a borrower is labeled a spendthrift. Why else would anyone need a loan? Perhaps as a hedge against inflation in a strategy emphasizing borrowing now and paying back later in inflation-eroded cheap money. Instead of being a poor money manager on the verge of financial ruin, a borrower might be cleverly enjoying goods and services now and deducting the interest charge (the cost of borrowing) from her income tax.

Governments borrow, secure in the knowledge that tax collections will enable them to meet their obligations, while at the same time borrowing will enable them to provide the services citizens have contracted for. Corporations rely on the sale of their goods and services for the cash flow to pay off their debts. Borrowing by individuals, governments, and corporations can be smart money management.

Borrowers have an important function. One cannot admit this until emotions and misunderstanding are stripped from the topic of borrowing. Borrowers are needed to permit the medium of exchange (money) to do its job. "Aha!" you say, realizing that borrowing creates new capital through granting the borrower credit that is spent for some purpose. There is nothing moral, immoral, or personal about it. Borrowing and lending are business transactions.

In an ideal society, the credit equation would consist of borrowing plus lending. Ours, a real society, requires regulation by the government. Our equation is Credit = Borrower + Lender + Government.

Ideally, the borrower's sex and marital status are of no consequence to the transaction. All borrowers ought to be equal. Likewise, borrowing from one bank ought to be just like borrowing from another. Unfortunately, in our society, the borrower's sex and marital status frequently have determined whether a loan application was approved.

The determining factor in obtaining credit *logically* would be the ability to fulfill the loan agreement conditions. Will the borrower be able to repay the loan within the agreed-upon time limits? Can the borrower pledge as security something equal in value to the money borrowed? Will the loan be repaid if something should happen to the borrower?

The Government. Governments have long been mediators in disputes between borrowers and lenders. Governments play the role of negotiators and regulators of financial transactions. But only in recent years has government taken on additional responsibilities in financial matters. Important legislation enacted in 1974 was designed to make it illegal to discriminate in granting credit. The legislation includes provision for enforcement by appropriate compliance agencies.

On October 28, 1975, the Federal Equal Credit Opportunity Act (ECOA) became effective. This law states:

> it shall be unlawful for any creditor to discriminate against any applicant with respect to any aspect of a credit transaction on the basis of . . . sex or marital status.

Working hand in hand with the ECOA is the 1971 Fair Credit Reporting Act, which requires creditors to explain rejections of credit within 100 days if an applicant inquires about why credit was denied.

We will focus on the ECOA, since it deals directly with issues important to women. The government requires that ECOA notices be prominent on materials that lenders provide to potential borrowers. There are two required notices:

Equal Credit Opportunity Notice

The lender may provide the applicant the Equal Credit Opportunity Notice on this page (Federal Reserve Board Regulation B, 12 CFR 202, 4 (d). The Equal Credit Opportunity Act, 15 U.S.C. 1691 et seq. prohibits discrimination against credit applicants on the basis of sex and marital status. Beginning March 23, 1977, the Act extends this protection to race, color, religion, national origin, age, whether all or part of the applicant's income is derived from any public assistance program, or if the applicant has in good faith exercised any rights under the Consumer Credit Protection Act. The applicant should note that *the lender must provide the notice* here, on an application form, or on some other separate sheet of paper. *This notice provides the name of the lender's supervising agency.* (Italics added.)

Notice
Required by Equal Credit Opportunity Act

The Federal Equal Credit Opportunity Act prohibits creditors from discriminating against credit applicants on the basis of sex or marital status. The Federal agency which administers compliance with this law concerning this bank is the Comptroller of the Currency, Consumer Affairs Division, Washington, D.C. 20219.

The first gives general provisions of the law, and the second cites the compliance agency for a specific lending institution or creditor. A list of compliance agencies for financial institutions, stockbrokers, credit card companies, and retail stores is given in Figure 6–1.

Our aim is to secure fair and equal treatment, so it is appropriate to say that we favor and support prudent lending practices by institutions and realistic borrowing by consumers. Prudent financial policies and practices benefit the nation. Unfortunately, both sides—financial institutions and their customers—will need to improve their performance to achieve this goal. Until then, the government may be working women's best ally where credit is concerned. Before deciding whether you agree, let's look at two faces of credit.

FIGURE 6–1 Compliance Agencies*

For Banks:

Comptroller of the Currency
Consumer Affairs Division
Washington, D.C. 20219

or

Federal Deposit Insurance Corporation
Regional Director for the region in which the nonmember insured bank is located

or

Federal Reserve Bank
serving the district in which the state member bank is located

For Savings and Loan Institutions

Federal Home Loan Bank Board Supervisory Agent
in the district in which the institution is located

For Credit Unions

National Credit Union Administration
Regional Office serving the area in which the credit union is located

For Stockbrokers

Securities and Exchange Commission
Washington, D.C. 20523

For Credit Card Companies (except those handled through banks) and retail stores

Federal Trade Commission
Regional Office in area of operation

*From "Credit Rules That Give Women a Fair Shake,"
Changing Times: The Kiplinger Magazine, May 1977,
pp. 13–15; "The Equal Credit Opportunity Act and
Women" (Washington, D.C.: Federal Trade
Commission, Equal Credit Opportunity, 1977);
Consumer Handbook to Credit Protection Laws
(Washington, D.C.: Board of Governors of the Federal
Reserve System, 1978), p. 44.

TWO FACES OF CREDIT

Face One: How Credit Can Be Seductive

Credit is a promise—the promise of fulfilled dreams now, without effort. A wallet full of credit cards used impulsively can be disastrous and irresponsible. The cure can be easier: Cut up and dispose of the credit cards. Or learn how to live with them, within your means. We'll focus a bit on credit cards while remembering that these illustrations of mini-credit are not the main point.

Credit cards can appear in the mail by magic. They give the holder power. So do similar but not identical charge accounts. (One can have charge accounts at stores giving a 90-day grace period before adding a service charge; one can have charge accounts at stores whose customers must guarantee a minimum amount of trade annually, etc.) These forms of credit make life's goodies so easy to get. And since we only ride life's merry-go-round once, we want our share of its better things. Besides, some of us feel good about ourselves when we get something special, while others feel that we ought to be good to ourselves. Still others want what they want immediately and will let tomorrow take care of itself. Those are rationalizations. There are pressures, too, some carefully planned by motivational researchers who con us into spending.

We think we are acting freely . . . until the bill comes and we panic, overextended, overexpended on every credit card and charge account. Perhaps credit cards should carry a warning: "This item may be hazardous to your health. Handle it with care." We've heard so many horror stories. And, like most women, we've experienced the credit crunch and know that self-discipline is hard to learn.

Those are the smaller, seductive aspects of credit. Taken singly, they are not terribly important. Macy's does not tell Gimbel's what your monthly balance is, nor does Visa investigate your Texaco balance. But there are agencies that make checks about your credit behavior possible. Now that women can and do have accounts in their own names, credit bureaus keep tabs on them and watch their response to the heady power of virtually limitless available credit.

Face Two: How Credit Can Be Used Responsibly

The second face of credit is the one where you are in control of how you are going to choose the creditor you'll honor with your attention and patronage. This is the delicate matter of building up your credit rating. Building a credit rating is something all women need to know about so that they can function as fiscally responsible adults. It's time this topic came out of the closet and into the clear light of day.

Another closet topic that deserves being aired and put to rest is that banks and bankers are not used to lending money to women and minority group members. Some banks feel that they can continue behaving as they formerly did—namely, by operating under one set of rules for potential male borrowers and using another set for potential women (and minority) borrowers. Well, they can't. It's against the law. Then, too, women (and minority group members), now an economic force to be conjured with, are turning out to be good money managers. They are better at handling money than they or bankers expected. But knowledge about money cannot be inherited; it has to be learned by each individual. Both women and bankers need to be aware of today's economic conditions.

Today's woman needs to know how to build credit, and about one credit rating—hers. We all have values assigned to us which determine how good our credit rating is. Many of us remain unaware of our credit ratings, assuming that business is fair; we also assume that money has no sex. Most of us assume, in addition, that credit institutions all share the same advantages and disadvantages. Nothing could be further from the truth.

Starting with gasoline credit cards, all-purpose credit cards, or store charge cards, we find that these are available to women in their own names, providing they can pass the required credit check. It is easy to be accepted as a credit customer for many credit cards and charge plates. You fill out an application, and within six weeks a plastic invitation to help the economy is in your hands. You have some credit, but the issuer does not know whether you are a good credit risk. Part of your subsequent credit rating depends on how promptly you, as card holder, pay your bills, how recently you have moved (related to how up-to-date your credit rating is), and whether you check with a credit bureau to find out what your credit rating is.

All metropolitan areas have credit bureaus. You can find the closest one by telephoning your Better Business Bureau. Good advice was offered by Leonard Sloane in "What's in Your Credit File?"[1] Sloane and other experts consider checkups on your credit rating almost as important as regular physical examinations. You might give this idea serious thought and then follow it up with action. If there are errors or omissions in your credit rating, you are the only person who has a genuine interest in correcting them. Anyway, nobody can do it for you.

Impulsive buyers generally have poor credit ratings because they stretch themselves out of shape financially month after month. Then, too, when a bill is not completely paid within a month after billing, an interest or service charge is added to the unpaid balance. Impulse buyers thus find themselves poor credit risks saddled with lots of extra charges.

Other buyers are poor readers or just too trusting. Read each credit card agreement carefully. It must inform you of the annual service charge and the monthly one. Whatever the standard charge, it is a high price to pay for credit. (By contrast, bank loan costs vary with economic conditions and type and length of loan, but banks are unlikely to extend credit to you unless you demonstrate a high credit rating or have a substantial deposit with them so that your loan is protected.) The new legal provisions governing borrowing provide advantages to nonworking and recently employed wives. They also provide equal advantages to nonworking or newly employed husbands. To do less would be sexist. The new provisions have potential impact upon working women. They may find themselves responsible for other people's debts. You might find yourself paying a spouse's bills, too. Contrary to popular myth, not all bad credit risks are female. There are plenty of tales about husbands and ex-husbands who were able to transfer responsibility for their debts to wives and ex-wives.

Before entering into a credit agreement with a store, find out whether you would be comfortable supporting a business with its philosophy. Where you have credit says something about you. So, before signing an agreement, be sure it really is to your credit.

We are ready to turn from credit cards and smaller forms of credit to the larger transactions—loans. You might pause here to reflect on the money myths provided in Figure 6–2. They may serve as a guide. When one of the myths describes you, action is required on your part.

NOW ABOUT THAT LOAN

There are two basic reasons for wanting a loan. The first is needing the money; the second is less obvious. You may find it as crazy as I did the first time it surfaced. In 1946, my mother announced, "I just borrowed $5000." "What for?" we asked. She said, "To put in the bank." "You borrowed $5000 to put in the bank?" "Yes, it seemed like a cheap way to build up my credit rating," she answered. It was, and it worked. The next year, when she did extensive remodeling, my mother got her loan the day she requested it. Needing money and building up your credit rating work together, if they can. You must have a good credit rating to make that possible. And borrowing today is not a cheap way to achieve tomorrow's good credit rating, but it is an effective method.

There are some cautions. Married women can cosign notes with their husbands and thereby improve their credit rating from none to one

FIGURE 6–2 Grim Fables for Our Times

_____	1. Women and children don't want money and don't need to know anything about it.
_____	2. Women generally are poor credit risks.
_____	3. Women control most of the United States' wealth.
_____	4. Working women can easily make loans to finance homes in their own names.
_____	5. Most working women check their credit rating every two years.
_____	6. Few working women know anything about the stock market and other kinds of investments.
_____	7. A working woman cannot borrow money from a bank unless she has a cosigner, preferably a male.
_____	8. It isn't feminine to know anything about money.
_____	9. Women do not get a feeling of power from handling money and other assets effectively.
_____	10. Working women rarely know their financial worth.

Check the statements that are typical of your views. What correctives can you apply to improve your situation? Begin today; it is to your advantage.

dependent upon how the loan was repaid. The risk is that if you cosign a note, you are legally responsible for its repayment; cosigners are equally liable. What happend to one young couple who borrowed $14,000 from the husband's parents and signed a note, is that the husband died suddenly. The in-laws demanded payment, and the bereaved wife luckily managed to pay it. But can you imagine how she felt? Though such events are unusual, one must realize that when risks are taken there is always a possibility that one will have to pay the piper.

Do You Look Like a Good Risk?

In the abstract, a job, a savings account, few outstanding debts, a telephone (preferably in your own name), and no children in college should make you a fine credit risk. It helps if you make regular deposits into your savings account and if your bank provides full service. If you have dealt with the same bank for years and can address some tellers by name, so much the better. You need to possess integrity, a sense of humor, the patience of Job, and luck to get your credit where you want it. We are talking about the place from which you borrow and the amount you are able to borrow.

Let's suppose you have done all of the things mentioned, and a big opportunity has arrived. You need far more money than your credit card will permit you to borrow to take advantage of that opportunity. You know that it will be more expensive if you wait another year. So you are ready to talk business with the boys in the pine-paneled den. (There may be a woman banker there, but don't expect her to make special allowances for you. "Business," as Charles Chaplin remarked in a movie, "is a ruthless business.")

C-WORTHINESS

What to Do at the Bank

Once you decide to go to a bank, three tasks await you:

1. Finding the right bank for your loan
2. Doing your homework
3. Building your case

The simplest thing is to run through the elements a creditor and a potential borrower need to be familiar with. To begin, we take a look at the banker's Cs—capacity, character, and collateral. Then we examine three additional Cs—checklist, confidence, and contingency plans.

Capacity, Character, Collateral[2]

Figure 6–3 consists of a checklist. It covers the creditor's three Cs—capacity, character, collateral, and more. *Capacity* refers to your ability to repay a loan. Typical questions might be whether you are working, whether you owe money elsewhere, and what proportion of your assets are already earmarked.

Character answers the question of whether you are as good as your word. A potential creditor may want to inquire about your past credit performance from other lenders. Are you regular and prompt in repayment? How long have you lived in your present location? How long have you worked for your present employer? In other words, how stable are you? And do you manage your money well?

Collateral refers to what you own that is marketable. Cash and items that could be converted into money are collateral. Items such as

FIGURE 6–3 Checklist for Getting a Loan

1. The purpose of the loan (you already have decided this):

   a. *Home improvement,* adds to property value.
   b. *Educational expenses,* should add value to person receiving training.
   c. *Travel or vacation expenses.*
   d. *Invest in securities,* may add to or diminish in value.
   e. *Investment in real estate,* may grow or remain stable these days.
   f. *Miscellaneous,* emergencies, gifts.

2. The amount of money you wish to borrow:

   a. *Do you have collateral to secure this loan?*
      Can you *put up as security* a fully owned car, securities, real estate deeds, appliances, an original Picasso, a bank book? Used fur coats and most used jewelry might be rejected.
   b. *Is the loan size requested reasonable for the purpose?*
      A $25,000 request for getting an M.A. in Education is different from the same amount for a B.A. in Business, but neither is reasonable. Yet $25,000 for medical school tuition and expenses might be too low a figure. Loan size tells a banker whether you have done your homework. In the educational expenses example, your requests lets the banker know whether you have checked out other funding sources first (state scholarships, educational opportunity grants, etc.).
   c. *What do you currently owe (indebtedness)?*
      Are these obligations being met as planned? (Or have you defaulted, say, had your furniture *repossessed?*) Bankers are not interested in hard luck stories; they are looking for good risks. Bankers want to know if you can manage additional borrowing without squeezing your income. Bankers want to know if there is evidence of impulse buying.
   d. *How can you improve your chances?*
      Persons who have just gotten a promotion or a large raise and who can provide six months of figures on expenditures for rent, food, clothing, entertainment, charity, loan payments, and savings would be seen as good loan prospects. Have the figures with you. You may not need to show them.

3. Finding the right bank for your loan:
   a. *Prior experience with this bank.*
      Money is tight. If you have a savings account or a checking account at this bank, you know and trust the bank. If the banker there knows you by name, you feel comfortable there. If you do not use your savings account there as a checking account, the bank probably has no negative feelings about you, unless your hobby is bouncing checks. People who try to avoid service charges by having a savings account on which there are several transactions monthly are not playing fair with the bank; the passbook

FIGURE 6-3 (Continued)

makes this quite clear. People who bounce checks are not desirable loan customers.

b. *Talking to your banker.*

What will the loan cost? Can you have it insured for a small additional fee? Is there a prepayment penalty if you are able to pay the loan off early? Is there anything else the banker should tell you about borrowing this money?

c. *Before taking the first loan offered, comparison shop.*

Visit at least one other bank and compare advantages and disadvantages of what is offered. Think about the way you feel about each bank. Banks vary in services but also in the interest shown you (a bank willing to spend time on a $5000 loan now will be even more helpful in the future when your needs are greater). Did you notice that there was a woman vice-president of this bank? (If there is, women customers are likely to be valued and well treated.) If all of the women employees are tellers or business machine operators, you might well receive poorer service than a male customer seeking the identical loan.

4. Just in case it doesn't work.

Have contingency plans.

Don't have all your hopes in one place; you may be turned down, disappointed. Plan realistically. Think of alternative ways of obtaining the loan you need. Could you borrow part of the amount for a shorter period to establish credit and then refinance? Could you devise your own loan package using insurance, savings, and a smaller loan?

---

paid-up life insurance policies, unmortgaged real estate, government bonds, securities, assessed collections, and so on, are collateral. They can secure a loan, for they serve to assure that you will repay it. If you don't pay, you forfeit the collateral, and the bank does not lose on the transaction. Collateral is always worth more than the face value of the loan. The government regulates the collateral percentage of the loan. For instance, if collateral had to equal 130 percent of the loan's face value, you would pledge collateral worth $13,000 to secure a $10,000 loan. The creditor keeps your collateral until the loan is entirely repaid. While this may seem neither fair nor trusting, once you have borrowed money and repaid it you have a credit rating. Then the bank from which you borrowed serves as your gold-plated credit reference. Like falling in love, getting a loan is better the second time around—one is more relaxed about it.

Checklist

We are now ready for the credit seeker's first C—that *checklist* you've been examining in Figure 6–3. You will have to tell a loan officer why you need to borrow money, exactly how you plan to use it, when you will need it, and what you will provide as collateral. The checklist will help you. As you would be the first to notice if someone came to borrow your money, the desirability of making loans for the purposes outlined varies from secure to risky.

The checklist doesn't cover everything. My first big solo loan went to pay my income tax. Nobody in the bank wanted to know how incompetent my accountant had been or how stupid I was to stick with him as he goofed my federal return annually. What the loan officer wanted to know was that I needed $13,500 on April 15 and how I would repay both the principal and the interest.

The loan officer knew I played the stock market because he had made purchases and sales for me. He knew when I made money and when I didn't. He could even tease me with, "When are you going to give us some *real* business?" And I could answer, "You mean like that time you bought me $250,000 worth of government securities instead of the $2500 I ordered?" Still, I felt no bank would lend me as much as $13,500.

My women friends, independent borrowers, were requesting between $3000 and $5000. I was scared, certain to be turned down. That left some unpleasant alternatives: I would go to jail for tax evasion, or I could devote my whole salary (after withholding taxes) to paying off that income tax plus the accumulated penalties. There were no other ways to clear my debt to the American government.

The loan officer surprised me. He provided a complex financial form to fill out. Then he said the bank would accept my loan and not to bother to fill out the whole application. I would need to give him collateral when I got my loan check. Getting that loan was a relief, though the government was really making me pay. Now I could do the same for the bank—pay. A horrid future, one sure to teach me some important lessons about credit, loans, and accountants . . . if I survived.

Then there was the matter of interest. My loan was for 1 percent over prime. My loan officer explained that the prime rate is set by New York banks and is the lending standard for the United States. The prime rate is related to (is higher than) the Federal Funding Rate, which establishes the rate at which banks can borrow money. In inflationary days, prime rates rise whenever you blink. By the end of my loan year, I had really been "primed." Prime rates can decrease, too, theoretically. They didn't for me, so I had lots of interest to deduct from the next income tax return my marvelous new CPA prepared.

There's something else about interest rates: While credit cards and charge accounts have fixed service charges for bills remaining unpaid after 30 days, bank rates vary. We've been talking about effective rates of interest—what you actually pay—not about the quoted rate—what the loan officer quotes you as the going rate—which can fluctuate with the money market or can include additional charges.

There are installment loans with fixed interest rates. Such loans are more expensive than the one I got, to start. Their advantage is that you know what your cost will be on each portion of the loan. The amount never varies. Loans like that, the type usually offered by banks, can be bargains in inflationary times. Since their interest rate is fixed and the loans tend to be long-term transactions, like mortgages, the borrower comes out ahead in the long run. For example, our mortgage, which seemed incredibly expensive in 1968 at 6¼ percent, now ranks as a fabulous bargain.

In addition to remembering about collateral, current indebtedness, reasonableness of loan size, and documenting your recent expenditures, you will want to keep in mind that you are a customer. Caveat emptor— "Let the buyer beware"—applies even in the conservative banking business.

Bankers, like doctors and lawyers, will only give you the service you want; you are responsible for letting them know what they can do for you. Do ask questions, even if you preface them with, "I don't know much about borrowing money. Would you explain what a prepayment penalty is?" As it may seem complicated and forbidding, you could follow a loan officer's explanation with, "Have I got it right? A prepayment penalty is . . . ?" just to double-check. Before leaving home to see your banker, write down the questions you want answered. Loan officers will be glad to answer them; it makes them feel superior, and everyone likes that.

Confidence

If you are confident that you deserve the credit requested and pass the capacity, character, and collateral screening, you may find yourself in the bank's debt for some time. To maximize your chances, try creditor role playing, putting yourself in the banker's position, because it helps to increase your *confidence*. Creditor role playing helps you to be clear, brief, and unflustered by what may seem like nosey, personal questions about your finances. In your role playing, focus on being flexible, businesslike, and innovative. Get a friend to play borrower as you take the banker's role. Ask a few bankers for advice on presenting yourself effectively for the loan you need.

You might do so well with the first bank that you are immediately tempted to accept the loan offered. Since banks compete with one another, that may not be your best move. Sometimes, even when rates are identical (and they may not be), services and atmospheres vary. What makes you feel comfortable is an important personal matter, especially in something as intimate as finance. Look until you find it. For all of these reasons, it is a good idea to make contingency plans. These are plans you may use if your basic plans do not succeed. On the other hand, just having contingency plans may help you to be relaxed yet businesslike and may lead to unexpected ease in achieving the credit you desire.

Contingency Plans

In a real sense, *contigency* plans are your ace in the hole. If you are turned down for a loan, how else can you get the money you need? We call this making contingency plans. Suppose you need $5000 and the bank will only lend you $3500. Where will the remainder come from? Could you borrow it from a family member? On a credit card? Could you pawn something? Or could you, as the checklist asks, borrow part of the amount for a shorter period of time to establish credit and then refinance? What are the relative costs of different combinations? Contingency plans are alternative strategies to make sure you get what you want and need, and at the lowest cost.

Summary of C-Worthiness

We've outlined what you need to do to get a loan—the homework you have to do, finding the right bank, and building your case. We've provided a checklist and clues to confidence, which included sizing yourself up and evaluating your capacity, character, and collateral. Finally, contingency plans were suggested.

You may be of sterling character, a full-time, long-time employee of the U.S. Mint, debt-free, stable as gravity, and still you may not be granted the credit requested. If you are refused by more than one bank, short money may not be the reason.

ENSURING ACHIEVEMENT
OF YOUR LEGAL RIGHT TO CREDIT

You cannot exercise a legal right without knowing that you possess it, nor can you assess enforcement of a law unless you test it. It sounds simple. One expects the world to be nice and people to be full of good will and good faith. That's the opposite of the notion that everyone is about to do you in. Truth lies somewhere in between. Not everyone wishes you well, and it may be a good idea to understand what good faith means since good faith governs many transactions. For instance, when you leave your shoes to be repaired, you expect them to be fixed without damage to the leather. The shoemaker expects you to come back, pay for the work, and take away your shoes. When good faith is not exercised, negative reactions can result.

I used to expect good faith, good will, and good citizenship to prevail. Then I grew up and learned about sex discrimination. Some good things may be omitted or not practiced fully when the person with whom one interacts is female. It isn't like saying that good citizens obey the laws and bad citizens don't. It doesn't always happen that the lawbreakers get punished swiftly. Beliefs like my old ones lead to rude awakenings, especially when women expect laws about creadit to be upheld.

Credit and What's in a Name

Once I almost missed a flight when the slow, surly ticket writer asked, "Miss or Missus?" I said, "Miz." He said, "How do you spell it?" "M—s." He said, "M—s? How's that Miz?" I said, "Look, you're not paying for the ticket; I am. So what difference does it make to you?" He finally took my credit card. That harassment was a foretaste of what many women experienced when they tried to get their rights under ECOA.

Ms., Miz, Miss, Missus may seem a small matter against a backdrop of financial institutions and governmental regulation; to me, "what's in a name" is very important. The put-downs concerning women's remarkable indifference to what's in their names have large negative effects when these same women attempt to obtain credit. Single women have less conflict about what to call themselves than married women do. The society can attach childish nicknames to them or use diminutives of their given names, but it cannot name them as possessions of a male human being. That is what happens to many otherwise adult, married women.

Married working women frequently lose opportunities to achieve credit because they are identified as Mrs. even when their own first names follow the title. I would like to suggest that some credit accounts (at banks and elsewhere) be established by Penelope C. Jones instead of by Mrs. David X. Jones or Mrs. Penelope C. Jones. Single women could also benefit from setting up some accounts without any prefix to their names. Failure to insist on one's own name along with one's own credit can be disastrous; it lets creditors view one as a child rather than as an adult woman. Nobody feels guilty about not lending to a child; certainly no bank can be expected to.

Few women realize that no law denies them the right to select the name by which they wish to be known. Only custom leads us to accept the tag society pins on us. Women, like men, can pick and use a preferred name as long as they do not use it with the intent to defraud. Women who use Mrs. in addition to their first names make tentative, hesitant credit statements.

Insist That Your Own Name Be Credited

It is harder for women to get credit, no matter what name they use, no matter how great their contributions to society, no matter what laws are on the books, than it is for men. Demonstration of lack of equal credit opportunity is not enough. Even my fantasy of sending 25,000 women investigators in marathon relays through the banks of Chicagoland applying for large loans would not make it easier for women to obtain credit. So I began thinking about credit problems that could be tackled effectively by individual working women. Let's turn to strategy.

Acting in Your Own Behalf

Women who get what they go after are often asked how they did it. Women sometimes explain, "Nobody told me I couldn't." Others say, "It was the thing to do, so I did it." They may be telling the truth. I think, though, that they were good observers and did things similar to those they saw working for others.

We can learn a lot from women who have a positive approach. The women who were successful in getting what they wanted because of their expectation that it would be forthcoming, because they took advantage of available opportunities, and because they used methods they knew would work, have given us tools to apply to our own problems. Their strategic outlooks can help us act in our own behalf.

It is time to summarize what has been said so far. You expect to be granted credit, but credit is denied. What do you do? You can complain in writing first to the concern that turned you down, or you can get a check on your credit rating, or you can find a cosigner who would make good on the loan if you were to default. We are going to look briefly at complaint letters, credit rating checks, and cosigners. The first two are things you will probably have use for. The last—cosigners—you may decide to wean yourself away from.

Complaint Letters and Your Line of Credit

If credit is denied you, the potential creditor is required to explain the rejection of credit. Of course, that information won't be volunteered; you have to ask for it, perhaps insist on it.

We mentioned earlier that the 1971 Fair Credit Reporting Act requires creditors to explain why credit was denied. The ECOA also requires creditors to explain denial of credit. The creditor must explain in writing in 30 days or you can sue for damages. A rejected applicant ought to inquire in writing and keep a carbon of the letter. The ECOA prohibits sex discrimination in granting of credit (including marital status discrimination).

Here is a personal example. It concerns a major credit card I hold in my own name. Once a year, I am informed of my new line of credit—the maximum the credit company thinks I can handle. When my new card arrived a few years ago, my credit limit had been increased. About that time a male colleague, who earned less than I, mentioned his new line of credit with the credit card company. His new line of credit was much higher than mine.

I protested in writing to the company making them aware of my knowledge of ECOA. They sent me a form to fill out. I returned the blank form and reminded them that the burden of proof of non-discrimination was theirs, not mine. My letter ended with an offer "to refer my correspondence to an impartial body if I have not received satisfactory notification by" and gave a date. It was clear that the credit card company was going to have to reconsider my credit line. Here's how it went:

During a 45-minute long distance call in which a whole sideshow of evasions were resorted to with pseudo-politeness, I was told, "We don't usually give credit lines of $3000." "Oh, yes, you do, too," I said. "My friend has one, and he'll tell anybody who asks." "Well, when we checked your credit, there were no references to support a credit line like that." Imperiously, I asked, "Just *whom* did you check my credit with?" She told me.

Finally, the credit line was raised 50 percent. It remained far below the credit line extended to my male friend. However, I had learned that if you've got the goods, you can get the credit. You may not use it, but if you don't have it trouble is sure to find you. I also learned something about safeguarding my right to credit. I had not been sloppy but downright ignorant. I didn't know anything about who ran the credit checks.

Anyone could concentrate on building a good credit rating and be just as foolish as I was in neglecting to determine if anyone had noticed, had recorded what a financial whiz I was. Nobody had noticed or recorded my stellar fiscal performance. Slips like that can undo lots of good work.

Credit Rating Checks

Margaret Daly suggests making an attempt to keep one's credit rating current.[3] You may not be aware that approximately 2000 credit-reporting bureaus exist nationwide. Creditors subscribe to these bureaus but are not required to report to them. Furthermore, and supporting Daly's suggestions, these bureaus sometimes make damaging mistakes. I had gotten caught in those damaging mistakes. No credit-reporting bureau had complete information on me. Errors of omission made me appear uncreditworthy. I remedied that. After discovering that nobody is required to report my credit rating to a bureau, I requested a file disclosure. I am the only person who can request a disclosure of my file. I checked up on the reporting of accounts on which joint credit reporting had been requested by asking in person at the bank holding the mortgage, and asking for changed reporting by department stores. This method of building a credit rating is open to married women under the ECOA. What I really wanted to know was why I had been denied additional credit by Visa/Bankamericard. I was entitled to this information without charge, even though I already had a Visa/Bankamericard credit line.

So little came back from the credit-reporting bureaus that I had telephoned to find out why my various charge accounts and transactions were not listed. The answer was, "Oh, ma'am, they don't report to us. Why don't you try _____ ?" In the blank was the name of yet another credit-reporting bureau. So, short of policing each credit card and charge account to find out which credit-reporting bureau it used, I would get nowhere. Maybe that was the idea.

There was a simpler solution. I explained the situation to my friendly banker. He made some credit inquiries about me with each credit bureau. He then assured me that neither file had bad marks on me. That bit of information is not easy to get about yourself. My friendly banker said, "That ought to make you look good *and* interesting." Incidentally, my worst rating was on a slightly delayed payment on a joint account. All of the accounts in my own name were in fine shape. I realized that often we are unaware of what behaviors we are being judged on.

Daly concludes that if you follow the rules (requesting an explanation of denial of credit, updating your file) and the credit bureau refuses, you may sue the bureau for failure to reveal the contents of your file. If you are merely curious and want the credit bureau report, you can request it. It may cost you a few well-spent dollars.

Cosigners

Steadily employed women who need to borrow money for large purchases sensibly go to banks for loans. Then the good sense evaporates. Banks ask women without a satisfactory credit rating to produce a cosigner for the loan. That cosigner, for married women usually turns out to be the husband; for unmarried women it is the father. That's silly and unfortunately extends the stereotypes of the childish woman incapable of thinking about money and the flighty woman untrustworthy with money.

If a bank insists on a cosigner, ask a woman relative or friend to cosign your loan. By the way, dealer financed car purchases do not require cosigners. Thus, buying a car on the installment plan improves your credit rating and your mobility.

If you are buying a house with a co-owner, both of you should sign the mortgage agreement. For safety's sake, both of you should be insured for the full amount of the loan. Term insurance, which decreases in value each year until the loan is paid up, is a relatively inexpensive way to protect yourself. Term insurance would pay off the mortgage if you became unable to. If you feel that fully insuring both cosigners is excessive, consider insuring each for half the loan amount. I'm blushing now: Nobody considered insuring me in 1968. Since then I've met my half of the payments, so an accident to me would have been catastrophic.

Today women are sometimes perceived as good credit risks; they often are *excellent* credit risks. The view of women as creditworthy will improve as more women use credit wisely and responsibly. You can help by knowing how and when you need a cosigner. Then you will be making decisions about your credit options.

The idea of credit for women is becoming less threatening. Many women see it as a game, a challenge. Figuring out alternative ways of obtaining credit, then testing them is fun, and successful. More women everyday are getting the credit they need.

OTHER SOURCES OF CREDIT

You may have additional credit assets which can be used alone or with the credit sources already discussed. Three often overlooked credit sources are insurance, social security and joint credit reporting (for married women). If it applies, each can round out your creditworthiness.

Insurance

When trying to scrape together the down payment for a house, consider all of the collateral available to borrow against. For instance, if you have whole life insurance, the borrowing possible on your insurance policy can mean the difference between successful financing and missing it by a hair. If you are in your twenties, whole life insurance can be a good investment. Let's spend a moment distinguishing between life and term insurance.

Term insurance is protection purchased for a given length of time. Over that span, your policy decreased in value and in the protection offered. Meanwhile, the risk you insured against diminishes. After 15 years of mortgage payments, much of your indebtedness has been repaid. You only need protection for the remainder, which decreases monthly. However, your mortgage term insurance payments do not change.

By contrast, whole life insurance grows in value until—if you are lucky and long-lived—you have a paid-up policy as good as cash. Such a policy is an asset, usable as collateral for a loan.

Whole life insurance is a good buy for young adults because: (1) life insurance premiums are computed according to life expectancy charts, (premiums rise as you get older, but by then you've paid up a big part of the policy). (2) You build up equity as you pay up the policy and as your dividends (if left in the policy account) begin to earn interest. You could apply the dividends to your premium payment, thereby reducing your payments and the rate at which your insurance account grows. Either way the insurance account matures, and within ten years you can borrow against it (for as long as you choose) at the same low interest rate. Term life insurance policies are never paid-up. One cannot borrow against them. (3) Whole life insurance should be part of every working woman's protection package, but by itself is not enough.

To enhance their security and credit worthiness, working women should have both short- and longer-term financial plans. A basic plan involves regular, small savings deposits until the account reaches $1000, which is the minimum for money market mutual funds. These funds are federally insured and pay high interest. When savings reach $2500, they can then be transferred either into a higher-interest bank money market fund or to a longer-term certificate of deposit with a guaranteed interest rate. Certificates of deposit can serve as loan collateral (and continue to earn interest), but if redeemed before maturity there is a substantial interest penalty. Bankers consulted agreed that many options usable as sources of credit opened up when liquid assets reached $2500. They also cautioned that conditions change rapidly—so do options available—and each banker suggested consulting with a banker before making your decision.

Social Security

You may have overlooked a psychological source of credibility and credit. If you have been working for a number of years but haven't established credit accounts in your own name, consider your social security account. It bears witness to your industry, energy, and enforced frugality. Have you checked your social security earnings record within the past two years? If not, get a postcard now and turn to figure 6–4. Because of the statute of limitations, corrections in your social security earnings record must be made within three years, three months and 15 days.

You cannot be certain that an employer deposited money withheld from earnings in your social security account unless you check. Don't be a believer when you can be sure. Your inquiry will be answered with infor-

FIGURE 6–4 Requesting Your Social Security Earnings Record

**YOUR SOCIAL SECURITY
RECORD**

If you want a statement of your
social security earnings, please fill in
the other side of this card.

In the space marked "Social Security
Number," show your number *exactly*
as it is shown on your social security
card. We need your correct number
to identify your record. If you have
more than one social security number
give all of them.

You do not need to pay anyone to
help you get a statement of your
earnings. There is no charge for this
service.

Be sure to put a stamp on this card
before mailing it.

SOCIAL SECURITY ADMINISTRATION

P.O. BOX 57

BALTIMORE, MARYLAND 21203

FORM OAR–7004 (2-71)

☆ GPO : 1971 O - 417-324

REQUEST FOR

STATEMENT

OF EARNINGS

SOCIAL SECURITY NUMBER →			

DATE OF BIRTH →	MONTH	DAY	YEAR

Please send a statement of my Social Security earnings to:

NAME { MISS MRS. MR. } _____

STREET & NUMBER _____

CITY & STATE _____ ZIP CODE _____

*Print
Name
and
Address
In Ink
Or Use
Type-
writer*

SIGN YOUR NAME HERE
(DO NOT PRINT)   _____

Sign your own name only. Under the law, information in your social security record
is confidential and anyone who signs another person's name can be prosecuted.
If you have changed your name from that shown on your social security card, please
copy your name below exactly as it appears on your card.

mation about your account and a booklet explaining current social security regulations.

But here's the point: you can impress a potential creditor by saying,
"I've got a social security earnings record that lists $102,000 through
1982; I haven't been working just as a hobby. Without mentioning how
long it took to amass that earnings records, you can add, "Obviously, I

had to work during my childbearing years." You persevered and survived, and the potential creditor knows it. A chat with your personnel officer at work might reveal other pleasant surprises about your credit potential. Ask if you have overlooked something; it costs nothing to ask.

Joint Credit Reporting

A final way to gain credit concerns married women only. Married women have long been overprotected regarding credit. While married, their credit is joint with their husbands as if the unit included only the male householder—even when the wife is the major earner, as when the husband is going to school. Ending this is as simple as signing your name, and that's what it takes. Figure 6–5 presents a sample document.

ECOA made credit discrimination based on marital status illegal. If both spouses are responsible for an account then both are entitled to have that credit information included in their individual credit reports. This right ensures that credit histories will be available to divorced or widowed women.

This regulation took effect in June 1977. The provision is unpopular with banks. No financial officer in our investigations (in Appendix B) mentioned it. However, the banks' lack of enthusiasm won't deter women from achieving good credit ratings and building up their credit.

Although our discussion has focused upon ways and means of obtaining the credit you desire, you may still encounter problems. If money grew on trees, people wouldn't go to banks for it, they'd get ladders and pick some. This chapter has given you glimpses of where sex discriminatory practices occur. (Reading Appendix B will further increase your awareness.) You may have had your eyes opened, or you may have felt sophisticated all along. Either is to your credit.

ADDITIONAL INFORMATION SOURCES

Free items to send for:
The Equal Credit Opportunity Act and . . . Women

Federal Trade Commission
Equal Credit Opportunity
Washington, D.C. 20580

FIGURE 6–5 Amendments of ECOA Effective in 1977

NOTICE

CREDIT HISTORY FOR MARRIED PERSONS

The Federal Equal Credit Opportunity Act prohibits credit discrimination on the basis of race, color, religion, national origin, sex, marital status, age (provided that a person has the capacity to enter a binding contract); because all or part of a person's income derives from any public assistance program; or because a person in good faith has exercised any right under the Federal Consumer Credit Protection Act. Regulations under the Act give married persons the right to have credit information included in credit reports in the name of both the wife and the husband if both use or are responsible for the account. This right was created, in part, to ensure that credit histories will be available to women who become divorced or widowed.

If your account with us is one that both husband and wife signed for or is an account that is being used by one of you who did not sign, then you are entitled to have us report credit information relating to the account in both your names. If you choose to have credit information concerning your account with us reported in both your names, please complete and sign the statement below and return to us.

Federal regulations provide that signing your name below will not change your or your spouse's legal liability on the account. Your signature will only request that credit information be reported in both your names.

If you do not complete and return the form below, we will continue to report your credit history in the same way that we do now.

When you furnish credit information on this account please report all information concerning the account in both our names.

Account Number | 5 | 2 | 1 | 1 | | | | | | | |

_____

Print or type name now on account

_____

Print any additional name to be reported

_____

Signature of either spouse

_____

Address

_____

City   State   Zip

Consumer Handbook to Credit Protection Laws

Publication Sevices
Division of Administrative Services
Board of Governors of the Federal Reserve System
Washington, D.C. 20551

Women: To Your Credit

From your nearest Commercial Credit Corporation Office, *or*
Director, Publication Relations
Commercial Credit Corporation
300 St. Paul Place
Baltimore, MD 21202

Pick up a copy of *Alice in Debitland* at you bank, or write for it from:

Publications Services
Division of Support Services
Board of Governors of the Federal Reserve System
Washington, D.C. 20551

NOTES

1. Leonard Sloane, "What's in Your Credit File?" *Parade, Chicago Sun-Times,* January 20, 1978, p. 12.

2. *Consumer Handbook to Credit Protection Laws* (Washington, D.C. Board of Governors of the Federal Reserve System, 1978), p. 14.

3. Margaret Daly, "Check Out Your Credit Rating," *Better Homes and Gardens,* May 1977, pp. 240–44.

Passage of the ERA will tend to cut down on the bureaucratic fumbling in equal rights laws that we now have. It would simplify the process and keep us from fighting law by law the 800 federal laws that are discriminatory.

JEAN MAACK, ERA Illinois (Chicago)
as quoted by Verna Jones, "A Matter
of Survival: Feminists Will Pick up
Where ERA Leaves Off," *Suburban
Trib*, January 30, 1980.

Elaine Donnelly, a prominent Michigan Republican and a member of the Reagan–Bush campaign's "Women's Policy Advisory Board," says that the Equal Rights Amendment is as "dead as a doornail" and will remain so under Reagan's administration.

American Association of Women in
Community and Junior Colleges
Newsletter VI, no. 2 (Winter 1981): p. 4

Déjà Vu
and Overview
the exhibition game
of the Equal Rights
Amendment

THE EQUAL RIGHTS AMENDMENT: AMERICA IN TRANSITION

Mindset

June 30, 1982, was an important date for American women. On that day the extended deadline for passage of the Equal Rights Amendment (ERA) ended. On July 1, 1982, American women might have had thoughts like these: If equality under the law were a reality in the United States, an Equal Rights Amendment would be unnecessary. If there were no sex-based discrimination, everyone would have supported the ERA. That this did not happen bears witness to the fact of pervasive sex discrimination.

The ERA issue is not "dead as a doornail." There has been continuous activity culminating in presentation of another ERA to Congress. Working women need to be informed about the ERA's contents, and about its history, defeat, and probable revitalization.

This chapter provides grist for your mental mill and direction for your thoughts. But an explanation of the title is in order. The French déjà vu means "seen before" or "old hat." In this chapter, what we ought to know about is an earlier women's legal rights issue, namely getting the vote. We review that issue to emphasize similarities in the struggles for achievement of women's suffrage and equal rights. Perhaps by examining history's lessons, we can avoid repeating its errors.

The historical aspect is also part of the title's overview. Background for the ERA is found in several constitutional amendments whose implicit and explicit omissions serve as a foundation for the 27th Amendment— the ERA. In addition, overview includes speculation plus informed opinion about what an ERA's effect might be.

Finally, "the exhibition game of the Equal Rights Amendment" invites you into the arena, or, more actively, onto the field. Having read this far, it is assumed that your preparation for tackling this crucial working women's issue qualifies you to play, coach, and star in the exhibition game. If you don't win this time—as working women didn't in 1982—you can be better prepared for next year's exhibition game.

Our objective is to whet your appetite, get you thinking and then active in achieving your equal legal rights as a working woman in the U.S. The ERA issue could be described as a rose with the usual complement of thorns. I for one am willing to pick it and to cultivate the plant. Are you? This chapter should help you to decide.

Why might a contemporary married woman be concerned about the ERA? Because she is also likely to be a working woman. If she is married, she may have worked in several states, all having different laws affecting women. Suppose she had been a married, resident wage earner in Nevada who purchased a home with her earnings—that house could only be listed in her husband's name. Thus he would have sole control over her house. I lived and worked in Texas where I could not dispose of my assets without hubby's signature, but he could sell anything either of us owned without my signature. Perhaps that has changed. All states have laws which would be affected by passage of an ERA; these laws are important to every working woman, especially important to married women.[1] Few wives can predict where they will move next. They would do well to worry about lack of one national law affecting women.[2] I have moved from New York to Connecticut to Maryland to Massachusetts to Virginia to Texas to West Virginia to Illinois without knowing the myriad rules and regulations. You can bet I long for one nation, indivisible, under one ERA.

ERA Status Retrospective

A Civil Service Commission report indicates orderly progress under state era laws. It supports era, suggesting that principle might function as well as a constitutional mandate.[3] The report stated that nationwide women's status was generally bleak, but that the 14 states which had passed era laws or state constitution amendments had made strides in important areas. Among these, only Illinois and Virginia failed to pass the ERA by December, 1978, the original ratification date. The report's conclusion emphasized the need for the ERA to "signal that sex discrimination is no longer acceptable in our nation's laws, policies and practices".[4] Passage of state era amendments in Illinois and Virginia may be related to ERA's defeat in those states. Had they ratified ERA, only one additional state would have been needed to pass the amendment.

What Does the ERA Say?

The proposed amendment states:

Section I: Equality of rights under the law shall not be denied nor abridged by the United States or by any state on account of sex.

Section II: The Congress shall have the power to enforce, by appropriate legislation, the provisions of this article.

Section III: This amendment shall take effect two years after the date of ratification.

Translated, the ERA says that two years after ratification (passage by three-fourths of the states), sex discrimination will be illegal throughout the United States. But the legal issue is deeper, vastly more complex. The introduction to *Impact ERA* points out that the "equal protection clause" of the 14th Amendment has never been explicitly extended to sex.[5] Thus, sexual equality is debatable under American law. Further, lack of a ratified ERA to clarify the "equal protection clause" embroils us in a Catch-22 situation. The sex discrimination victim must prove that sex discrimination is illegal and that it has taken place. This Catch-22 is comparable to the treatment received by many rape victims. They are assaulted; then officers of the law insinuate (or bluntly state) that they "asked for it." Some victims are told, "You enjoyed it," while others are subjected to lie detector tests (which are inadmissible as evidence in court).

American women's current legal status with regard to sex discrimination is bizarre. In effect, women are unpersonned, called unpleasant things if they protest their treatment, labeled as aggressive if they win; whatever women do about sex discrimination, they become pariahs. ERA ratification would have eased the psychic strains, clarified the legal issues, and provided a rational substratum. Such a rational substratum is found in the words of the Equal Rights Amendment, which reminds us that sex is not a valid legal reason for removing a citizen's right to equality before the law.

One ERA, 50 *Eras*

A basic difference exists between the ERA and 50 eras. We should have learned it during Prohibition when an amendment (the 18th) supported by few people passed yet took a dry eternity to get repealed. Apparently much of the consternation over the ERA arises because state laws can easily be repealed; state constitutions can also be rewritten and revised. State equal rights amendments and other state anti-discrimination laws confer far less protection than a federal ERA would, have no guarantee of stability, and are in effect only within the borders of the state. Constitutional amendments and federal laws take precedence over state laws. The former are in effect nationwide. Another distinction exists between enactment and enforcement: a law that has not been enacted can neither be tested in court nor enforced. Therefore, the ERA lacked opportunity for testing.

The spring 1978 map shows that some states having no era—Idaho,

Nebraska, and Tennessee—first ratified the ERA and then voted to rescind. To rescind means to "cancel, take back, repeal." However, the rescissions were not accepted. Kentucky also ratified the ERA and then rescinded, but the rescission was vetoed. Indecision and wavering on ERA indicate how successful ERA opponents were in arousing fears about potential effects of the ERA on American culture. Few ERA proponents emphasized potential reactions to its defeat.

For inclusion in the Constitution as the 27th Amendment, the ERA required ratification by 38 states. When the ERA deadline was extended until 1982, 15 states—See Figure 7-1—had not ratified the amendment.

Two non-ratifying states—Illinois and Virginia—have eras. Thus women in 13 states have no legal protection against sex discrimination other than the statutes and federal laws discussed elsewhere. One might assume that states having neither eras nor similar laws are lax in enforcing antisex discrimination laws.

Customs, stereotypes, and myths have fueled popular fears and led to this outrageous example of differential treatment of American women.

FIGURE 7-1 Hugh Haynie, *The Courier-Journal*, Louisville, Kentucky, 1978.

"Okay, back in the water, lady! We've magnanimously extended the time for your marathon swim!"

There are myths aplenty already, but the ERA and working women are fertile fields for creating new ones. A sample collection of work myths subtly implying the ERA's harmful effects are presented in Figure 7–2. Challenge yourself by trying to find factual evidence to support them. You might start with examining information available from the Women's Bureau of the Department of Labor.

When we move from myths to the map—in Figure 7-3—we observe many state differences in the amount of protection from sex discrimination women can claim. The map reminded me that women in non-ERA states might benefit from learning about the ERA. For instance, why did Alaska, where men outnumber women, ratify the ERA, while several states where women are the majority did not? Why, when the press repeatedly asserts that the American majority supports passage of the ERA, does it fail to occur? How can the amount of legal protection from sex dis-

FIGURE 7–2 Work Myths

1. The family is the main interest of more than half of America's working women, the married ones.
2. These married working women have no ambition.
3. Because they are smaller than men, women need to be protected on the job.
4. Women are not interested in careers; they only want jobs.
5. Even when women have careers, they really are more concerned with their personal development than with the career as a way of life.
6. Because working mothers are responsible for their children, they have higher absenteeism rates than men.
7. Everyone knows that women only work for pin money for extras.
8. More manual dexterity enables women to do well at and to like tedious, repetitive jobs.
9. It is a big mistake to let men and women mingle on the job; in places where men and women work in the same department, efficiency drops rapidly.
10. Men do not perform well when their supervisor is a woman.
11. Women do not perform well on the job when their supervisor is a woman.
12. Most of the power and wealth in America is controlled by women.
13. Women are more people-oriented than men and are less mechanical, which is why they do not make good doctors or engineers.
14. Women are more moral than men by nature and should not be corrupted by the world of work.
15. Working mothers tend to produce juvenile deliquents instead of normal children.
16. Married women take jobs from men.
17. Women don't want promotions or job changes; they like clerical jobs.
18. Women wouldn't be happy in "men's jobs" and shouldn't compete for them.

186

crimination be reducible to where a woman lives? Figure 7-3 illustrates the protection American women can obtain under anti-sex discrimination legislation. It currently varies by region: quite a lot on the West Coast and in the North, virtually none in the South and Southeast. American anti-sex discrimination legislation resembles a kaleidoscopic picture. Pieces fall willy-nilly resulting in an unfinished picture. Summarizing: no American woman has adequate legal protection from sex discrimination and some women remain entirely unprotected. The map represents our behavior; it depicts the crazy quilt of man-made laws. Further, it informs us how America really feels about its working women.

The Congressional Issue

Why were the 27th Amendment's words perceived as so dangerous? One view is that the ERA proposes something radical—real equality for all Americans; that is insufficient explanation for the delays and constraints. Timing probably was more influential. Here is the ERA timetable:

1923: First introduction of the Equal Rights Amendment to the Congress by Alice Paul, its author. Her eighteen words were, "Men and women shall have equal rights throughout the United States and every place subject to its jurisdiction."

1972: Introduction of the amendment to the states for ratification with seven-year time limit set by Congress.

1979: March 22—deadline for ratification.[6]

1982: June 30—final deadline after extension of ratification deadline by Congress.

1982: July 1—make a new start.

Paul died in 1977, 54 years after introducing her amendment. Her proposal to Congress came 3 years after American women were enfranchised. A rapid review of events during the intervening years may increase our understanding of Congress's remarkable unresponsiveness to women. Naturally, Congress, like our judicial and executive branches, acts slowly, deliberately, and only when response is inevitable. Such caution has helped our government to endure, but caution can be overdone.

Shortly thereafter the depression absorbed America's energies, then came World War II. Women worked during these emergencies, but afterwards they were expected to be back in their kitchens living "normally." Perhaps the unwillingly sheltered mothers of post-World War II families spread an unexpected gospel along with the peanut butter and

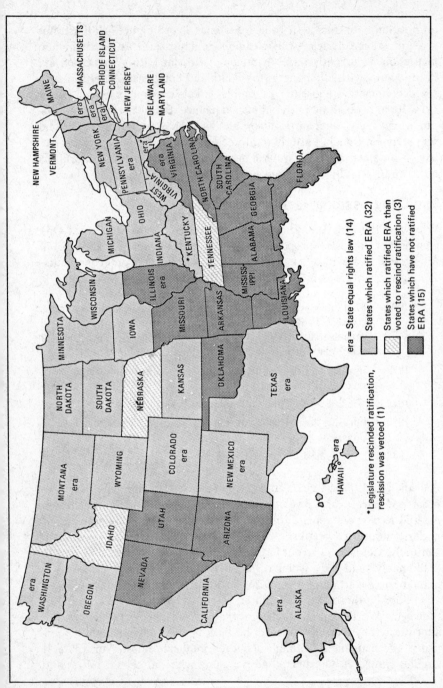

FIGURE 7-3 1978 ERA Status Map.

era = State equal rights law (14)

States which ratified ERA (32)

States which ratified ERA than voted to rescind ratification (3)

States which have not ratified ERA (15)

*Legislature rescinded ratification, rescission was vetoed (1) jelly, for somehow the seams of the status quo raveled. Our postwar babies grew up protesting everything: undeclared wars, inequality, customs, laws, and their elders' attitudes. Some grew into the women of the 1960s and played important parts in promoting social change. They shocked us into realizing that from the nation's beginnings American women have not enjoyed equality.

So much for capsule history. No alert American citizen during the 1970s could have labeled pleas to end sex discrimination by Constitutional Amendment a new idea. Peter Gabriel Filene, an authority on sex roles, reports that during the early 1970s it appeared that the Feminists would be victorious.[7] After passage of civil rights legislation, Filene continues, legal equality became an accepted principle, but its practice was not assured. Congress proposed the ERA and sent it to the states for ratification during the 1970s. But Congress also orchestrated the subsequent stalemate, and the ERA's defeat.

After 1975, the ERA's defeat seemed certain. That outcome was insured by the three-year extension of the ERA ratification deadline which Congress granted in 1979. The ERA extension raised the hopes of proponents while calming the anxieties of opponents.

Working women who expected the ERA to be passed for them by legislators were living in Wonderland or Oz. They misunderstood the informal network of Congress; they forgot that Congress is a workplace whose labor force craves continued employment. Congress responds to economic and political realities which tailor American opinion by wielding formidable power.

We working women apparently are not yet fully aware that participatory democracy is our greatest hope, our best challenge. But women—some of our ancestresses—once were. Review of the legal rights struggle that engrossed them may help us renew our courage and purpose.

COMPARATIVE CASE HISTORY: "GIVING" WOMEN THE VOTE

The 19th Amendment to the Constitution of the United States in 1920 gave American women the right to vote. Organized activity toward this goal began July 14, 1848, with an announcement in the *Seneca Falls County Courier*.[8] Women were invited to a two-day Woman's Rights Convention to discuss the rights of, and matters affecting, women. The convention, held in a chapel, drew capacity crowds of 300. Chairperson the first day was Mr. Mott. His wife Lucretia Mott spoke the second day but her speech was overshadowed by remarks of a respected local matron, Elizabeth Cady Stanton. Stanton read a *Declaration of Sentiments and Resolutions*—a document containing feminine pronouns, modeled after the *Declaration of Independence*.

The *Declaration of Sentiments and Resolutions* opened with statements of men's repeated injuries to women. These injuries included denial of the franchise, passage of sex-discriminatory laws related to property, civil rights (for married women), and wages. Women had to agree to be obedient to their husbands; their occupational pursuits were rigidly controlled by men and consisted of poorly paid jobs. Likewise, the male-dominated church and state limited and circumscribed woman's participation. Although the vocabulary of these points made in the form of resolutions differed from current usage, their intent was abundantly clear.

The assembly unanimously accepted everything up to the ninth resolution exhorting women to achieve the vote as "their sacred right." This plank brought divisiveness and ambivalence into the open. It was inaccurately suggested that God had ordained the present order (including disenfranchised American women) and His will was to be obeyed.[9] The Seneca Falls women persisted. They held another convention the same summer. The idea of woman's suffrage gradually spread.

Stanton and Susan B. Anthony together continued the battle for 50 years.[10] Maybe strength of character begets longevity; Stanton's political memoirs were called *Eighty Years and More: Reminiscences 1815–1897*.[11] Nevertheless, 72 years of concerted action devoted to gaining the basic right of democratic citizenship was far longer than the average American woman's life expectancy.

Did you notice the peace and tranquility with which this section began? "The 19th Amendment to the Constitution of the United States in 1920 gave American women the right to vote." Nobody "gave" the women of America the vote. They *fought* for it. They may have finally worn down the opposition. Maybe "giving in" took place to restore domestic and national serenity.

American women saw five constitutional amendments pass from the time they first politely requested suffrage, yet women were disciplined and accepted the prize with dignity. Not so we who have voted since we reached the legal age; we have been less verbally restrained.

The argument, presented by Congress when women petitioned in 1865 to be included in the 14th Amendment, seems unreasonable and irrational today. Congress said, in effect, "Wait your turn." Let's review the contents of this crucial amendment, beginning with Section 1:

> All persons born or naturalized in the United States, and subject to the jurisdiction thereof, are citizens of the United States and of the state wherein they reside. No state shall make or enforce any law which shall abridge the privileges or immunities of the citizens of the United States; nor shall any state deprive any person of life, liberty, or property, without due process of law; nor deny to any person within its jurisdiction the equal protection of the laws.

This would have been sufficient to grant women the vote in July of 1868, had the legislators stopped at the end of Section 1. Citizens have citizens' rights, among which the franchise is primary. Furthermore, the 9th Amendment informs us:

> The enumeration in the Constitution, of certain rights, shall not be construed to deny or disparage others retained by the people.

Its companion, the 10th Amendment, states that:

> The powers not delegated to the United States by the Constitution, nor prohibited by it to the states, are reserved to the states respectively, or to the people.[12]

Thus, from 1791 to the end of Section 1 of the 14th Amendment of the Constitution, only social custom barred women from the national ballot box. It was a potent force, not backed by legal proscription, until women attempted to receive their legal rights. No laws relating to women's voting behavior had been enacted since the early nineteenth century (except in New Jersey); nor did the matter arise in formal legal debate until after the Civil War when women petitioned Congress to enfranchise them along with the emancipated (male) slaves. Congress refused.

Section 2 of the 14th Amendment is given below, with the precedent-setting portion italicized:

> Representatives shall be apportioned among the several states according to their respective numbers, counting the whole number of persons in each state, excluding Indians not taxed. But *when the right to vote at any election* for the choice of electors for President and Vice-President of the United States, Representatives in Congress, the Executive and Judicial offi-

cers of a state, or the members of the legislature thereof, *is denied to any of the male inhabitants of such state*, being 21 years of age, and citizens of the United States, or in any way abridged, except for participation in rebellion, or other crime, *the basis of representation therein shall be reduced in proportion which the number of such male citizens shall bear to the whole number of male citizens 21 years of age in such state.*

A bitter person might reflect that being born female in the U.S. was then equivalent to the male crimes of inciting rebellion and committing felonies. This quaint idea, implicit in Section 2 of the 14th Amendment, makes plausible one black woman's fury. In 1868, she stated that a white master had been exchanged for a black one, and that constituted no emancipation.

Women like Susan B. Anthony voted anyway. Some were jailed for it as she was. Nor had women received formal citizenship by 1872 when the first woman U.S. presidential candidate ran, nor when women first went to jail for their cause and began to play politics seriously.[13]

The amendment for woman's suffrage was first introduced in Congress in 1878. Drafted in 1875 by Anthony, it read:

The rights of citizens of the United States to vote shall not be denied or abridged by the United States or by any state on account of sex. Congress shall have power to enforce this article by appropriate legislation.

Those interested in details of the militant suffragist movement will find a history by Doris Stevens fascinating.[14] Actively involved women represented the gamut of American society. Among the 500 imprisoned for woman's suffrage between 1913 and passage in 1919 were: doctors, actresses, DAR members, librarians, college graduates, young women, grandmothers, wives and daughters of elected officials. When a large group jailed for picketing President Woodrow Wilson was given a presidential pardon, the suffragists refused the pardon, insisting they had done nothing wrong, and they were forcibly ejected from jail.

The rhythm of the struggle for woman's suffrage varied. Times of enthusiasm and enterprise were interspersed with quiescent periods. Wyoming became a suffrage state in 1869, followed by Utah in 1870.[15] Colorado in 1893 and Idaho in 1896 also had women voters. By 1917, there were four more suffrage states. In some cases the vote in both state houses was unanimous; in others women achieved suffrage by a slim plurality. Tennessee, on August 18, 1920, became the thirty-sixth state to ratify the amendment. Wisconsin and Michigan, on June 10, 1919, had been the first and second states to ratify.

What strikes us today is the number of women who fail to exercise the power of the ballot. Do they realize that a voter is a person, a person with power? A voter has control of her person, her property, her mind, and her destiny. Everyone was expected to vote—including every woman—yet that didn't happen.

Nor were other predictions fulfilled; ratification of the 19th Amendment didn't cause family life to disintegrate, nor did women become depraved. Culture flourished; America's standard of living rose. Why, then, has the achievement of women's suffrage been somehow demeaned? Will the ERA run a similar course requiring nearly 75 years to ratify? Will the ERA become law, as a formality, after customs have changed drastically by reaching gender equality?

Paralleling suffrage, the odds are that no enormous changes will come with passage of the ERA. However, focus on the ERA already has brought some changes in the kind of sex discrimination practiced. Progressive employers, law abiding in their policies toward pregnancy and childbirth, may discriminate in other ways that cut off opportunities for working women. For example, by such discriminatory acts as: (1) rejecting qualified women who, although willing to relocate for job advancement, do not announce that they are married; (2) expecting women scholars competing for fellowships to be subservient to male candidates and to be tolerant when asked sexist questions; and (3) openly asking prohibited questions which male applicants are not asked, such as, "How would your family feel if you took this job?" Obviously, an effective way to cut off advancement opportunities is to bar certain candidates from employment. Women have endured such treatment for decades. Would the ERA offer substantial help in such matters?

WHAT THE ERA IS INTENDED TO DO

An Equal Rights Amendment is not just a women's rights bill; it is a human rights bill. The ERA's intent is to require that the law treat men and women equally. This can be accomplished in two ways: by extending laws that already apply to one sex to both, or by finding them unconstitutional on the grounds that they deny equality of rights to one sex.

After passage of the ERA, men and women would be treated the same way in legal matters, as persons, as individuals. But an ERA has nothing to do with personal matters (such as who takes out the garbage and who can use the toilet). The ERA deals with legal status only.

Earlier we considered the merits of eras versus ERA and concluded that an ERA could more effectively promote working women's legal rights. An underlying concern is dealt with in an August, 1980 *Working Woman* article; "ERA: a question of human rights" notes that failure to ratify ERA could imperil all of the legal gains American women have made since 1920 when they were enfranchised.

Working women have not achieved workplace equality, the article reminded, thus could lose most; working women need to consider the ERA and its relationship to the political climate. There have been strong, consistent indications that the Reagan administration not only opposed the ERA but proposes to undo the civil rights progress that had been made.

There are also indisputable indications that diminishing government enforcement of affirmative action laws and regulations was part of the Reagan administration's policy. It is predicted that further weakening of the enforcement powers of the Office of Federal Contract Compliance Programs will lead to numerous additional lawsuits. The number of cases awaiting trial grew during the Reagan administration. Apparently dilatory tactics—of weak enforcement, and glutting of court dockets—will prevail, delaying the impact of significant decisions, and encouraging further erosion of compliance with affirmative action regulations. Such results would be disastrous and demoralizing for the nation's working women.

Furthermore, to create the impression of favoring equal rights, the Reagan administration placed many women in visible—and vulnerable—positions where they often were tokens. Some public scandals (e.g. the Environmental Protection Agency) resulting in resignations of the appointees have occurred. The Reagan administration has publicly praised itself for appointing many women but has not assumed responsibility for failing to provide support to them, or for the damage that all women suffer when any highly placed woman "fails" and leaves her job.

If you apply the criteria of Chapter 4 to the Reagan administration's affirmative action program, you must conclude that the Reagan administration, far from providing support for women's equal rights, undermined women's progress in countless ways. Yes, an exceptional woman, Sandra Day O'Connor, was appointed the first female Supreme Court justice in history. She appears to be in every way a peer of the other justices. But "one swallow doesn't make a spring." The Callisters and Hatches, the 50 state committees Reagan suggested and supported (as alternatives to a national equal rights initiative), charging them each with weeding out their own state's discriminatory laws, do not inspire confidence. They are part of the déjà vu picture: the return to states' rights strategy fools no one. It surfaced in 1914 during the woman's suffrage contest when the president of the National Association Opposed to Woman's Suffrage sent Woodrow Wilson a letter warning that the 19th Amendment "would take from the different states the deciding power of the voters."[16] Or worse yet, it would permit a few obstreperous women to pester the legislators continually about women's suffrage. Contemporary conservative women's groups opposing the ERA, and using the same tactic, have received Reagan administration support. Women's suffrage was nevertheless achieved, and we predict that equal rights will also be achieved.

When an Equal Rights Amendment is ratified, changes will occur gradually. The two-year grace period following ratification provides ample time for state legislatures to make the changes required in their state laws. It also provides time for the federal government to make the legal modifications required by the ERA. The laws would be rewritten or revised (or removed) in terms of function rather than in terms of sex; any modifications would be permissible, provided there are no distinctions based on sex. State legislators are capable of producing laws that conform to an ERA yet protect women who need protection.

While all aspects of life that are currently regulated would be examined after passage of the ERA, we are primarily concerned with employment—how the ERA would affect working women. First:

> The Equal Rights Amendment would restrict only governmental action and would not apply to purely private action. *It would not affect private employment*; it would prohibit discrimination by Government as an employer—federal, state, county, and city, including school boards. . . . It would require equal pay for equal work for employees of Government.[17]

As the League of Women Voters succinctly expressed it, while federal efforts to end discrimination based on sex have since the mid-1960s produced some improvements, "the effort to end employment discrimination is fundamentally inadequate," and the ERA would have been a "well-known remedy . . . would provide an accessible . . . permanent remedy."[18] The advantages of enacting an ERA for working women would include removal of the necessity that a sex discrimination victim provide proof thereof; demonstration of workplace sex discrimination would suffice. The ERA would end state and federal legal disjunctions; there would be one law affecting governmental action. A single law would make it unnecessary to learn about many statutes, regulations and compliance agencies. Passage of an ERA would also give working women a psychological and social boost and would encourage them to use the rights that working women have been afraid to test.

Some Specific Examples
of ERA Effects

Using a case study approach, an article entitled "The ERA—What Would It Really Do?" cites loci of potential ERA impacts on women: Title IX and single-sex schools; the Equal Pay Act of 1963; Title VII of the Civil Rights Act and the Equal Employment Opportunities Act of 1972; battered wives; the right to support; the right to (marital) property; the Equal Credit Opportunity Act of 1974; the right to alimony (which would call for recognition of the homemaker's contribution and equitable property division); the right to child support; the right to pensions; the right to inheritance (IRS and state taxation would have to be reviewed after passage of an ERA to ensure that each spouse's work was equally evaluated).[19]

We will outline probable effects of an ERA upon three of these:

1. Title VII of the Civil Rights Act, and the Equal Pay Act
2. Title IX of the Education Amendments
3. The Equal Credit Opportunity Act

These will be discussed in the context of federal legislation, regulations, executive orders and state laws.

Title VII of the Civil Rights Act, and the Equal Pay Act. There currently are many inconsistencies among the states regarding protective legislation, minimum wages, maternity leaves of absence, and maximum hour laws. In some instances both sexes would benefit from an ERA; in others males would be the prime beneficiaries (maximum hour laws cover women only in most states), while removal, chiefly of protective legislation, would help working women most. Sex-discriminatory "protective" legislation, which was being dismantled when Title VII became effective, would continue to be removed until all of the archaic, unconstitutional laws were gone. Beneficial legislation would be extended to both sexes under an ERA. For instance, only in Alaska is the state minimum wage higher than the federal minimum wage. This is important to working women; the federal standard would become the accepted one with passage of an ERA, and since the government never reduces state minimum wages, the Alaska rate would become the national standard.

Inequality of men's and women's earnings would be directly addressed by an ERA, thus providing impetus for recognition of women in the marketplace. That could help change women's attitudes toward themselves and their work. An ERA could assist mightily in removing gender from work, thus extending Title VII by eliminating sex discrimination in the workplace; meanwhile, the Equal Pay Act would be extended by removal of sex segregation from occupations and hence sex-based salaries and wages. After passage of an ERA, participation in its enforcement by working women is a vital ingredient in making changes occur.

Title IX of the education amendments. Title IX does not affect single-sex educational institutions; an ERA would, if they discriminated on the basis of sex. The League of Women Voters tells us, "With some public pressure, good regulations, and vigorous enforcement, Title IX could really make a difference."[20] We have concluded (see Chapter 5) that Title IX is a beginning but has far to go. For instance, Title IX has *not* been vigorously enforced. Passage of an ERA would shift responsibility for enforcement of Title IX to the states through legislatures and the courts.

Passage of an ERA would enable women working in education (and students) to have a greater role in shaping educational policy. This would include affecting the presentation of men and women in textbooks, in counseling, and in curricula, particularly in the nontraditional and emerging vocations.

The Equal Credit Opportunity Act. It is extremely difficult to prove that credit was refused because of one's sex. Sex discrimination in granting credit is specifically prohibited by the Equal Credit Opportunity Act. Passage of an ERA would extend the federal prohibition against setting higher requirements for loans requested by women than by men. Such regulations now in effect for government agencies (such as the Small Business Administration, FHA, VA) would be extended enabling women to obtain credit needed to establish businesses. Courts might determine that federal regulation warrants ERA extension to them. The effects of subsequent increased enterprise by working women could help us all.

Other possible changes. ERA passage would alter the sex-based determination of property ownership and unequal punitive provisions (some states make an adulterous wife—but not an adulterous husband—forfeit property rights). That women will lose child support is a myth that needs debunking. The fact is that women have no marital right to child support, and most jurisdictions have been lax about collecting child support from errant fathers. Collection of child support awards should improve under an ERA. Battered wives, contrary to popular belief, would gain considerable support when an ERA is passed. All laws upholding different standards will become unconstitutional; in addition, an ERA would override laws in states giving lenient treatment to brutal husbands.

If you are interested in helping to secure these rights, you may find the material provided at the end of this chapter useful.

Unresolved questions about ERA. Until an ERA is passed, there will be unanswered questions. While it seems likely that women would be eligible for military draft, it seems equally likely that women with dependents would be exempt and that the same selective service standards would apply to men and women.

It seems unlikely that the ERA will lead the country to a disastrous political orientation, such as communism. But failure to pass an ERA may increase working women's frustration and despair.

An ERA would promote equality in criminal laws by mandating identical sentences for identical offenses. It is not likely that laws concerning rape would be affected.

The final question remains whether working women can translate the enormous symbolic and legal potential of the ERA into actuality. That's a job for all working women. To help you get involved, a choices for action checklist (see Figure 7-4) presents a program for participatory democracy. It is your invitation to play in the exhibition game. You're ready and have done the warm-up exercises.

Until then: a reprise. Two years ago the ERA was defeated because too few states ratified it. A new ERA was introduced to the House of Representatives, and will undoubtedly reach the Senate. I hope that by 1995 the United States will have enacted an Equal Rights Amendment. Maybe we can speed the process; it shouldn't require the 72 years needed to achieve women's suffrage.

I recall talking with a working woman who had been in Washington, D.C., observing Congress when the ERA was sent to the states. She said, "I felt as if we had won a battle, that everything would be all right. I felt that way for a little while; now I'm tired of fighting." And her words re-

FIGURE 7–4 Choices for Action: Participatory Democracy

Circle the letter in front of each activity that is typical of you.

1. I regularly read
   a. one daily
   b. more than one daily
   c. a Sunday
   newspaper
2. I regularly read
   a. two
   b. more than two
   newspapers having different political viewpoints.
3. I belong to a nonpartisan organization such as
   a. the League of Women Voters
   b. (fill in name)
   c. (fill in name)

   and regularly

   a. attend meetings of this organization
   b. participate in study groups
   c. have held a local office in the group
   d. have held a state office in the group
4. I am a registered voter and
   a. vote in national elections
   b. vote in state elections
   c. vote in local elections
5. I work for a political party
   a. only in national campaigns
   b. and have been a delegate to one or more political conventions
   c. and am a precinct captain
6. I have basic knowledge of the law,
   a. Constitution, federal
   b. constitution, state
7. In the last year, I have communicated my views on issues to
   a. a senator
   b. a congressman
   c. a state senator or assemblyman
   d. county or local legislators on the following issues:
      (list them)
8. I have held elective (public) office at the following level:
   a. town or municipal
   b. county
   c. state

FIGURE 7–4 (Continued)

9. My activity in participatory democracy next year will be
   a. informational:
   b. political:
   c. citizenship:
10. My participatory democracy goals, as a working woman next year, are:
    a.
    b.
    c.

Mark your calendar for today's date. Also mark it for 3, 6, 9, and 12 months from today. Check your progress at those intervals. Modify your activities (9 above) and goals (10 above) as appropriate. Use as many additional sheets of paper as are needed.

minded me of when my youngest child was being born. I told the doctor, "I'm tired. I've had a long day. I don't want to push any more." The doctor, a brisk woman, said in a no-nonsense voice. "You must."

That is what all working women have to do.[21]

ADDITIONAL INFORMATION SOURCES

Places to call or write if you would like to help pass an Equal Rights Amendment:

ERAmerica
1525 M Street, N.W. Suite 206
Washington, D.C. 20036
(202) 833-4354

National Organization for Women
425 13th Street, N.W.
Washington, D.C. 20004
(202) 347-2279

National Federation of Business and Professional Women's Clubs
Attention: ERA Coordinator
2012 Massachusetts Avenue, N.W.
Washington, D.C. 20036
(202) 293-1100

The League of Women Voters
1730 M Street, N.W.
Washington, D.C. 20036
(202) 286-1770
(Check your local phone book first for a chapter near you.)

Other things you can do:

1. Support your local pro ERA group.
2. Send a small contribution to a pro ERA group in a state that has not passed the ERA.
3. If you live in a state that did not ratify the ERA, write to your state senators and representatives. Tell them why you support reintroduction and passage of the ERA.
4. Praise, support, and patronize businesses that support ERA. Use economic sanctions against ERA opponents, and tell your friends why you are not patronizing these businesses and establishments.
5. Participate in public hearings for the ERA and task-oriented and education-oriented pro ERA coalitions.
6. Become expert and vocal on the ERA issue.

NOTES

1. Community property is a legal concept. In some states it means that even when husband and wife are equal owners of their joint property, the husband manages and controls that property. States having well-defined community property laws are Arizona, California, Idaho, Louisiana, Nevada, New Mexico, Texas and Washington; these laws vary: In some of the states women, since 1972, have been permitted to manage their own earnings. It should be noted that community property is accumulated after marriage. If one spouse is rich and neither spouse works, no community property arises, while the rich spouse remains rich.

The contrasting legal concept is that of separate property, encompassing 42 states and the District of Columbia. Separate property means that neither spouse has a legal right or interest in the partner's earnings unless a specific gift is made or joint ownership is specified. A major criticism of the separate property system is that it ignores or devalues the wife's unpaid contribution to family property.

2. For a rosier view of state eras, see "ERA—Let the Record Speak," in ". . . To Form a More Perfect Union . . . " *Justice for American Women* (Washington, D.C.: National Commission on the Observance of International Women's Year, 1976), pp. 26–28; "In Pursuit of Equal Rights: Women in the Seventies," League of Women Voters, 1978, pp. 19–20. A list of state eras and the dates when state constitutions included provisions that equal rights or equal protection may not be denied on account of sex, are found on page 19 of the latter publication. They are, alphabetically, Alaska, 1972; Colorado, 1972; Connecticut, 1974; Hawaii, 1972; Illinois, 1971; Maryland, 1972; Massachusetts, 1976; Montana, 1973; New Hampshire, 1975; New Mexico, 1973; Pennsylvania, 1971; Texas, 1972; Utah, 1896; Virginia, 1971; Washington, 1972; and Wyoming, 1890. See footnote 46 on

p. 27 of the publication for more detailed information about state eras in Illinois, Utah, Virginia, and Wyoming.

3. "State ERA Laws Spur Reforms, Report Finds," *Chicago Sun-Times*, December 12, 1978, p. 7.

4. *Ibid*.

5. The Equal Rights Amendment Project of the California Commission on the Status of Women, ed., *Impact ERA: Limitations and Possibilities*. (Millbrae, Calif.: Les Femmes Publishing, 1976), p. 7.

6. Eighteen constitutional amendments, some containing volatile ideas, have been ratified without deadlines. Although not required by the Constitution, deadlines have been the final section of each amendment since the 21st. Congress (not Alice Paul, its author) added the deadline to the 27th Amendment.

7. Peter Gabriel Filene, *Him, Her, Self: Sex Roles in Modern America* (New York: Mentor, 1976), p. 208.

8. Miriam Gurko, *The Ladies of Seneca Falls: The Birth of the Woman's Rights Movement* (New York: Schocken Books, 1976), p. 96 *ff*, provides an excellent account of the convention and the *Declaration*. The announcement from the *Seneca Falls County Courier* is reprinted by Alice Felt Tyler, "The Rights of Women," in Barbara Welter, ed., *The Woman Question in American History* (Hinsdale, Ill.: Dryden Press, 1973), p. 80. For additional details, see Elizabeth Cady Stanton, *Eighty Years and More: Reminiscences 1815–1897* (New York: Schocken Books, 1971), chapter IX.

9. In colonial times, ownership of property conveyed voting privileges in New England, New York, and New Jersey. Barbara Mayer Wertheimer, in *We Were There: The Story of Working Women in America* (New York: Pantheon Books, 1977), informs us that women were not specifically disenfranchised except in Georgia, South Carolina, Pennsylvania, and Delaware after the Revolution. They merely were not specifically *en*franchised. In New Jersey, all residents over 21 years old who owned a stipulated amount of real property and who had resided in the state for a year were able to vote until 1807, p. 50. Tyler, in "The Rights of Women," p. 77, notes that women did vote for a while after the Revolution in Virginia. Gurko, *The Ladies of Seneca Falls*, p. 24, cites the following years for *removal* of women's right to vote: New York, 1777; Massachusetts, 1780; New Hampshire, 1784; New Jersey, 1807. Women were able to vote in several of the territories until they became states. Women voters had to meet the same eligibility tests as male voters. Presumably, in voting to join the Union, these women unwittingly disenfranchised themselves.

10. Tyler, "The Rights of Women," recounts the pressures on Stanton, who was the speech writer of the movement while Susan B. Anthony delivered the fighting

words. Stanton was a conscientious mother as well as a stalwart women's rights advocate. According to Tyler, in Stanton's exchange with Anthony, who remained unmarried, there are several letters from Stanton about overwhelming time demands on her from the suffrage movement. In one letter, Stanton threatens to have another baby unless suffragist demands are moderated. Stanton concludes, "Now, be careful, do not provoke me to that step!" p. 81. Also see Stanton's dedication of *Eighty Years and More.*

11. Stanton, *Eighty Years and More,* is an important source for those interested in the history of women's rights.

12. The textbook used for quotations from the Constitution was Michael Krasner, Stephen G. Chaberski, and others, *American Government: Structure and Process* (New York: Macmillan Publishing Company, 1977). The index of the book fails to mention FEPC, any of the legislation or agencies beginning with the word *equal* (for example, Equal Employment Opportunity Commission), and affirmative action and even women are absent from the index. This book is dedicated to two persons with feminine first names. Such omissions in a publication appearing during International Women's Year are extremely odd. One wonders about such omissions from a book bearing the imprimatur of the publisher who had the president of Radcliffe College write the laudatory foreward to its *Creating Positive Sexual and Racial Images in Educational Materials,* a handout available to authors and teachers. A textbook ought to tell it as it is and as it ought to be, not the way it was "in the good old days."

13. Julia Davis, "Victorians thought her a downright scandal—as she was," *Smithsonian* 8, no. 7 (October 1977): 131–41, describes the activities of Victoria Clafflin Woodhull, nominated in 1872 by the Equal Rights Party. Victoria Woodhull, her sister, and others ended up in jail. However, Woodhull championed a number of interesting causes, among them socialism and free love. Davis comments, "She died at 89 in her chair, having refused to go to bed for four years lest she die there," p. 141.

14. Doris Stevens, *Jailed for Freedom* (New York: Schocken Books, 1976). At least read the Introduction and Appendix 6.

15. Utah ratified the 19th Amendment half a century before it became the law of the land. This is an example of how politics and economic interest create strange bedmates. The leaders of the Mormons are astute political maneuverers and have been since the inception of their denomination. Likewise, they have been most conservative where women's rights are concerned. They supported woman's suffrage when it was an unpopular cause because they needed the votes of women in their territory to gain their political objectives. This is ironic, yet furnishes a cautionary tale. For an update on the actions of Idaho's Mormon Judge, Marion Callister, who ruled in December 1981 that the ERA deadline extension was not valid, see "Poetic Justice for the ERA", *The New York Times,* January 27, 1982,

p. 24. In "Reagan and the ERA" *The New York Times,* January 8, 1982, one of Tom Wicker's columns states that conservatives of Reagan's administration committed actions that weaken states rights, the Constitution, and the checks and balances built into the United States' legislative, executive, and judicial structure. Among Wicker's charges are that of having "flouted the twice-expressed will of the legislative branch of government." Judge Callister did not prevail. The issue became moot when the ERA was not ratified by the deadline date. Women are going to have to be more alert to inconsistencies displayed in pursuit of power and profit motives. When something makes little obvious sense, women are going to have to learn to ask, "Who does this benefit?" and, "In what way?"

16. Allan J. Lichtman, "The Grand Old Ploys," *The New York Times,* July 17, 1980, p. 25.

17. "The Equal Rights Amendment—What It Will and Won't Do," (Washington, D.C.: Citizens' Advisory Council on the Status of Women, U.S. Department of Labor, August 1970), p. 2.

18. "In pursuit of equal rights," pp. 6 and 19.

19. Jill Newman, "The ERA—What Would It Really Do?" *Woman's Day* 43, no. 2 (November 1, 1979): 56–63 and 152.

20. "In pursuit of equal rights" p. 8.

21. While readying this book for production, I read "House Panel Approves Born-Again ERA Proposal," *Chicago Sun-Times,* November 8, 1983, p. 13. The expectation for full House passage prior to adjournment on November 18, 1983, was defeated by six votes. The original wording was retained.

Most cases never get to court anyway . . . . So the question is: how much can you scare the other side?

ERICA JONG, *How to Save Your Own Life* (New York: New American Library, 1977), p. 245.

Time was when, if you aspired to some high public office and they found out you belonged to a private club that wouldn't admit women, you had to apologize to the dominant culture and quit the club in an act of public dudgeon. Well, no more . . . . The Republicans' Attorney-General-designate, William French Smith, belongs to the famous Bohemian Club of California, which not only excludes women but is being sued on that account by the California government . . . . Mr. Smith is . . . not planning to quit . . . . The President-elect belongs to the Bohemian Club, and he's not quitting either. Even the Vice-President-elect and the Secretary-of-Defense-designate are members . . . .

"Changing Times (asides)," *The Wall Street Journal*, January 7, 1981.

Curtain Calls, Winning the Pennant, and the Cost of Your Ticket

THEMES FOR HIGH DRAMA

Mindset

We have examined the major legal aids available to contemporary working women. We have not put them onstage against the backdrop of today's multithemed drama. Two prominent workday themes are change and management. Our focus in this final chapter is upon these themes, first separately and then together. Change is spotlighted; then management is center stage. Finally, the management of change is featured.

Economic, political, social, and legislative contexts are sketched to provide background for working women's options. These props—the economic, political, social, and legislative contexts—are not static either. We experienced the impact of these changes when the Equal Rights Amendment was not ratified and again when a woman was appointed a Supreme Court justice. Against the backdrop of change, two state governors who were women no longer hold that office. Meanwhile, another harbinger of change is found in the many working women who have been successful in establishing and managing high-technology businesses. Nor, you might conclude, is the changing scene we live in marked by consistency.

Changes occur with such speed that it is difficult to be prepared for all of them. One tends to concentrate either on the nearby or on the distant. In the first case, one may be in danger of missing the large drama. In the second, emphasis on the faraway or on the future can lead one to overlook crucial shifts on the local (workplace) stage.

This chapter outlines a variety of decisions, any or all of which may confront the working woman. Some possible outcomes of the action choices made are explored. The outcomes, as in all transactions, are related to the inputs. That's "the cost of your ticket" part of the title. It sounds scary, but it need not be. After all, you get to choose the show or the game you play in or star in. It is your show from here on out, symbolized in the title by "curtain calls." You get to take all the bows. And the expectation is that you will play superbly in the workplace game. You will soon be "winning the pennant." Both "winning the pennant" and "curtain calls" are reminders that you know how to achieve what you want in the workplace. But *you* must decide how, when, where, and why you participate.

Of course, each working woman will face these workplace challenges and the opportunities of change and management in the light of her own experience, goals, and values. Facing new events is vastly superior to reacting to them. That's additional mindset for this chapter: to prepare you to take advantage of new opportunities in the workplace, to assure that your choices for action move you closer to your workplace goals and that you close the book saying with conviction, "Yes, I can."

Change and Motion

Today's working women realize that change takes place whether they like it or not. Wise working women try to take advantage of change and to do so in a constructive, positive way.

Today's changes, particularly technological developments, have reshaped our educational patterns, leisure activities, lifestyles, and, most fundamental, our expectations.

Technological developments have changed our ideas about speed and motion, about our universe, even about ourselves.

We are viewing these issues as themes of high drama, of comedy or tragedy. Awakened expectation is the substratum of the themes, the drama, even of our motivation to participate in it. How are working women's generalized expectations faring?

Let's look briefly at judicial or political, cultural, and economic change and motion as they influence working women.

Moving right: the Supreme Court (judicial or political). My reactions to events may be harsh, so I checked with a lawyer. She agreed that the Supreme Court had moved right. But she asserted that the Nixon appointees behaved like monks; their perceptions were cloistered, unworldly:

> They don't know what the world is about. When the abortion case came up, Burger went home and asked his wife and daughter how he should decide. Luckily, they were on the side I agree with.

Suppose Sandra Day O'Connor, the woman appointed to the Supreme Court, asked her husband and sons how to find in a crucial case. We'd never hear the end of it.

It remains that the Supreme Court has not recently lived up to its main tasks of interpreting and defending the Constitution.[1] The Nixon appointees, "strict constructionist" justices—Powell, Blackmun, Rehnquist—and Chief Justice Burger, are almost a majority. The addition of Reagan's appointee, O'Connor, ensures a conservative outcome of landmark cases for the next two decades. This probably means less constitutional protection and less freedom for every American.

Changes in constitutional interpretation will have a ripple effect at state and local levels, felt particularly by individual citizens. Powerful business and industrial interests will tend to prevail over individual citizens and group concerns. It is already possible to cite examples on the books affecting our lives and work.[2] Conservative landmark decisions after 1970 include reversals of progressive, broader constitutional interpretations and erosion of individual rights guarantees. In one case, it almost appears that this is especially true for individuals who are not white males.[3]

One apparent result of Supreme Court performance since 1970 is a lackluster enforcement of federal laws by federal agencies, particularly in workplace issues involving sex discrimination. There have been many instances when the Justice Department, the Office of Civil Rights, the EEOC, and other compliance agencies failed to act to combat sex discrimination or to investigate complaints promptly while protecting informants and victims from job harassment. We have already given some examples; they do not occur in a vacuum. One is tempted to wonder whether this Nixon Supreme Court shares Nixon's contemptuous views of the Constitution, as illustrated by his behavior and words when Watergate burst. But one must assume that one is observing nine justices of good faith and great power acting according to their consciences. Making that assumption permits some optimism about constitutional interpretations.

But the future will not become judicially brighter unless working women act on Martha Griffiths's suggestion and vote only for those political candidates who promise equality in the marketplace.[4] Remember that the people we elect confirm the lifetime appointments of Supreme Court justices; acting on that can help working women gain real equality under the laws of the land and in the interpretation of the Constitution.

Moving righteously: an old tune replayed (culture). The crisis of confidence arises when I talk to competent, active working women. One insists, "It's a man's world." Another, noting the trivia I deal with on workdays along with tasks on the job description, asks, "Would a man in your position be expected to do what you do? Put up with what you put up with?" While I have not yet answered yes, I am certain that a male in my position would never receive the tirades I have. Another told me she had expected her prestigious position to be "mostly glory, but it's lots of hard work and long hours." A fourth working woman, who holds an important job but got caught in a wage freeze this year, in a wistful moment admitted, "I've been doing this job for six years. That's too long. I'm tired of it." All of these women work hard, are positive about their work, and are successful at it. Yet from time to time they express the same doubts. The gnawing question seems to be, "Is the prize worth the struggle?" I feel it is; you probably do, too.

These statements and questions mean that a sense of futility lies dangerously close to the surface. They reflect change in our national mood. We also notice it among groups of nonworking women. There is more favorable talk about domestic servitude as the ideal state for womankind. Women espousing this view believe absolutely in the righteousness of traditionalism while forgetting that righteousness is best defended by just laws justly enforced.

Perhaps someday soon, women holding divergent views can be objective, can agree to disagree, and can manage to work together. Then, having overcome divisiveness, women can pause long enough to reflect that equality does not mean identity, that differences can be equally valuable in a society as diverse as ours. That day, women will have moved toward a truly righteous society.

Moving toward lower expectations (economic). Even with high unemployment, high interest rates, and a high degree of uncertainty, approximately one-half of the U.S. population has experienced only affluent times. But today's young adults—the recent high school and college graduates—have borne the brunt of shock waves of diminished expectation. Many of them have not found jobs, even though they are well trained or trained in fields where manpower shortages exist. Jobs are hard to find. Whole industries (for example, steel and automobiles) are moving toward robotics, displacing countless workers. Such basic change and motion may be accompanied by altered political, economic, and personal behavior; self-protective behavior may be the outcome. That behavior may be conservative compared to what the individual formerly displayed.

Economic behavior also alters. When threatened by possible loss, working people protect their jobs without liking them better than before.[5] Chances for advancement decrease. Groups denied opportunities to prove themselve are found incompetent without being tested; that is the essence of prejudice—prejudging. It underlies sex discrimination. As expectation diminishes, sex discrimination and illegal actions tend to increase and to become overt. Women, minorities, and young workers suffer most. During times of low expectations, working women may have to rely on their wits, ingenuity, and patience. But they need to remember that stellar performance is most likely to win applause and other offers to perform.

Nobody said dramatics were easy. These themes (moving right, moving righteously, moving toward lower expectations) sketched external conditions that working women currently face. The themes may also function as backdrops for the conflict, the action. Working women's performance remains to be described after some new casting. Women directors are among those taking curtain calls, receiving gilded statuettes. That calls for a new perspective.

PITCHING, NOT CATCHING

Working women have emerged from the handmaiden position. The major civil rights legislation helped them get ready for some pitching, even to head up some teams. Less athletic, equally ambitious working women chose directing and practiced that role.[6] Four examples of motion, symbolically tracing the route from catcher to pitcher, from player to director, follow. We've called them moving from the pawn's position; moving: relocation and staying put; moving across; and moving up.

Moving from the Pawn's Position

Now we switch temporarily from baseball and theater to chess, a game subtle in its moves. There are more pawns than other pieces on the chess board; pawns are expendable and often sacrificed. Working women, long marketplace pawns, are gaining experience in chess strategies called the bishop's, rook's, king's, or queen's role. Women are becoming skilled marketplace chess players, achieving their share of chances to say "checkmate" and make it stick.[7]

Working women seeking ways of exchanging pawn positions for more rewarding ones have turned to education in unprecedented numbers: to prepare for more challenging work, to aid in self-assurance and assertiveness, and to signal availability for better jobs.[8] Education helps the working woman to emerge as an adult; no one would dare treat her as a workplace pawn.

Attitudes are crucial to change of this kind. Changing one's own attitudes may be more difficult than taking one's own sex discrimination case before the Supreme Court. Attitude change may be the most difficult, most engrossing personal challenge. Happily, one instantly recognizes success; one reacts differently. One has achieved an important victory. It may be that the important first step in attitude change for working women is to begin growing a thicker skin, learning how to take remarks and criticism in the workplace in proper perspective (objectively, as they are often meant) rather than personally as before. You can do it. You can move from workplace pawn to a position in which you call some of the plays. One play literally deals with the question of moving. Our motions take us there next.

Moving: Relocation, and Staying Put

Before relocating, I read about relocation.[9] I learned that a growing number of women professionals were willing to move for career advancement; some companies even helped spouses find work. Most working women—married women, women with dependents—are geographically stable. Many single women haven't given relocation serious thought, while divorced and widowed heads of households find thinking about relocation exhausting and threatening. Rethinking may transform relocation into the greatest miracle since fire was invented.

The captive workforce theory speaks powerfully for relocation; its parallel is "coolie labor"—cheap, imported labor. Today, the cheapest legal labor in the workplace is geographically stable womanpower.

Even with a law-abiding employer, a woman employee is unlikely to improve her economic status dramatically if her employer knows that she must remain in her present position or that there are replacements available at beginning wages. The woman in the captive workforce is the workplace's invisible woman, and loyal service does her little good. By relocating, she is suddenly visible, energetic, courageous, known to have something on the ball. The impact of being chosen to locate elsewhere—even if she helps the choosing along—makes her a sought-after employee.

Relocation can result from a transfer, transfer and promotion within the organization, or a position in a new organization. A geographic move across one or more states, or an ocean, is usually involved.

Moves shake one up and cause rethinking. That's not all bad! Relocation forces necessary self-evaluation. The new turf happily balances the new realizations. New turf provides opportunity to redesign oneself, an easier task as an unknown newcomer. In other words, you have an out-of-town tryout stage on which to enact your new script. Incidentally, you have occupational strengths, or you wouldn't have been offered the job· you wouldn't have relocated without expecting to feel comfortable in the new setting. The offer to relocate was hardly made because of your sartorial with-it-ness; you were picked because of your past performance and future potential. Upon relocation, you need time to become an integral part of the new scene. It requires hard work, concentration, and being yourself. All in all, relocation is a time-defined education. However, you are expected to be oriented soon, ready to get on with the job.

Relocation is a challenge; you emerge stronger for having faced it, more fully your own person. Many working women could benefit from these experiences. Nevertheless, relocating is only one route to truth and occupational self-fulfillment. The same outcomes can be achieved by other means.

Working women who stay put don't stop moving. Although they remain on the same job, they can be preparing for another, actively looking, busy with satisfying concerns. One of my friends said, "They may be on a fishing trip, but their bosses haven't a clue." When the big one bites, such working women may leave their jobs on short notice, with good reason, for superior situations. It happens every day. The stay-put woman may fool you, or she may *be* you.[10]

Moving Across

An improved position may involve a lateral or sideways move; title and duties may remain the same, but some factor—perhaps salary—has motivated you to switch jobs. Working women know that pay is accorded to the job as a mark of importance and approval and as a sign of perceived value to the organization.

I suspect along with Ruth Halcomb that working women tend to confuse their salary and their worth as human beings.[11] This confusion creates workplace problems, adds fuel to inflation, and promotes job changes. So do internal workplace conditions like those mentioned in "Is It Time to Leave Your Job?"[12] The job change factor list includes unsatisfactory working conditions, being overworked, being underpaid, being passed over at promotion time, being bored, and being the indispensable woman.

Moving across may be a solution if you and your job are mismatched—if you are not learning anything new. Wise men have always known this; they make frequent lateral moves, on the way learning about other organizations in their field and meeting people who may prove helpful. Working women make fewer job moves than working men do. Maybe moving across is something working women can learn about from working men.

The reasons for men's lateral job moves may be similar to those working women face. But working men tend to act upon them. For example, a male interviewee was asked whether his superiors knew he was job hunting. He said, "Oh, yes. I wouldn't apply anywhere without letting them know." Later, someone asked, "Why do you want to work here?" "Well," the candidate replied, "when I mentioned this interview, I was told my job would end December 31." You can draw your own moral, but you'll agree that a lateral move was one possible solution.

If you are being eased out and sense that a lateral move is indicated, hold your cards close to the vest and prepare your hand. Have a placement file set up at your college, university, or employment service, and keep it current. See that your placement file contains a recent, functional résumé plus recommendations from any organization at which you have worked for two years (full- or part-time). Have your referees send their letters to the placement file. If you do this regularly every two years, then when a change is indicated you won't worry about your credentials or that your supervisor will learn you are looking. You can concentrate on doing your job well and doing your job search superbly. When you've accepted a new job, you'll give notice, and you might receive a farewell party.

Internal lateral moves are something else. Another department may offer you a better future. Once the transfer is made, you'll need to learn skills required in the new department before further advancement. An internal lateral move may happen if you and the supervisor work well together; you may be invited to switch departments. Or lateral moves may be part of a management training program designed to produce leaders who fully understand an entire unit.

Internal lateral moves provide information about the organization's attitudes toward working women, enforcement of the law, and efforts being made toward equal employment opportunity and affirmative action. Such information can guide your career decisions. Sampling an organization from various positions can answer important questions about your future there. If you like what you see or if you've had enough, you may be ready for the next step.

Moving Up

The heady, dizzying feeling, the marvelous self-importance, increased pay (and enormously increased taxes), heavy responsibility, utter loss of femininity, masculine office . . . you get the picture. It's ecstasy; it's paralyzing.

"What am I doing here?" or "This is blown out of all proportion; it shouldn't have taken so long." Do not be alarmed by these thoughts; routine will set in soon. Enjoy the peak experience; then come back to earth.

However, the higher you go, the more decisions you must make: what job needs to be done, how, by whom, when, why. Each decision produces outcomes for which you will be held responsible. (That's the cost of moving up.)

Your responsibility is to get jobs done. No one cares how many hours you work at night or on weekends. You get the blame (called accountability) if a job is not done right and not done on time. However, you can delegate responsibility to those you supervise. Failure to delegate generally results in overall failure. Learning how to delegate and to provide the needed resources helps you to overcome the worst pitfalls. When you delegate responsibility and the authority required to discharge it, you will be a successful, upwardly mobile working woman.

Besides "making it," you become the focus of other working women's expectations. Your mere presence arouses these expectations. Suddenly you've become a miracle worker, a walker on water. You are on both sides now. A woman moving up the career ladder is visible, vulnerable, and guardian of the legal rights of other working women who look up to her.

You have two major jobs to do. Each requires skilled performance and constant objectivity. Being up there means you've got an effective work style which you will continue to refine. But you may need help in your other role as a leader of working women.

Successful working women find themselves on a new pedestal. It feels a mile high sometimes, at other times an iota from rock bottom. Experiences as a ranking woman employee illustrate these extremes. You are introduced to a board member, who says, "I am delighted to meet the new *lady* VP." You bite your tongue, refrain from saying, "I was hired for my skills, not for my manners." An entry-level woman confides that she has been waiting to see "what you looked like." You hope she means what you are going to do for women employees, not whether you measure up to her notions of fashion. A supervisee is terrified of older women; anyone over 25 qualifies. A male supervisee with powerful political connections believes flattery is more effective than doing his job. Your boss treats you as if you were a quarterback, and you have trouble making the first down. Secretaries test your perceptions. Do you realize they run the place since they control paper flow and its storage and know where everything is? You are still new to the game. It doesn't seem alarming that the bellhops are taking over the hotel. Maybe they'll manage it better than . . . oops! You're one of *them* now.

People begin to play pranks on you or tell you jokes. You're in. You're about to get off that pedestal and join the other workers as a mere mortal. It's time to gather the forces and forge a new union—time, that is, to join those having a vested interest in promoting legal rights of women and minority group members at your workplace. You ought to be there whether or not you have any interest in other women's economic fate or how the laws are enforced. After all, you are a woman and one in a successful, tiny group. Your working women colleagues may be an unexpected crew, but what matter? Stick with them.

Efforts at promoting a fair shake for women and minority group employees are a form of moving up—prime moving—that tends to be overlooked. It may be more important in the long run than the promotion of individual women to the higher echelons.

As Charlotte Farris said:

> One half of the population cannot be successfully liberated from sex-stereotyped expectations and choices unless there is an equal effort to liberate the other half.[13]

Upwardly mobile working women, therefore, have two roles beyond what they won in the casting call: they have tacitly agreed to embody liberation from sex-stereotyped expectations and choices and to teach others these behaviors. That's a mighty tall order.

DEFINING THE FIELD FOR PLAYS

All games have rules and offside plays. One offside play is sexual harassment; being out of bounds doesn't prevent its occurrence. While none of us likes to face this topic, it is in our interest as working women to be up to date about sexual harassment in the workplace and what can be done about it.

How a working woman interacts with her supervisor may be related to sexual harassment. But some supervisor–supervisee situations are impossible. Others can be improved. And all such situations are governed by game rules and theatrical principles, as are all work roles. On the field or stage, you are most effective when you manage yourself well and continue to improve. Sexual harassment makes your career development doubly difficult to accomplish.

The next section provides helpful ideas on why sexual harassment is not a joke at all but rather is epidemic in the workplace; how it breaks myths; and how to combat it.

Sexual harassment remains a forbidden game, but I doubt much progress will be made against it until working women master the art of negotiation.

Forbidden Games: Sexual Harassment

Sexual harassment used to be considered a joke or an employer's prerogative. Two examples, from scholarly study of the dirty joke and from a working woman/student, clarify this stereotyped, sex-discriminatory attitude.[14]

The joke goes beyond the employer's dream of surpassing the "take a letter" routine. While superficially mild, it is basically vicious: A boss who always polished his car with his wife's discarded lingerie found none in the ragbag one Sunday. On Monday, still upset, he asked his steno what happened to her panties "when you wear them out." The embarrassed young woman answered that if she could "find them afterward, I put them in my purse." That sample was 1952 New York City vintage. The first person account from Chicago, 1978, is more serious:

> I worked as a legal secretary for Mr. J. Along with my normal secretarial duties, I was expected to boost his ego and play his games. He also invited girls up to the office after hours to perform sexual activities. Mr. J. had made advances toward me which I turned down. After a month of obvious tension between us, I was fired, not by Mr. J. but by a law student clerk whom he authorized to do this. Because of my sex, Mr. J. felt he had the right to push himself on me; and because he was my employer he somehow had the idea my body was his from nine to five.
>
> Working woman/student, 1978

The working woman/student who reported this went on to say that Title VII of the Civil Rights Act of 1964 would have provided her with legal recourse had she known about it. The view she expressed has been adopted by the EEOC, namely that sexual harassment is sexual discrimination and that Title VII "guarantees female employees . . . a working environment free of (discriminatory) intimidation."[15]

Widespread workplace sexual harassment has been documented in federal government agencies—in the Departments of Health, Education, and Welfare; Labor; and Housing and Urban Development to mention only three. Suits have been filed against the Environmental Protection Agency, the Justice Department, former Attorney General William Saxbe, and the male employees of Western Electric, Johns–Manville, Bausch and Lomb, Public Service Electric and Gas Company of New Jersey—since 1975. Nor is the academic establishment exempt; Yale University and schools in the University of California system have been sued for sexual harassment by female students and employees. Some states have moved to make sexual harassment illegal; others have found officials of state agencies guilty of sexual harassment.[16]

The worst state agency violator who came to notice was the administrative manager of the Springfield, Illinois, Fair Employment Practices Commission, who was suspended because he sexually harassed female employees and then retaliated against them by preventing job advancement when they refused his advances or protested against them.[17]

A legal action taken by sexually harassed working women was won in Oakland, California, by two former waitresses against a union leader. The judgment for $275,000 was awarded in a nonjury civil trial. Damages were to be paid by the Hotel and Restaurant Employees and Bartenders Union Local and Ray Lane, union leader. Lane refused the women union jobs when they rejected his sexual advances.[18]

Multiplying these examples of sexual harassment by thousands gives some measure of the prevalence of and social sanction for such events. More women are now admitting sexual harassment. Those working women who talk about sexual harassment are acting to combat it. Their actions clearly indicate that working women do not condone, encourage, or enjoy sexual harassment. Figure 8–1 presents myths about sexual harassment; each is followed by factual information. Weigh the myths and facts against your experience.

By definition, sexual harassment takes place when a person in power uses control or influence to coerce a worker into sexual relations. Most often, if *she* refuses, *he* may use his power to affect her job or job prospects negatively. Because of power imbalance, the working woman objecting to or refusing to comply with the suggested sexual behavior may face serious risks. She may be unable to quit her job. Psychological hazards combine with economic risks when a working woman is sexually harassed. Who would believe her rather than her male supervisor? If she complains, she risks being negatively labeled or having her coworkers

FIGURE 8–1 Myths About Sexual Harassment*

Myth:	Sexual harrassment only affects a few women.
Fact:	Several surveys have documented the widespread nature of sexual harassment. In one study, 88 percent of the respondents said they had experienced one or more forms of unwanted sexual advances on the job.
Myth:	Sexual harassment is rare on the campus.
Fact:	Women have only recently begun to talk about the long-hidden problem of sexual harassment of students, staff, and faculty. Fear of ridicule, a sense of hopelessness about the problem, and a feeling that it's a "personal" dilemma have kept the problem concealed.
Myth:	Women should ignore sexual harassment when it occurs.
Fact:	In one survey, 33 percent of those reporting sexual harassment tried to ignore the unwanted attentions. In 75 percent of these, the harassment continued or became worse. One-quarter of the women who ignored the sexual propositions received unwarranted reprimands from their bosses or had their workloads increased.
Myth:	If a woman really wants to discourage unwanted sexual attention, she can do so. If she's sexually harassed, she must have asked for it.
Fact:	Many men believe a woman's "no" is really "yes," and therefore do not accept her refusal. Additionally, when a man is in a position of power, such as employer or teacher, the woman may be coerced or feel forced to submit.
Myth:	Most charges of sexual harassment are false. Women use these charges as a way of "getting back" at a man with whom they are angry.
Fact:	Women who openly charge harassment are often not believed, may be ridiculed, may lose their job, be given a bad grade, or be mistreated in some other way. Women have little to gain from false charges.
Myth:	Sexual harassment is not harassment at all. It is a purely personal matter between men and women. It's a fact of life.
Fact:	When a woman is coerced by a professor or her employer, she is not always in a position to readily reject such overtures, or if she does, she may face adverse reactions. Several courts have ruled that sexual harassment on the job constitutes sex discrimination under Title VII of the Civil Rights Act, and in some instances have awarded damages to women. Whether sexual harassment against students constitutes sex discrimination under Title IX of the Education Amendments is now under litigation. Regardless of the legal outcome, students face a chilling climate for learning if sexual harassment is permitted or indirectly condoned.

*This section was adapted from a pamphlet, "Sexual Harassment at the Workplace," published by the Alliance Against Sexual Coercion, P.O. Box 1, Cambridge, MA 02139. From *Sexual Harassment: A Hidden Issue,* courtesy of The Project on the Status and Education of Women of the Association of American Colleges.

make light of the sexual harassment. Already a victim, now she has to cope with feelings of helplessness and confusion. Psychosomatic ailments, a common outcome, are costly for all concerned.[19]

Sexual harassment consists of verbal comments, invitations, gestures, propositions, or actions that treat workers as sex objects rather than as employees. Women in nontraditional jobs face the greatest sexual harassment risks, which can include acts of physical violence.[20] Figure 8–2 lists actions that may be included in sexual harassment.

What can you do about sexual harassment? In 1977, the advice to a victim was to avoid confronting or accusing your sexual harasser. Instead, work for an internal transfer. As a last resort, suggest that you'd rather not work for him because of a personality clash.[21] That advice wouldn't work because men would believe the woman was leading her boss on. Politely copping out doesn't work either. Who would believe anyone doing good work should be transferred? Conversely, a woman doing good work would want to remain to reap the benefits. Personality clash, ha! What's wrong with you? Did the boss spurn your sexual advances?

A legal feature on the radio acknowledged the innocence of such advice. The 1980 commentator, a lawyer, suggested that women sexually harassed on the job should do the following:[22]

1. Protest loudly and repeatedly. Make sure you are heard.
2. Follow oral protest with written memos.
3. Get witnesses.
4. Keep working, thereby protecting your unemployment compensation.

FIGURE 8–2 What is Sexual Harassment?*

Sexual harassment may include *any* of the following:
- Verbal harassment or abuse
- Subtle pressure for sexual activity
- Sexist remarks about a woman's clothing, body, or sexual activities
- Unnecessary touching, patting, or pinching
- Leering or ogling at a woman's body
- Constant brushing against a woman's body
- Demanding sexual favors accompanied by implied or overt threats concerning one's job, grades, letters of recommendation, and so on.
- Physical assault

*Courtesy of the Project on the Status and Education of Women of the Association of American Colleges, taken from *Sexual Harassment: A Hidden Issue*, p. 2.

Staying on the job until the case comes up or the complaint is investigated applies to residents of states where sexual harassment is not a condition of eligibility for unemployment compensation. For the conditions in your state, inquire at your local U.S. Employment Service.

Keep a diary of the harasser's actions, including date, time, place, and names of witnesses. If your organization lacks one, develop and use an in-house grievance procedure (helpful since most organizations would prefer to solve their problems "inside the family" rather than in court). If the organization drags its feet, consider filing a charge.[23] Consider filing a civil suit against the harasser. Use your influence with coworkers and the personnel department to gain inclusion of policy language in affirmative action plans and union contracts. It is strongly suggested that working women be advised of their rights and how to handle sexual harassment. (An excellent film narrated by Ed Asner and entitled "The Workplace Hustle" provides a good opener to discussion of the topic by male and female employees at all levels. A skilled moderator is essential.) If your state does not include sexual harassment as a condition of eligibility for unemployment compensation, alert women's groups and work to change the law.

While pamphlets and training help, working women need to know about agencies like the Alliance Against Sexual Coercion and the Working Women United Institute (addresses provided at the end of the chapter).[24] Management must be made acutely aware of the cost of sexual harassment (absenteeism, unemployment compensation costs, lower productivity, health insurance), of its anachronistic character, and of its illegality. The support of management is vital in the elimination of workplace sexual harassment.

Every working woman can help to eradicate sexual harassment. Your awareness can help; you can label sexual harassment and stop it fast by being willing to support those whose victimization you observe as a witness and by refusing to tolerate sexual harassment. There is one warning: Be sure of your grounds. Don't charge sexual harassment unless your complaint falls within the guidelines in Figure 8–2.

By pulling together, we can make a reality of the working woman–student's closing statement:

> It would have given me great satisfaction to show Mr. J. that I wasn't the "dumb blonde" he thought I was, and that no one has the right to abuse other people without suffering the consequences.

The Basic Power Game: Negotiation

While it would have given the working woman/student great satisfaction to show her boss how smart she was, she didn't do it. She thought about it. Today, working women are being advised by lawyers and affirmative action officers to negotiate.

Part of the reasoning behind this terrifying idea ("Who, me, negotiate? I don't know how") is that if we retain power and control over ourselves we can relate to our supervisor (and to our harassers) as an adult. Adults do not retreat meekly when looked at crossly. So, learning to negotiate includes unlearning old ways of relating to those in authority, especially when one's rights as a working woman have not been respected. That's doubly hard because the supervisor's task includes responsibility for ensuring respect of all supervisees' rights.

Another part of the reasoning behind the emphasis on negotiation by working women is to bring employment issues, grievances, failure to respect employee rights, and violation of the laws into the open. This serves a dual purpose. The wrongs don't fester and further harm the working woman by increasing her self-doubts and reducing her self-confidence; the negotiation approach permits keeping records of the magnitude of various misunderstandings, problems, and violations. Tallies can also be kept on successful strategies, those producing workable solutions.

Negotiation emerges as a management approach, one often related to management of change. Frequently the negotiation script deals with the accomplishment of a job change. The working woman, for instance, learns that she will not be rehired when the current contract expires. She is shocked, angry, bewildered, but rarely surprised. Her friends advise her to negotiate.

Here is a typical negotiation scenario, or play-by-play. The rejected working woman uses all of her workaday energies to do the daily tasks she formerly enjoyed. She does not want to be fired for nonperformance, but she secretly believes no one has ever shared the disgrace she feels was visited upon her by nonrenewal. Her emotional paralysis gradually recedes and she begins making notes. That first step follows her wallow in self-pity and the slough of despond.

Her rejection may concern a salary dispute, harassment, unfair employment practices, philosophical differences, or any other workplace issue. She will continue to be troubled by it until she realizes that she must initiate action in her own behalf. That action frequently is negotiation.

Alas, most of us have been taught *not* to stand up for ourselves. Now, negotiation strategy advises us to stand up for ourselves and to do it nondefensively, nonthreateningly at the very time when we are at our occupational nadir. It may be the tallest order of our work lives. Besides (as we keep insisting), we don't know how.

We go back to the friend, affirmative action officer, or lawyer. There we hear what other working women have done successfully in similar situations. That gives us a little courage. With the friend's guidance, we specify how we have been wronged and what correctives we desire.

If, for example, it becomes clear that we have not been correctly or legally compensated during the past year, we might outline how the organization would benefit by having us on salary rather than the current hourly wage. We would show how this change would be an economy for the organization. We would offer another alternative. Instead of extra compensation, we would agree to an extra week of paid vacation to make up for the underpayment. Our friend would rehearse us until the roles became completely familiar.

At the meeting (or, in the jargon, "at the confrontation") both we and the supervisor, prepared to be flexible, would give a little and receive a lot. That is an example of a cooperative negotiation resulting from an error everyone wants corrected.

More commonly, however, working women benefit from negotiation when they want an error corrected but the organization is not concerned about it. A typical example is that of negotiating either a reassignment or a resignation. This kind of negotiation is appropriate when, for whatever reason (except plant shutdowns or items covered by a collective bargaining agreement), your organization decides to dispense with your services in your present position. You would probably not be in an entry-level position if you found yourself in this circumstance. More likely, you would have been promoted once or more, would have been performing well, would have decided that your career future was with the organization, when a ground shift took place and you were caught up in it. One type of ground shift is a reorganization of the entire unit caused by the entrance of a new managment team with new personnel, policies, and ideas. You would be labeled as part of the old order. You would be slated to go with the rest in a clean sweep or house-cleaning operation.

You could decide to go, or you could decide to let the chips fall where they may. Working women formerly relied heavily on these options and bravely bore their negative consequences. Now there is another alternative. You could decide to exercise initiative and open negotiations with your supervisor.

As in the earlier example, you would rehearse with your friend or with your lawyer (or affirmative action officer if the issues involved warranted it) the conditions of a settlement acceptable to you. Here is an example. A woman dean at a liberal arts college successfully served her three-year probationary contract. She expected to receive a permanent contract for another three years when the president resigned. It was late in the academic season before a new president was appointed, but he had selected the dean he wanted. The woman dean was not reappointed. She decided to negotiate and offered conditions that would enable her to find a new, equivalent position. The liberal arts college agreed to a negotiated settlement that gave the dean one year's salary, one year's continued use of a campus house for herself and her family, one year's use of her title followed by "on leave," and other assistance (such as recommendations) in finding a new position. By the end of the agreement, the dean was successfully settled in a new position. If she had not negotiated, she would not have had the freedom, energy, or peace of mind to pursue a new occupational opportunity.

Here is another example. Helen, a social worker who had a heavy case load, decided to attend an important conference held partly during working hours. She registered for the conference several weeks in advance. Then she went to her supervisor, giving him plenty of notice. She said, "Mr. Thomas, I am going to attend a conference on women family therapists the second week in July." He responded, "I'll see if it's possible and let you know, Helen." She said, "Mr. Thomas, I'm not sure you heard me. I am going to attend a conference on women family therapists the second week in July. I'm letting you know now so you can arrange to have my intake hours covered. I will inform my clients, of course." He said, "That conference sounds like a good idea. You may pick up some good new techniques."

You may recognize some of the negotiation approaches my friend Helen used. She made sure, without becoming emotional, that Mr. Thomas got the message: Helen was going to the conference. That point was nonnegotiable. Helen was also paying for the conference, was willing to share what she learned, and was putting a lot of her time into attending it. She was asking Mr. Thomas to provide a little coverage for the intake hours, to give her permission to miss those hours (and her regular hours) without prejudicing her employment. Had Helen backed down, had she offered to cancel her conference registration, everyone would have lost. As it worked out, Helen, Mr. Thomas, the organization, and future clients all benefited.

Negotiation, then, represents an objective problem-solving approach. It also is a new, confident attitude that signifies that a compromise satisfactory to both parties can be reached, even when one of the parties is a working woman. One could also characterize this new workplace willingness to negotiate—to ask for something one wants, to give something the other side wants, and ultimately to agree amicably—as indicative of the change and motion women are experiencing in the workplace.

Working women are using negotiation, and they are thinking about how and why it works. Two main reasons come to mind. First, working women are taking an active, participatory stance when they negotiate. They are clearly signaling that the issues are important, that their work is important, and that they are important. Second, both parties to any negotiation are aware that below the surface of their calm and cordial confrontations lies the law. Negotiation is a quasi-legal approach. Yet, should either side fail to live up to the agreement reached, the matter could become a legal confrontation. Both sides wish to avoid that. However, it does no harm for the negotiating working woman to keep in mind what she has learned about her legal rights and their protection and about her legal obligations, too. She can be certain that those with whom she negotiates are doing the same. For these reasons, she may decide to have her lawyer accompany her to the negotiation sessions. This option—that of legal counsel—is open to the other side as well.

All things considered, then, the willingness and ability to negotiate (when necessary) are acid tests of the working woman's talents for managing herself within the milieu of change and motion. I'd wager she does quite well; I'd bet she's doing better all the time.

But what happens when change, motion, self-management, and romance coincide in high-level workplace settings? While we generally advise working women to find their amusements far from the workplace, Cupid does sometimes have irresistible persuasive powers. It is not always possible to separate business and pleasure. Sometimes they can even be managed together, over an obstacle-strewn course.

The following is presented as a modern morality play to illustrate the new look of managing yourself.

Managing Yourself

This true story has the kind of third act one finds when a talented working woman and a powerful boss play their drama for a business community audience. You can interpret what happened, realizing it is probably more related to stress and social pressures in high places than to sex.

William Agee, 42, chairman of the Bendix Corporation, hired Mary Cunningham, 29, upon her graduation from the Harvard Business School. Mary rapidly rose to vice-president. Tongues began to wag. Yes, obviously, she and Agee were close friends, and her responsibilities expanded. Yes, males slightly offstage were hostile and jealous. Jealous males can be as vicious as "catty women."

To this plot add the volatile mixture of Cunningham's gender and managerial skills, Agee's divorce, and Cunningham's separation. Soon Agee informed employees that his close friendship with Cunningham in no way affected evaluation of her performance.[25]

Shortly after this announcement, Cunningham requested a leave of absence. The Bendix board gave her a vote of confidence instead. Ten days later, Cunningham resigned.

Since then, Cunningham and Agee have married. Cunningham, now a vice-president for Seagram Ltd., is taking an upaid summer leave to write a book. Agee is currently unemployed after resigning from Allied Corporation (Bendix Corporation's parent) with a $4.1 million "golden parachute" deal. During the years since they met, Agee has often been headlined for his aggressive merger activity, which has caused new highs in corporate nastiness and resentment. Cunningham, who meanwhile has concentrated on the marketing of wines, will use her breather to fill us in on her meteoric ascent at Bendix and her romance with her boss there. One cannot resist quipping that while marriages are made in heaven, mergers are engineered on earth. After curtain fall, you are invited to evaluate the theme, the action, and the props featured in this modern morality play.

Empathize. How would you have managed yourself under similar circumstances? Would you agree with Jacoby that "no one cared when women were 'only secretaries' and could be replaced like disposable parts," but that it is quite different when the vice-president and the boss are inseparable?[26] Or do you believe that what you do during and after work is nobody's business but your own?

Many working women will have to answer similar tough questions as women—few now, more later—rise to the top. Suppose a woman president and a male vice-president were entangled. Society might have difficulty with such out-of-role behavior, representing double nonconformity. Relax. It will be a few years before that combo hits the *Sunday New York Times Business Section*.

OTHER SOURCES OF POWER

Few people studied how working women behaved and were treated before the Women's Movement. We now know that women are reluctant to ask for help in performance situations, tend not to recognize or to use available help, and tend to reject help while overemphasizing sex discrimination. Three interpersonal solutions for working women's problems—modeling, mentoring, and networking—have received much attention recently. So far, this source of potential power has hardly staged a political production; however, its effects have been felt in the workplace and in the courts.

Another power source is women's experience with foundations and on corporate boards. Foundations fund (or fail to fund) projects capable of increasing knowledge about women and creating awareness about conditions affecting working women. Corporate boards could integrate the views and ideas of women consumers; until recently they have been slow to accept women representatives in their policy-making councils. Corporate power sources and foundations are largely virgin territory.

The final power source we deal with is private enterprise. It includes thoughts about working for yourself, dual-career families, and related ideas. Private enterprise means juggling high-priority segments of your life until they form a meaningful, satisfying, workable whole. It implies individuality, ingenuity, detemination, and, for working women, enforcement of the current laws, plus enactment of the missing pieces. Private enterprise involves fine tuning and lots of stamina. It involves working with others and the ability to go it alone. A character in Amanda Cross's *Poetic Justice* voices that aspect of private enterprise when she notes that "women are liberated the moment they stop caring what other women think of them."[27]

Private enterprise is your ultimate choice for action; you shape it in your image, realizing that your winnings will be in direct proportion to the calculated risks you take.

Modeling, Mentoring, and Networking

Modeling. Modeling resembles role playing, which has been mentioned throughout this book. The difference is that in modeling your performance may be guided by someone who demonstrates the action and then helps you until you can do it alone. Driving lessons are an example. But modeling does not always require formally guided practice. You can watch and learn. Playing school is an example. A student driver is a highly motivated learner eager for the rewards of a license, independence, and power. By contrast, playing school emphasizes the imitative aspect of modeling. The teacher's purpose is to impart knowledge, but kids readily learn the power game later demonstrated in their play. These examples illustrate both the conscious practice aspect of modeling and its unconscious side. Formally guided practice is under the model's control; however, learners gain knowledge by observing a model, and this incidental learning may not be what the model intended.

While you are trying hard for job mastery, you do what the nearest successful occupant does: you follow your leader. The available modeling may involve a total performance (leadership style), a superficial manifestation (dress code or group slang), or a partial performance (closing a sale). As there are models conscious or unconscious of their role, so there are learners who work at and others who seem to absorb what the model has to offer. A model's power is believed to originate in the ability to give or withhold rewards. Therefore, the person who evaluates you and holds this power over you may become your model.

Mentoring. Models may not be trying to teach; mentors usually are. Mentors can be found at all levels of all organizations. Marilyn Moats Kennedy defined a mentor as someone who teaches you the ropes and is a political person.[28] You and the mentor share an objective: your competence. Kennedy referred to five kinds of mentors: informational mentors, godfathers, peer mentors, external mentors, and retirees.[29] Each kind of mentor can be helpful in certain situations. An informational mentor can confer power on you. Secretaries do this when they provide information. Godfathers hold top positions and take care of you so that you are obedient and rise. Peer mentors, your equals in status, cooperate with you. External mentors know your field but work for a competitor. Retirees can be good mentors because they have plenty of time to concentrate on you and your career. Since there are no all-purpose mentors, every working woman needs an array of mentors.

Mentors can serve in another way: They can keep working women and organizations from sex discrimination confrontations. To this end, some organizations use the development of subordinates as part of their executive performance evaluation.[30] These organizations reward both mentor and subordinate for superior performance.

Where do you find a mentor? Most working women pick their mentors. They select mentors two or three levels above themselves, perhaps in a related part of the organization. While your supervisor makes a handy model, choosing that person as a mentor is not recommended.

Working women once had difficulty finding mentors. Nowadays, men are willing mentors while women managers often have a commitment to mentorship.[31] And when women managers take an interest in a woman newcomer, it doubles the impact. The mentoring is helpful and encouraging, but the cultural mentoring—the introduction and explanation of the work environment—may make the difference between a well-oriented working woman and one who regards her work environment in a detached, passive way.

Networking. Modeling and mentoring usually involve working people of unequal status. In networking, equals gather to use their power for a constructive purpose; women collectively have a lot of power. Women may form a network to ensure that the laws against sex discrimination are enforced within their workplace. In nationwide organizations, networks concentrate their energies on activities designed to provide direct benefits for those involved. Mary Scott Welch has reported extensively on networking within the communications industry.[32] She demonstrates that one woman may not be listened to, but a group is hard to silence or ignore. Networks may cut across organizations while maintaining an occupational thrust. Women Employed, the Chicago office workers network mentioned in Chapter 2, is an example.

Networks give their members strength, protection, and direct communication links. Network happenings include dissemination of information about job conditions such as salary data (particularly wage disparities between men and women workers) and promotion disparities (all advancement goes to men). Organizations would prefer having such data remain secret. Without networks, it would, and organizations within an industry could continue to violate the law, secure that nobody would every find out. Networking has ended that strategy.

For instance, it was difficult for a real network—a nationwide one, NBC, where "networking" started—to ignore responses to a questionnaire answered by a large number of women employees who detailed their sex-discriminatory workplace experiences. After many fruitless attempts to negotiate with top management failed, the Women's Committee for Equal Employment Opportunity at NBC filed its complaint with the New York City Human Rights Commission and later sued NBC. The women's committee won. Their victory will provide (1) job access up to the vice-presidential level, (2) pay boosts to the average salary level for males in the rank to accompany each promotion of a woman. The women's committee must now see to it that the settlement is fully implemented by NBC.

Gains are gains only when effectively monitored. Victories must be implemented and must become part of organizational policy. When rape, abortion, incest, adultery, and stupid females disappear from the soap operas, when ordinary women are portrayed as doctors, police officers, and dignified housewives rather than as aberrant comic figures or as sex symbols, I'll believe that NBC has lived up to its part of the bargain about employing women writers, program directors, and so on.[33] That has not happened yet.

While your organizational network is essential, you can also benefit from a personal network, which can function as a career aid when needed. A personal network is composed of widely different people, who need never meet, yet each can give you something vital.

My personal network contains family members, lawyers, a college president, a stockbroker, teachers, professors, secretaries, state and county government members, and numerous friends. I keep in touch with these people whom I like and respect; if I needed their help, it would be there. Likewise, if they needed my help, I would be there. Members of my network have often supplied the missing piece—information, a job recommendation, a pat on the back.

We've seen how modeling, mentoring, and networking protect working women from being alone and isolated in the work world.[34] If you have included modeling, mentoring, and networking among your choices for action, pause now and pat yourself on the back three times.

Foundations, Corporate Boards, and Community Groups: A New Stage

Foundations, corporate boards, and holding office in community groups are additional alternative sources of power. The foundations used to be overlooked by women and women's groups when they sought to implement a project. Today women are learning how to write research proposals, to do research, and to obtain funding. These are skills sought after in the marketplace. A grantswriter with a good track record (several hundred thousand dollars' worth of funded grants) is a powerful person. She is promoting women by demonstrating their competence in a nontraditional endeavor and by the topics chosen for her efforts. Her stock in trade is at an all-time high since grant competition has grown while resources are shrinking. This trend is evident in government grant approaches under the Reagan administration. There is high probability that government grants—a large source—will continue to shrink.

Women foundation managers—and there are enough of them to have an organization—would do well to help working women and their organizations learn about obtaining grants. There is much more, however, to "grantspersonship" than obtaining funding for a proposal. Of course, one has to start with an idea, write a proposal, submit it, and hope it will be approved.

Women's organizations need to commit themselves to completing the project, if funded, before they consider applying for a grant. Requests for money are inextricably linked with responsibility to complete the project. Doing less is close to fraudulent. Unfortunately, when women accept a commitment and then flub up or fail to perform, it remains worse than when men exhibit identical irresponsible action. Male flubbers do not arouse the same expectations as female flubbers. By contrast, men are expected to succeed; women are expected to fail. We need to make it impossible for anyone to feel that a women's group's successful project completion is a fluke. Such thinking, like always expecting a male to succeed, is sexist.

If you take the proposal route, upon project completion, consider offering yourself as a candidate for the foundation's advisory board. Foundations welcome links to the community; few think of having working women as members. What's in it for you? Strengthening your ties to the foundation, performing a community service, new experiences and colleagues, initiation into a different stage of decision making, another kind of credit for your résumé, a springboard to those corporate inner sanctums that working women have trouble penetrating. That's quite a lot to achieve in addition to the satisfaction and experience of completing your project.

After serving as a foundation board member or as a community group board member, you may be invited to serve on a corporate board of directors. (Recently, 18 percent of newly appointed corporate board directors have been women.) If you were invited and accepted, you'd be in a position to end annual corporate report statements like the one in "Summary Report," Annual Meeting of Stockholders, Baltimore Gas and Electric Company, April 22, 1977, which stated that the absence of women on the board of directors was the result of the difficulty "encountered in finding representative women" with "business experience, particularly in the financial field." But the company was "looking forward to our first woman director." The 1981 corporate report revealed that this wish had been granted—a woman director had been found.

There are multitudes of qualified women who have not given any thought to serving on corporate boards. Are you one of them? Are you motivated by rewards of prestige, hard work, money, and the ability to make important contributions affecting millions of women?

Are you willing to question the practice of excluding women from U.S. corporate boards?[35] Did you know that one way of camouflaging the exclusion of women from corporate board membership seems to have been to count executive secretaries, who took minutes at meetings, as board members?[36]

Internal promotion is one route to corporate board status, so vice-presidents in these corporations came under close scrutiny. In 1977, of 804 vice-presidents in a survey of some *Fortune 500* corporations, nine, or 1.1 percent, were women. It is unlikely that a woman will become president of a *Fortune 500* company in the foreseeable future, nor will there be many internal promotions to corporate board status among the working women at *Fortune 500* corporations.

Nevertheless, corporations are looking for people who have served on boards; who have prestigious positions, functional specialties, and financial understanding; who are well known nationally or professionally, or in the corporate world; who can function as team members; and who are familiar with their industry or corporation. Additional qualifications include having time to serve and knowing a board member personally. While most working women are unlikely to know corporate board members personally, a well-structured personal network may help.

Board members meet four or more times a year, attend the annual stockholders meeting, and act as overseers for the corporation. Board members serve on committees. Women board members tend to find themselves on the executive pay and auditing committee, today regarded as cosmetic rather than as a crucial committee.[37] The executive or financial committee is more important. If appointed to a corporate board, insist on meaningful committee assignments; then discharge them ably.

You are a likely corporate board candidate if you are an engineer, industrialist, scientist, mathematician, or manager at the vice-presidential level having responsibility for multimillion-dollar budgets and hundreds of employees.

If this discussion of the foundation, corporate, and community sources of power has whetted your appetite, begin planning your training. It takes time. Start by taking a leadership role in one of your current organizations. Work up to board membership. Serve on several different kinds of boards—that's the best preparation for those having the time and energy. One day a corporate boardroom door may open to your knock.

Experience gained through board memberships of nonprofit organizations may also qualify you for public office. Consider that in your action plan. Few women are in high elective office, and their number is dwindling, although there are potential replacements in training. More women are in high appointive offices that resemble the boards of corporations. These options may also be adjuncts to your career.

Private Enterprise

We are now ready for our final alternative source of power: private enterprise. We have defined its individual options to include owning one's business and one's own business (illustrated by being part of a dual-career family). The thread tying together private enterprise options is self-determination. Perhaps identifying, achieving, and then maintaining self-determination is the greatest challenge today's working women face.

For working women, especially the married ones, self-determination may be a double career whammy. The traditional pattern had the wife docilely giving up her career, though seething within, at her husband's whim or transfer. Today, other methods assist in handling the new stresses resulting when both partners have positions they want to keep. Occupational schedules to fit the partners' needs are being worked out, and domestic arrangements have become more flexible. Such solutions are part of the most private enterprise. Working women deserve applause for the imagination they have brought to bear on dual-career problems. Private enterprise has also lightened the load for many single parents who are working women. Another new solution lies in recent efforts to provide equal job opportunity and treatment for dual-career couples wishing to have families. The Kellogg Foundation in 1980 made a large grant and Exxon Corporation made a small one to the Career and Family Center of Catalyst for the study of problems of couples who want careers and children.[38] This study examines corporate reactions to problems of dual-career families in which the corporate worker is the career woman.

Results from the Career and Family Center studies may help assuage the guilt almost invariably carried by working women in dual-career marriages. Women partners in these marriages may benefit most from the research by learning of the trade-offs that others in similar marriages have found workable.

For those other persevering working women, those whose aims are closer the the original definition of private enterprise, there are other challenges and opportunities. By implementing Yankee ingenuity, by going into business for themselves, these women demonstrate optimism, confidence, and willingness to work hard in order to come out ahead. This form of private enterprise represents a new outlook for working women.

A few years ago when I was teaching management courses, a growing proportion of the ablest students said their objective was to own their own businesses or to work for themselves. Today, substantial help is available from governmental agencies such as the Small Business Administration and through women's groups. The new emphasis on private enterprise by women provides another strategy for working women, another power source. Those finding private enterprise appealing make comments like, "Nobody said I couldn't, so I went ahead and did it." They knew they could. So can you.

TAKE YOUR BOW

A day will come when you may stand in front of the footlights and bow humbly as friendly strangers clap thunderously. Or you may bring in the victory clinching point for your team and thus become the most valued player. Either way, you will give the lion's share of the reward—applause or trophy—to all those who helped make it happen. You don't need wonderful trappings, those crutches, any more. What's important is that *you've* done it. That's the memory to cherish and draw strength from later, when the cost of your ticket is again uppermost.

A Personal Word and an Invitation

We all know that there are rites of passage, baptisms by fire, flingings of the gauntlet—in everyday English, challenges. Some are painful—flauntings of the law, for instance. There is male inability to treat you as an equal partner or to take you seriously as a coworker. We working women can differentiate between talk about equality and behavior indicative of it. We know, though, that whatever the hazards, we will meet the challenges.

That is included in the cost of my ticket, along with deciding how I want to accomplish my constructive goals and then proceeding over ground untrodden before. I may not get to the top level; I may decide I don't want to, but I will accomplish my goals. You can achieve yours, too. And this may help. Once, long ago, I read a poem by Marianne Moore about getting across a swamp.[39] The poet said she'd figure out a way across that swamp if the listener could tell her why she ought to cross it. I read that poem again and think I have an answer. As both the listener to and the author of my life's poems, I see challenges as the substance of my life, meeting them as reward enough. Sure, I *can*, if I set my sights high enough. I believe *you* can, too.

It may take me longer, cost me more effort, or require more growth than I think I am capable of. But there are inner resources to exercise and strengthen. There are external resources waiting to be called upon. Many of these have been explored in *Yes You Can*; as many more have been left for you to discover, test, share, and enjoy.

True Ending: True Grit?

This book was started a long time ago. At that time I wouldn't have dared to predict my experiences. But during the three years in which most of my spare time was devoted to *Yes You Can*, I have undergone many changes, and so has this book. During those 36 months, I have been part of a commuting couple, mostly living alone in upstate New York where I worked. During those months, when my exciting, demanding, worthwhile, challenging workday ended, sometimes very late at night, I came home, changed clothes, and, sick or well, began the job I didn't apply for—getting this book done for you. During those months, without my intervention, my oldest granddaughter learned to speak and to swim, surely excellent portents; my second granddaughter and first grandson have entered our environment. I hope you can make their workday world better than ours has been.

Who knows what will happen next? I don't. But I think I made the right decisions: to gamble on myself, to do some trail blazing, to work toward rather than to go to court for my legal rights, and to help other working women achieve theirs.

Turnabout is fair play. It would be satisfying to hear about your experiences, the challenges you've faced, the problems you've solved, and which laws have helped. The *final* last word is yours.

ADDITIONAL INFORMATION SOURCES

To read:

Lin Farley
Sexual Shakedown.
New York: Warner Books, 1980.

To contact:

Alliance Against Sexual Coercion
P.O. #1
Cambridge, MA 02139

Working Women United Institute
593 Park Avenue
New York, NY 10021

About portrayal of women and girls over national networks·

ABC-TV
1330 Avenue of the Americas
New York, NY 10019

RCA
30 Rockefeller Plaza
New York, NY 10020

NBC-TV
51 West 52nd Street
New York, NY 10019

PBS-TV
475 L'Enfant Plaza, S.W.
Washington, D.C. 20024

Please send copies of all correspondence to:

Federal Communications Commission
1919 M Street, N.W.
Washington, D.C. 20554

Chairperson, National Association of Broadcasters
1771 N Street, N.W.
Washington, D.C. 20036

Copies of correspondence would be appreciated by:

California Commission on the Status of Women
926 J Street, Room 1003
Sacramento, CA 95814

For freedom, accuracy, and fairness in media:

National News Council
One Lincoln Plaza
New York, NY 10023

For information on corporate boards, write:

Catalyst, Corporate Board Resource
14 East 60th Street
New York, NY 10022

A Sexual Harassment Action Kit is available for a $2.50 check made payble to FOPW, accompanied by a self-addressed mailing label, from:

Women's Program Office
American Psychological Association
1200 Seventeenth Street, N.W.
Washington, D.C. 20036

NOTES

1. Laughlin McDonald, "Has the Supreme Court Abandoned the Constitution?" *Saturday Review*, May 28, 1977, pp. 10–14.

2. *Ibid.*, p. 10, refers to *Washington* v. *Davis*, in which a biased employment test was not considered racially discriminatory because there was no proof that it was intended to be racially discriminatory. McDonald calls the outcome "perhaps the worst decision of the past 80 years." He refers to constitutional defense and interpretation. John P. Mackenzie, "Dark Doings among the Judges," *Saturday Review*, May 28, 1977, cites a close call for the Miranda rule, which prohibits use of evidence obtained illegally by police threats, violence, or other misconduct,

against a suspect, pp. 18–19. What such decisions could mean to working women in a negative way is horrible to contemplate. Decisions in cases in which women are plaintiffs may provide an additional rude awakening.

3. The reference is to the *Bakke* case, in which a white male is victorious. He got into medical school after charging that denial of admission was prejudicial. Horowitz, a white female who had almost completed medical school, was not permitted to finish her studies and graduate with her class. She lost her case before the Supreme Court. (See, Figure 5-6.) Also see Riane Tennenhouse Eisler, *The Equal Rights Handbook: What ERA Means to Your Life and the Future* (New York: Avon, 1978). In Fancy 8, pp. 25–26, Eisler states that the Supreme Court has been moving backward since 1973, especially with regard to sexual discimination. Fancy 9, pp. 27–28, deals with logic in the Supreme Court, while Fancy 8 dealt with justice in that body. Eisler concludes that little justice or logic will appear in Supreme Court decisions related to sex discrimination and sex bias.

4. For the statement by Martha W. Griffiths, see "Requisites for Equality," pp. 146–54 in Juanita M. Kreps, ed., *Women and the American Economy: A Look to the 1980s* (Englewood Cliffs, N.J.: Prentic-Hall Inc., 1976). Griffiths suggests that women defeat legislators who practice discrimination: "Women's first demand of legislative bodies should be a guarantee that all dollars buy the same goods in the marketplace," p. 148. Something to think about; after that, something to act on.

5. The last chapter of this book was originally projected as "What to Do Until the Lawyer Comes." Today's situation does not warrant an excess of litigation. See Amal Nag, "Slipping Back: Recession Threatens to Erode Job Gains of Women, Minorities," *The Wall Street Journal*, January 7, 1980, pp. 1 and 12. More recently, recession has been supplanted by high interest rates and high unemployment; these economic features harm women working toward workplace and marketplace equality. The current economic recovery has not yet had profound effects on women's workplace fate.

6. Courses are a popular way of increasing one's motion from pawn to management or attempting that transformation. Some are overpriced and benefit the givers most; others are honest and helpful. It is wise to check with someone who has taken a course before you shell out for it. Ask the informant whether the course will teach you how to play the game or teach you real leadership skills. Avoid courses such as those cited by Meg Cox, "Courses for Women," *The Wall Street Journal*, October 1, 1978, p. 1, which either offer working women excuses or make unrealistic promises of success. Management women feel that self-analysis is the best first step. After discovering gaps or weaknesses in one's training, they recommend taking specific courses to remedy them. Courses also need to be taken to maintain and enhance one's strengths. For those on the lower rungs of the career ladder, a general course or workshop may be the answer. Most seminars are available in a tape cassette form in addition to the one- or two-day motel format. Such workshops may have titles like "Women in the Workplace." Once

you've begun to climb, the titles change to things like "Motivation for Managers." Such courses tend to be filled mainly with males. There also are invitational seminars for those new to a position; an example might be "Bargaining and Negotiating Skills for Middle Managers." At such gatherings you would learn important skills and meet a peer group with which you could grow over time. Alternative routes to the same knowledge are books, professional organizations, and friendly, generous colleagues.

7. Sherry Lansing, the former head of Twentieth-Century Fox Productions, is one of these women. She pushed through the highly successful movie *Nine to Five* over the objections of male producers. She worked on every phase of the production, aside from acting in it. The film grossed more than $38 million within 24 days of its release, according to an article, "Fox Studio's Woman Chief Smashes Mogul Stereotype," *The Wall Street Journal*, January 13, 1981, pp. 35 and 39, by Stephen Sansweet. Apparently, Lansing not only plays good chess but is also a mean scriptwriter, having done wonders writing her own script, too.

8. Chapter 1 offers an overview of how this is done. Chapter 5 deals with educational laws. You might like to read Rosabeth Moss Kanter's "How to Stop Being 'Stuck' and Use Your Power," *Working Woman*, October 1980, pp. 70–77. Take a few minutes to study the checklist Kanter provides on p. 70. Kanter cites protection from risk as a way of keeping women in low level positions. Earlier, Louise Kapp Howe in *Pink Collar Workers* (New York: Avon, 1978), and Margaret Hennig and Anne Jardim in *The Managerial Woman* (Garden City, N.Y.: Anchor Press/Doubleday, 1977), made the same observation but gave different illustrations of it. All these authors described the safe behavior of working women in contrast with working men's risk taking and self-promotion.

9. Samples from the late 1970s included "Labor Letter," a column that let me know that when women refused to move they could do dreadful harm to their career potential, perhaps even reducing it by as much as 50 percent, says an Amoco Production Company official ("Labor Letter," *The Wall Street Journal*, September 13, 1977, p. 1.) That seems unlikely; that firm probably was not anxious to hire career women. By contrast, the article noted that Shell Oil Company changed its plans to move a woman executive to Chicago when her fiancé was based in Houston; wedding bells soon rang. Liz R. Gallese referred to relocation for women managers as a "moving experience"; see "Moving Experience: Women Managers Say Job Transfers Present a Growing Dilemma," *The Wall Street Journal*, May 4, 1978, pp. 1 and 6. Gallese cited problems of commuting couples, one or both of whom have been relocated. A major problem is that it is expensive both to move and to travel back to where one's roots are. Married couples have the added expenses of two domiciles, filing separate state income taxes, and so on. Still, the number of commuting marriages grows and is no longer the oddity it was when we were still reading about Mary Wells Lawrence and her arrangement with her spouse. Gallese tells us that one of her women informants, a relocation

and placement specialist, feels that "women have a deep apprehension of moving." My own experience differed; there was a short period of apprehension about living alone.

10. A fictional treatment like Marilyn French's *The Women's Room* (New York: Jove/HBJ, 1977) makes it abundantly clear that staying-put women, whether working or nonworking, can move swiftly and suddenly to the total surprise of those around who have just not been paying attention.

11. Ruth Halcomb's article, "How to Get a Raise," *Working Woman*, June 1980, pp. 48–50 and 81, gives some good pointers. Try her strategy first. If it fails, then give serious thought to a lateral move.

12. See Mary Scott Welch, "Is It Time to Leave Your Job?" *Redbook*, August 1979, pp. 39 and 86–89, for helpful ideas to use in addressing your situation and deciding what to do.

13. Charlotte J. Farris, "Teachers: The Key to Unlocking Sex Equity," *Journal of the American Vocational Association*, April 1980, p. 19.

14. G. Legman, *Rationale of the Dirty Joke: An Analysis of Sexual Humor* (New York: Grove Press, 1968), p. 341. Jokes are reliable clues to people's fears and feelings. Check this book if you want to discover how men really feel about women. It is not a pretty story. Working women are not treated separately; it is almost as if they did not exist. For corroboration of my view, see Eileen Shapiro, "Some Thoughts on Counselling Women Who Perceive Themselves to Be Victims of Nonactionable Sex Discrimination: A Survival Guide," pp. 73–85 in *Proceedings of the Conference on Women's Leadership and Authority in the Health Professions* (San Francisco: University of California, June 1977), especially pp. 78–79. Much of the material deals with sexual harassment on the job; interpretations of Title IX have made sexual harassment on the job illegal.

15. *California Women*, April 1980.

16. "Government Is Working to Eliminate Sexual Harassment of Women Workers," *California Women*, April 1980, pp. 7–8; *The Chronicle of Higher Education*, March 24, 1980, notes that new EEOC interim guidelines make employers responsible for preventing sexual harassment; *Chicago Sun-Times*, March 24, 1980, contains an article entitled "Sexual Harassment" on p. 30. The same newspaper on July 20, 1980, on p. 20, reported that lower-paid workers were promised career advancement in exchange for sexual submission. Thirty percent cooperated, and 80 percent of them were advanced; of those refusing the boss, 93 percent were either frozen in their jobs or received low evaluative ratings. The story was captioned, "Survey bares widespread sexual harassment at HUD." (HUD is the acronym for the Department of Housing and Urban Development.) Additional information is found in Barbara Varro's "Sexual Blackmail on the Job," *Chicago Sun-Times*, March 23, 1980, pp. 2–3, and "State Job Sex Pressures Found," by Do-

lores McCahill, same paper, March 5, 1980. The New York State Assembly voted to make victims of sexual harassment eligible for unemployment insurance; the state senate did not vote on the bill. Many New York state agencies have no policies or procedures for handling sexual harassment. See Bob Vogel, "Few State Agencies Moving to Combat Sexual Harassment," and "Harassment Bill Dies in State Senate," *The Times Record* (Albany), September 1, 1980, p. B–9. In 1978, laws were pending in Wisconsin and California. Massachusetts provides unemployment compensation if the employer has created or permitted unbearable working conditions. The first book-length treatment of this subject was Lin Farley, *Sexual Shakedown* (New York: Warner Books, 1980, a paperback edition of the 1977 printing).

17. Michael Zielenziger's account stated that half of the clerical staff of the office was out on medical leave caused by the stress of sexual harassment. At least three women lodged allegations against Carl Flipper. See "Aide Suspended in Sex Harassment Case," *Chicago Sun-Times*, April 14, 1980, p. 9.

18. "Two Women Win $275,000 in Sexual Harassment Suit," *Chicago Sun-Times*, March 12, 1980. Also see Section 4, "Waitress," in Howe's *Pink Collar Workers*.

19. "Sexual Harassment: A Hidden Issue" (Washington, D.C.: Project on the Status and Education of Women, Association of American Colleges, June 1978) lists among psychosomatic results of student sexual harassment "insomnia, headaches, neck and backaches, stomach ailments, decreased concentration, diminished ambition, and depression," p. 3. Letty Cottin Pogrebin, "Sex Harassment," *Ladies' Home Journal*, June 1977, pp. 24 and 28, ascribes to working women victims of sexual harassment feelings of anger, upset, fright, guilt, self-consciousness, entrapment, defeat, and physical illness. Perhaps a large share of women's job absenteeism is caused by sexual harassment as note 17 above suggested. This link does not appear to have been explored. In spite of sexual harassment, however, working women generally have excellent on-the-job attendance. Also see Phyllis Chesler, *Women and Madness* (New York: Avon Books, 1972), pp. 247, 251, 270–71. This brilliant book has no entry under sexual harassment. Women weren't talking about it then, at least not to psychologists, psychiatrists, and researchers. Maybe they didn't know what to call it. Or maybe they believed the myths and thought they were responsible for it, perhaps the greatest mental health hazard of all. All of *Women and Madness* is germane to our discussion.

20. See Barbara Varro's "Factory Worker Lost Her Job—But Not Her Will to Fight Back," *Chicago Sun-Times*, March 23, 1980, pp. 3 and 17. The brave woman in question, Mary Louise Shulske, was in her mid-thirties when a male worker made lewd remarks to her, grabbed her breasts, and bragged of his exploits to fellow workers. She told him each time to stop. She reported him to the supervisor, who also witnessed this male worker's behavior. When she complained, she was fired. Her suit against the company went before a district court

in April 1980; that same month *California Women* noted that physical abuse was a sexual harassment risk for women in nontraditional jobs. That nothing had changed during the next year is documented by "When the Boss Wants Sex: Sexual Harassment Was Tolerated Once, Today It's Illegal," *Essence*, March 1981, pp. 82–92, 115, 138, 141. A chart on p. 82 tells how to handle the harasser.

21. Shirley J. Longshore, "Job Frustrations: How to Solve Them Quickly, Diplomatically, Out of Court," *Glamour*, October 1977, pp. 218–21, 320–24, gives other solutions, too. We've learned that being firm and polite isn't enough. Nor is spending one's entire workday in the ladies' room going to be a final solution.

22. Neil Chayet, "Looking at the Law," WBBM, April 20, 1980.

23. The EEOC and FEPC require filing within 180 days of the incident. Union members can file charges with the National Labor Relations Board.

24. The Alliance Against Sexual Coercion provides an information packet for a small fee. The organization provides legal and emotional counseling. Working Women United Institute, a research organization, is building a referral network of lawyers, counselors, and women's groups. This information came from Merrill Rogers Skrocki, "Sexual Pressure on the Job," *McCall's*, March 1978, p. 43.

25. Susan Jacoby, "William and Mary," *The New York Times*, October 19, 1980, p. F3.

26. *Ibid.*

27. Amanda Cross, *Poetic Justice* (Avon: New York, 1970), p. 106.

28. Marilyn Moats Kennedy, "Myths about Mentoring," an address to Women in Management, North Shore Chapter, Morton Grove, Ill., May 23, 1978. For a later, published version, see Marilyn Moats Kennedy, *Office Politics: Seizing Power, Wielding Clout* (Chicago, Ill.: Warner Books, 1980), pp. 187–209, The Politics of Mentoring—or Searching for the Wizard of Oz.

29. One could interpret the Agee and Cunningham experience in terms of the godfather–mentee relationship.

30. Catherine H. Scott, "Managers As Teachers," *The Wall Street Journal*, October 9, 1978, p. 20.

31. "Women Take up Mentoring," *Chicago Sun-Times*, November 5, 1978, pp. 9 and 12.

32. Mary Scott Welch, "How Women Just Like You Are Getting Better Jobs," *Redbook* 149, no. 5 (September 1977): 121, 176–78; and *Networking: The Great New Way for Women to Get Ahead* (New York: Harcourt Brace Jovanovich, 1980). For another view, see Arlene Kaplan Daniels, "Networking," *Comment* 10, no. 3 (March 1978): 2.

33. If you are not pleased with, or are pleased with, a portrayal of women or working women on TV, you might want to register your reaction. A list of places to write is provided at the end of the chapter.

34. I have purposely not mentioned "old boy" networks here. The omission is because of my view that too much reinforcement has been given to the notion of old boy networks, a catchy title for a firmly entrenched method of keeping women out of the power structure. In addition, I see little advantage to working women in establishing support groups directly patterned upon ones that have done working women so much harm. I am confident that working women can create networks that have much greater utility for them. Helpful hints abound in Patricia Brookes, "Plugging into the Old Girl Network," *Working Woman*, July 1977, pp. 26–29.

35. If you are ready for this activity, see the address at the end of the chapter. Corporations are not going to seek out women candidates, so you need to make your availability known. Do your homework before applying through the Corporate Board Resource or elsewhere.

36. Joe Cappo, "Women on the Move but Not Necessarily Upward," a talk to Women in Management, April 18, 1978, Morton Grove, Ill. The Chicago-based corporations included in the surveys were Sears Roebuck, Illinois Bell, Standard Oil of Indiana, International Harvester, Kraft, Esmark, Household Finance, First Chicago Corporation, Continental Illinois Bank, People's Gas, United Airlines, and Commonwealth Edison.

37. "Cosmetic" applies to the approach taken as well as to the industry. Since the industry is viewed as a women's industry, one might expect it to be easier for women to get on cosmetic boards and such boards might confer lower status than the automobile, steel, or advanced technologies industries. The issue is more complex, however. Since 1982, Sears, Roebuck and Co. has had three women (20%) on its board of directors. Avon, AT&T, IBM, United Technologies, and United Telecommunications, among others, have two female board members. Major corporations generally have 15 board members. Interestingly, power companies (utilities) have been slow to appoint women directors.

38. Judy Klemsrud, "Finding the Right Career–Family Mix," *The New York Times*, July 20, 1980.

39. Marianne Moore, "I May, I Might, I Must," *The Complete Poems of Marianne Moore* (New York: Macmillan Company/Viking Press, 1967), p. 178.

Appendix A
legal rights survey: preliminary results, fall 1978

Here is preliminary feedback on the Revised Lawful Law Fool Quiz taken by colleagues of students in the Effective Business Roles class. One hundred and forty employed men and women took time to respond to the questions. This preliminary report is for them. There were 47 men, 83 women, and 10 persons of unknown sex in the sample.

Taking the 20 items as a group, 62.0 percent of the answers given were correct. This compares with 70.9 percent correct answers given by an earlier sample to the original questions, some of which were changed in the revised form. Two differences in direction may explain the higher (9 percent) scores the first time: Students' responses were included, and students had studied some of the laws before taking the survey. Your student colleague will tell you that his or her quiz was collected in class and that no answers were given until your quiz responses had been turned in.

The 31 class members taking the quiz on time had an average score of 65.1 percent—just about the same as the colleague score.

Remember that on the basis of chance alone, when True–False items are involved, 50 percent of the answers should be correct. With 62 percent correct answers, we can say that there is some awareness about legal rights among the working people in the sample.

On the other hand, 38 percent of the answers were not correct. There is plenty of room for increased awareness about legal rights. There still appears to be uncertainty, confusion, or misunderstanding about some of our legal rights. For your group, four out of ten answers, roughly, are not correct.

First, let's see what most people were sure of. Just about everyone (97.9 percent) knew it was not legal to pay men more for doing the same jobs that women do. The law that set the stage is the Equal Pay Act of 1963. A few less people (93.6 percent) were aware that one needs to apply for promotion (if one wants to advance and has the skills for moving up), and that it is illegal to offer training to members of one sex (male) only. The provision here is Title VII of the Civil Rights Act of 1964. In case you are wondering, the low-level jobs, the ones that do not usually require additional training, are usually filled by women, while the jobs that require training are usually filled by men. The Civil Rights Act Title VII was enacted to end sex discrimination on the job. In your group a surprising number of people (87.9 percent) understand that a school's refusal to give out transcripts when ordered in any way except by written order of the person whose transcipts are being requested (or the person's guardian when the transcripts concern the work of someone under 18 years old) is not discrimination but a legal safeguard of the transcript namee's rights. The law here is the Family Educational Rights and Privacy Act, popularly called the Buckley Amendment of 1974.

Three-quarters (75.7 percent) of the group knew that it was more than rude for a bank or lender to ask a woman what she did to prevent conception. It is downright illegal and sex discriminatory (because men are not asked the same question when they apply for loans). The Equal Credit Opportunity Act of 1974 is the pertinent measure. Two questions achieved identical correct response rates (72.1 percent). One dealt with admissions quotas for women at colleges and universities, while the other had to do with the retribution an employer could exact from you if you filed a complaint about your unfair job treatment. Both types of action are prohibited by federal law. The first is covered by the Education Amendments of 1972 under Title IX, which forbids a wide range of types of sex discrimination in educational organizations; the second is outlawed by several provisions of which Title VII of the Civil Rights Act of 1964 is the best known.

The next group of items concerns matters that are not quite so obvious. For example, less than seven out of ten (69.3 percent) of the group were aware that another part of the Equal Credit Opportunity Act of 1974 forbids lenders from discounting a wife's earnings when loan limits are being figured out. Slightly fewer people (65.7 percent) were aware that the federal government has no law that forces employers to hire women for the better-paid jobs.* There are provisions for which employers could

*But there are executive orders from the president designed to accomplish this.

244

be brought to court for not hiring the best-qualified applicant (even if such a person happens to be female, black, over 65, etc.), but such allegations are very hard to prove. Further, only 65 percent understood that affirmative action does not mean a company must hire unqualified women and minority group members. Affirmative action means good faith hiring; the best-qualified applicants are not always white males, and the federal government is telling employers that it knows this. The only true statement was recognized by about three-fifths (62.1 percent) of those taking the revised survey. The item dealt with honorable discharge from the U.S. military service and assistance ever afterward in finding and keeping civil service jobs. The Veterans' Preference Act of 1944 provides substantial benefits to those who served. Some of those who served did so almost 35 years ago and are still obtaining benefits on the basis of that service. This provision is one of the few that has never been overruled. Few women and few blacks (male or female) are receiving Veterans' Preference benefits, largely because the majority of those who served were white and male.

A final group of statements was answered correctly by more than half of the people responding. Title VII of the Civil Rights Act was involved in a precedent-setting case in Pittsburgh in 1970. The defendant was a newspaper that used sex designations for its job advertisements. The newspaper was sued by NOW and lost. It is illegal and sex discriminatory to list ads as "Help Wanted Male" and "Help Wanted Female." The new laws have built-in safeguards. It is definitely not OK to plan to hire, train, and promote members of underrepresented groups. As an employer, if you say you will, you better do it, or you may face costly suits, back pay decisions against your firm, consent decrees, or end up training and promoting the underrepresented anyway. Both items recieved 57.1 percent correct answers. While you must, if you run a school, provide equal sports opportunity for male and female students, there is no law that says that sports costs must be identical for male and female sports. In the past, girls had far less opportunity to participate in sports than boys. Title IX of the Education Amendments of 1972 attempts to correct this. Having girls watch the boys play no longer qualifies as girls' physical education.

Exactly half of the respondents said that the sex discrimination laws had no teeth. The laws do have plenty of muscle. But there is a big difference between enacting a law—which is a congressional matter—and enforcing it—which is what citizens have to demand, support, and encourage. We have adequate antidiscrimination laws and poor enforcement of them. We are all at fault in this.

The last five statements produced mostly incorrect responses. There was little awareness of when the personnel manager had violated the employee's rights (42.9 percent) or how this had been done. The Privacy Act could be tested on this point, as could stronger laws. It is doubtful that a personnel manager or anyone else can legally place negative items about an employee in the employee's personnel file without notifying the employee, preferably gaining the employee's consent. There is a great deal in the laws about removing negative items already in the file after a specified time limit. Avid readers of the Constitution's 5th Amendment are aware that their civil rights are protected by this provision also. The Equal Pay Act of 1963 prohibits the practice of changing titles for the same work so men can be paid more. Only four out of ten (39.3 percent) knew that, and your employers were probably delighted with your ignorance since it saved them money. There is no federal law that makes all discrimination based on sex in the United States illegal. The Equal Rights Amendment would provide such a law but has not been ratified. There are laws of national scope covering various kinds of sex discrimination on the job, in pay, in educational matters, even in housing and loans. Only 37.1 percent of you know the importance of having one law that covers the entire country and makes sex discrimination illegal. It would be saintly if America's larger concerns set good democratic examples for the entire business–industrial–educational–military complex. They don't. Large companies, such as AT&T, have been prosecuted for discriminatory policies. The subsequent consent decrees have cost them millions of dollars. The fact remains that women in America, no matter how qualified and experienced, are very rarely promoted to top-level management, without having relatives high up in the organization, regardless of the organization's size. Several laws cited earlier impinge upon this aspect of inequality—31.4 percent were aware of it. The last item, which 17.1 percent answered correctly, was utterly absurd and ridiculous. It suggested that the applicant who has been offered a position ask to see the firm's affirmative action plan before accepting the job. Now, not all organizations have affirmative action plans, and few show them even to trusted employees.

We feel that folks guessed a lot, and wildly at that, on the last five items. We also suspect that beliefs and attitudes, rather than legal rights information, motivated respondents' answers. It also appears that there is a large area of confusion between what exists and what would be desirable.

We hope that this quiz has motivated you to find out more about what your legal rights are. To help you, we list some major provisions figuring in the statements that you evaluated:

The Veterans' Preference Act of 1944

The Equal Pay Act of 1963

The Civil Rights Act of 1964, Title VII

The Education Act of 1972, Title IX

The Equal Credit Opportunity Act of 1974

The Family Educational Rights and Privacy Act of 1974

The Equal Rights Amendment (first proposed in 1923)

Appendix B
the credit fieldwork experience

This brief report summarizes a pilot study done by working women/ students in late April 1977 in metropolitan Chicago, with followup in early 1978. The objective was determination of informational compliance with provisions of the ECOA, namely whether the government had furnished informational materials to all credit-granting institutions for distribution to customers and the level of bank awareness of the federal regulation.

Women investigators gathered material from ten banks and a large credit corporation. Six of the financial institutions provided booklets listing the required ECOA provision:

> It shall be unlawful for any creditor to discriminate against any applicant with respect to any aspect of a credit transaction on the basis of . . . sex or marital status.

One booklet also listed the compliance agency for its institution.

No bank officer mentioned the ECOA in response to any woman investigator's inquiry statement:

> In case I find my dream house soon, I'd like to know all about the laws and have any information you've prepared for customers on the questions of loans and credit. I'm really looking hard, and you can never tell when you'll find just what you want . . .

Perhaps our random sample was biased, our logic faulty. We knew the sample was too small, but we predicted a better response. We had figured that financial institutions volunteering their compliance agency would be in compliance with the law, because customers could report deviations. Those institutions not listing their compliance agency could also be reported when in violation; surely they knew that. However, we found that the financial institutions were ignoring the ECOA, or so it seemed.

One exception was a bank that gave out a Government Printing Office booklet with the ECOA notice blanked out. (We later received other copies with the notice intact.) We were given several copies of *Settlement Costs and You*, published by the Department of Housing and Urban Development (HUD), containing the ECOA notice on page 31 of that unreadable pamphlet. No reader would believe that HUD wanted average potential home buyers to learn about their ECOA rights.

When the women investigators' reports were examined, methods of evading ECOA compliance became apparent. Among them were:

1. Subtle sex discrimination by reduction to absurdity.

    . . . Regarding the issue of women's rights in credit, stressing that no account is taken that a woman is of childbearing age when she makes a request for credit, Mr. J. stated that, "Even if a woman was to come into my office and have a baby right there on my desk, I couldn't refuse her credit."

    I feel that the above remark was out of place and uncalled for.

2. Noncompliance *because* of the law.

    I spoke with a mortgage officer. . . . He was very candid with me in explaining that the bank was aware of the regulations but did not publish facts on the law because the law constantly changes.

3. Defense of specious fiscal policy to indicate compliance that is also specious.

    We are making a 25-year mortgage of $15,000 to a 65-year-old woman.

    For a house . . . 25 percent of your monthly gross income must cover mortgage payment, insurance, taxes, and any other major related expenses.

4. Bad will or feigned ignorance.

When I asked if they would count my salary along with my husband's, he said, "Of course. We have to because of the new rules—is it EEOC? Something like that."

Because the fieldwork experience had contained such a small sample, the project was expanded and replicated. This time, both informational compliance and sex discrimination in granting of credit were examined. Forty-five bank visits were made. For the informational tally, these new calls were pooled with the earlier visits. Twenty-one of the 56 visits made (37.5 percent) resulted in the ECOA notice, while three (5.3 percent) also included the compliance agency.

In the second study, women investigators attempted to assess the effects of marital status upon potential mortgage credit. Each woman investigator made two visits. At the first bank, she announced that she was single (unmarried, divorced, or widowed):

> I earn $13,200 and want a modest three-bedroom house at around $40,000. My real estate agent has a lot of houses that are just perfect for me.

She was free to reveal savings of $3792.57 and a pattern of regular deposits. She was to let it be known that she had been employed on the same job for at least a year, and she was to be courteous. While in the interview she was to ask for loan information:

> Any booklet about loans that the bank can give me so I can study it for a few days.

Upon leaving, she was to thank the loan officer and ask for his or her card:

> So I can talk to you again. You have been very helpful.

On the second bank visit—to another bank—she varied her statement:

> My husband had to work today, so he couldn't come with me. He asked me to come in and get information about home loans. Could you give me a booklet? We found the cutest little house that is only $65,000.

If the woman investigator is asked, she is to say:

> Oh, yes, I have a full-time job. I like my work even more after a year of doing it. I earn $13,200.

Identical savings were to be reported by the woman investigator in both conditions; in the "married" visit, she could indicate that *she* had the regular pattern of savings and deposits.

A credit form was supplied for recording each bank visit immediately upon completion. Credit form A is a sample of the "single" form; an identical form, labeled Credit Form B, was used to record "married" visits. See Figure B-1.

Findings included the following: All of the women loan officers and 70 percent of the men loan officers did *not* mention the ECOA; among all loan officers, 19 percent did mention the ECOA; 84 percent of loan officers who were assistant vice-presidents or held higher positions did *not* mention the ECOA; among all loan officers, 22 percent did mention the ECOA; 66.6 percent of the women investigators rated interview quality as poor, including equal numbers of male and female loan officers in their ratings; however, among the positive interview ratings (33.3 percent), 57 percent were received by male loan officers.

It is disappointing to record that the "married" women investigators fared worse than the "single" ones, being denied serious consideration by most banks visited. Typical responses to them included:

> He thought it was a joke. He thought my husband should come in and talk to him. I became too upset to ask about the law, and he never mentioned it.
>
> *and*
>
> The loan officer that I interviewed was very friendly as well as professional. However, he felt that we should not go into any aspects of the loan since my husband was not present. He informed me that I should give the bank a call when my husband and I could come in to discuss the details of getting a loan.

Because of the put-off received by "married" women, who were often required to wait for a long time in uncrowded banks to see a loan officer who then suggested a return visit "with your husband," projected "single" and "married" comparisons were not possible. We just did not collect enough information. What we learned was that women received less than businesslike consideration when they wanted to borrow money for purchase of a home.

Nevertheless, we did accomplish some interesting things. First, women went into the real world and determined for themselves what happens when they attempt to achieve credit on their own economic mer-

FIGURE B-1

Your name, please print _____   Date of call _____
Your signature _____   Time of call _____
                                                   Time you left bank _____

CREDIT FORM A

Classification of bank: _____
Name of bank _____ Address _____ City _____
Size (by total deposit) _____ Main _____ or Branch _____
Your informant: Your estimates of:
                               Informant's age: _____

                               Informant's ethnic group: _____

                               Informant's manner _____

                               Was informant male? yes ____ no ____

attach card here

Informant's reactions:
To size and purpose of loan: _____
_____

To amount of savings: _____
_____

To marital status of investigator: _____
_____

To occupational status of investigator: _____
_____

Investigator's reaction to inverview:
Using *excellent, good, fair,* or *poor,* rate the
Quality of the interview: _____
Sequence of questions loan informant asked: _____
Did loan informant mention the law? _____

Was your request treated seriously when you asked about a loan? _____
_____

If loan was refused, what reason was given? _____
_____

its, and we probably performed the first face-to-face test of ECOA bank compliance. One investigator reported:

> I was pleased with my own discovery that it is very valuable to shop around for mortgages, something I haven't given much thought to. Also, my own ability to be assertive, begin applying for loans, I believe I have the right to . . . I never thought about it before. I'm 19, and I believed the biggest strike against me was going to be my age. I see now that belief was incorrect. All in all I learned a lot.

Second, a method was devised that can be used by other interested women to assess the ECOA where they live and work. How well does ECOA function in their home area to prohibit sex discrimination and marital status discrimination in lending?

Third, our studies did pinpoint an important research question: How widespread is violation of the ECOA by banks and their loan officers when the potential borrower is a woman?

Index